PRAISE FOR
THE BARNA REPORT SERIES:

The Barna Report is essential reading for anyone who seeks to understand the changing religious scene in America. The contents provide grist for the preacher's mill, valuable data for denominational decision-making, and essential facts for congregational long-range planning committees. This new edition is a required resource for those responsible for preparing the churches for the new millennium.

Lyle E. Schaller
Parish Consultant, Yokefellow Institute

The challenge of understanding the culture we've targeted for ministry has never been greater. As the pace of change among contemporary adults continues to accelerate, the value of credible research on the beliefs that shape their reception to ministry is essential. Thank God for George Barna and his willingness to serve the Kingdom with this critically important contribution.

Bob Shank
Senior Pastor, South Coast Community Church

A pastor can make better decisions in church management when he has better information. *The Barna Report* will give him vital information on the attitudes, practices and religious beliefs of Americans outside of his congregation....This book is necessary for any pastor who wants to make management decisions to lead his church to grow, reach Americans and minister to his clientele.

Elmer L. Towns,
Dean, Liberty University School of Religion

The Barna Report gives us another tool to test our assumptions about our listeners. Our ministry team passed around our two copies of last year's version until they were worn out. *The Barna Report* is a great primer for preparing sermons that hit felt needs. It is also a valuable tool for testing our programs. And above all, once again, George adds content to our understanding of needy America.

Doug Murren
Senior Pastor, Eastside Foursquare Church

THE BARNA REPORT

AN ANNUAL SURVEY OF LIFE-STYLES, VALUES AND RELIGIOUS VIEWS

REPORT 1992-93

AMERICA RENEWS ITS SEARCH FOR GOD

GEORGE BARNA

AUTHOR OF **THE FROG IN THE KETTLE** AND **USER FRIENDLY CHURCHES**

Regal Books

A Division of Gospel Light
Ventura, California, U.S.A.

Published by Regal Books
A Division of Gospel Light
Ventura, CA 93006
Printed in U.S.A.

ISSN 1063-1437
ISBN 0-8307-1576-2

1 2 3 4 5 6 7 8 9 10 / E3.1 /KP / 99 98 97 96 95 94 93 92

Rights for publishing this book in other languages are contracted by Gospel Literature International (GLINT). GLINT also provides technical help for the adaptation,
translation, and publishing of Bible study resources and books in scores of languages
worldwide. For further information, contact GLINT, Post Office Box 488, Rosemead,
California, 91770, U.S.A., or the publisher.

CONTENTS

Acknowledgments   7

Introduction   9

An Overview of *The Barna Report 1992-93*   17

1. Close to the Heart: America's Values   23
   The importance of family, health, time and friends • A turn to religion and the Bible • Views on abortion • Is there absolute truth? • Women as leaders

2. Dimensions of Our Faith   43
   Accuracy of the Bible, and who reads it • The relevancy of sin and the Ten Commandments • The significance of Jesus Christ and the Christian faith • The power of prayer • Who is into astrology?

3. The Image of the Church   59
   The Church's tarnished image • Is the Church failing women? • Different images for Chrysler, Catholics, Democrats and others • Meeting the needs of families, the elderly and the poor

4. Acknowledging the Saints   73
   God as all-powerful • Self-described Christians • The rise of the born again • Believers and nonbelievers • The elusive evangelicals: habits, beliefs and politics

5. The Life of the Body   89
   Who is going to church? • Where we attend: decline of the mainline • Sunday's pews • Brand loyalty • Church shopping: American style • Where are the volunteers?

6. A Religiously Active People   99
Religious television and radio • Bible reading • Sharing our faith • Helping the needy • Donating our time and money • The continued rise of the small-group movement

7. The Ten Commandments   111
Where is Moses when you need him? • A people steeped in sin • Our loyalty to God • America's idols • The differences of the Christian life-style

8. The Nineties Life-style   123
What we read • Books vs. MTV • Religious involvement this week • Movie attendance • Making friends • Our social circles • How we give our money: church, mail, media and the telephone • Who is giving the most? and least?

9. Politics and the Issues That Motivate Us   135
The key issues for election 1992 • Protestants, Republicans, Catholics and Democrats • The top five issues • Abortion as a voting issue • The Bush influence • Who is registered to vote?

Closing Thoughts   153

Appendices   159
    Information About the Information:
        Research Methodology and Related Insights   161

    Data Tables Directory   173
        July 1991 Survey Tables   179
        January 1992 Survey Tables   227

    About Barna Research Group   321

Index   323

ACKNOWLEDGMENTS

This book is the result of a significant investment of cash, the gracious participation of more than 2,000 people who were interviewed for this research, a lot of prayer, many hours of hard work, and a heartfelt desire to help Christian churches and believers in the quest to change the world for Christ's sake.

My colleagues at the Barna Research Group lent their invaluable support on this project. Paul Rottler managed the data collection process, involving our team of interviewers and supervisors. Cindy Coats controlled the data tabulation effort. Ron Sellers acquired the sample. The rest of the staff—Gwen Ingram, Vibeke Klocke, Keith Deaville, George Maupin—protected my time while analyzing and writing this book. This is a gifted and special team of people that God has brought together to cooperatively pursue a unique ministry.

My wife, Nancy, also contributed heavily to this project. Not only did she give me up for yet another period of solitary confinement while I wrote the book, but she shouldered part of my normal work load both at the office and at home. Her enduring encouragement to serve God fully has been invaluable. I trust she will receive special blessings for her willingness to support my commitment to carry out the vision for ministry that God has provided me. Perhaps our new daughter, Samantha, is the first of those inimitable blessings.

Special thanks are also due to my friends and co-laborers at Gospel Light Publications. They responded energetically to the concept behind *The Barna Report* series and have forged new trails in Christian publishing by investing significant levels of time, money, talent and faith to get information into the hands of the people who do ministry. I commend their efforts and their heart to serve. My own life and ministry has been enriched by knowing and working with people such as Bill Greig, Jr., Bill Greig III, Mark Maddox, Kyle Duncan and the many other talented and godly people who have made Gospel Light a formidable ministry for more than 55 years.

INTRODUCTION

Where have you heard this command before: "Therefore go and make disciples of all nations"?

Of course, that is the well-known command of Jesus to His disciples, often called the Great Commission (Matt. 28:19). It was a challenging instruction to His closest followers, and one the Church today is still seeking to complete.

But how did Jesus expect that command to be fulfilled? Did He assume that conversions would be based upon strong-arm tactics, wherein we would twist people's arms until they cried "Uncle" and angrily accepted Christ as their Lord and Savior? Was He expecting nonbelievers to be confronted with a few magic words of wisdom and then just surrender everything they own in order to worship God and lead a life geared to serving Him? Did He really anticipate that in a marketplace of competing philosophies and theologies the typical adult would immediately see through the deceptions of false perspectives and determine that Jesus Christ was the only means to having an eternal relationship with God?

JESUS CHANGED LIVES BY MEETING NEEDS

The answer to these rhetorical questions is, of course, a resounding no. The most compelling clues we have are those drawn from an understanding of Jesus' own life and ministry. He always worked from a base of information about the people to whom He was ministering. He responded to their needs in unique and unexpected ways, providing real answers to the tough stuff of daily living. Jesus did not dispense traditional religious wisdom as did the Sadducees and Pharisees. The religious leaders of the day had a limited influence on people's lives because their responses to people's needs were predictable, pat answers. Their brand of religion lacked true power and influence because it was insensitive to God's reality.

Jesus stood out from the crowd of religious teachers because His wisdom keenly addressed the hurts and confusion of people. His response was invariably one of practical help for the person struggling with difficult circumstances. And His solutions were based upon a worldview that emerged from the values and principles for which He stood.

Jesus intimately understood the people He wanted to reach. He gave love and compassion to respond to each individual need. Although He had a divine agenda to fulfill, He did so within the context of the human condition. In other words, He was able to satisfy His own purposes for coming to Earth in human form by influencing people's lives in light of their own needs.

PAUL SETS ANOTHER EXAMPLE

The example set by the apostle Paul is strikingly similar to Jesus' example and equally compelling. Paul did not have the types of divine insights that may have inspired some of Jesus' responses to people. Yet, Paul consistently sought to understand the culture in which he was ministering, and changed his manner of outreach and speech to increase his chances of reaching people with the gospel. He spoke of the need to contextualize the message without compromising it.

Contextualization demands a street-level understanding of the people: how they think, what they value, the ways they live, what they believe and how they communicate. Paul's life was committed to serving God by loving people so much that he took the time to study how they lived and to figure out what he could do to most effectively present the truths of the gospel to them in light of their perceptions and customs.

That is precisely how we can be most effective in addressing the problems and needs of our world today. Being an agent of God is not merely accepting Christ as Savior, performing the religious rituals of the day and talking about how great God is to people who know Him and serve Him. A true ambassador of Christ is one who accepts the calling to minister to the world as Christ did. We need to love people so much that we take the time to understand them and respond to their needs.

COPING WITH A COMPLEX WORLD

But how can we be sensitive to what people's life issues are these days? The world has become much more complex than it was 2,000 years ago. We have more people, more rules and regulations, more temptations, more information, more opportunities for spending our money.

The beauty of living in a complex world is that God loves His people so much, He has allowed us to develop many means to understand our sophisticated environment. At times our senses are overwhelmed by the billions of bits of information that bombard us daily. But there are ways of capturing, managing and interpreting the signs and symbols of our age to arrive at some well-organized, accurate perspectives on the current conditions and future prospects.

A relatively recent innovation that can help us minister more effectively for God's glory is survey research. Developed in the first half of this century through the work of men such as George H. Gallup, Archibald Crossley and Elmo Roper, survey research has become a multibillion dollar business. You often hear or read the results of Gallup Polls or similarly well-publicized research studies. From such research you may learn about the President's current popularity, the proportion of adults who believe the economy is worse today than it was a year ago, or people's opinions about specific products and services.

Have you ever stopped to wonder if God permitted the pioneers of the research industry to develop their techniques so His people could better understand the minds and hearts of the population, thus bringing them to a personal relationship with Christ?

I believe God did precisely that. The talents of a small group of intelligent people were used to formalize a series of techniques that allow us to be in touch with the thinking, the values, the behavior and the hopes of the population. Although the research techniques developed by Gallup and his colleagues are most frequently used to advance businesses and other institutions, the greatest potential influence of such research is to enable Christians to more effectively and efficiently fulfill the Great Commission.

RESEARCH AS A MINISTRY TOOL

The Barna Research Group, along with a handful of other research companies, has been able to use research to focus on the needs, the hurts, the frustrations and the expectations of today's population. Rather than concentrating upon how to sell more doughnuts or what price people would be willing to pay for an improved lawn mower, we have produced information that can help you discover how to have a more significant effect upon the world for the glory of God. By analyzing people's perspectives and conditions you will be able to respond more appropriately according to the Great Commission.

Think of this book as a means of getting to know your mission field. If you believe that you, as a devoted follower of Jesus Christ, are called to reach the world with the gospel, treat the information contained in this volume as a resource that will enhance your ministry. The research described within these pages is designed to help you better understand how people perceive the world and what we as Christians might do to influence their thinking and help them accept Christ as their Lord and Savior.

TIPS ON USING THIS BOOK

How would such a ministry tool be used? Let me suggest that you read the book in pieces, perhaps a chapter at a sitting, rather than taking it all in at one time. After you read a section, stop and reflect on what you have just learned about today's Americans. Try to articulate in your mind the implications of that chapter's insights for your own ministry.

Each chapter contains an opening page, which highlights some of the most important or unexpected findings related to that chapter's subject. The bulk of the chapter follows, under the "What We Discovered" heading. Throughout the chapter are some tables and graphs designed to help you understand the text more thoroughly. As well, sprinkled throughout the nine chapters you will see references to the actual data tables from the survey results. This data is presented in the appendix at the back of the book. (See page 14 for more information about the appendix.)

The closing portion of each chapter suggests ways you, as a committed Christian, might translate this information into practical ministry activities. The brief outline of Action Steps is meant to stimulate your thinking, not to provide an exhaustive, rigid agenda. Use the insights and talents God gave you to think through how you can use your resources in a more effective and strategic manner, for His glory.

Most Christians find they have their greatest ministry influence on their friends and acquaintances. After you read a chapter, think about the people God has placed in your life, and how accurately you feel the research data describe the people to whom you wish to minister. Based on your perceptions, think through some of the ministry applications of the information. Commit yourself to know your circle of contacts intimately enough to understand how they are similar to or different from the population at large, as described in this book. Then, reach out to them in ways that are based upon your enhanced understanding of how they think and behave. Use the insights in this book as a springboard to reach your world for Christ.

For Instance...
In last year's edition of *What Americans Believe,* one of the key findings was that two-thirds of the American adult population does not believe there is such a thing as absolute truth. What difference does that make to you?

Let me respond by relating the effect it has had on my personal ministry. First, I now realize most people do not believe in absolute truth, which partially explains why the approach I had been taking to share my faith with nonbelievers—i.e., basing much of my discussion upon information contained in the Bible—had limited potential. Because the typical American does not see the Bible as a source of objective, reliable truth, basing my evangelistic arguments on the Bible is neither sensible nor likely to be fruitful. The research taught me that I have to be more sensitive to the viewpoints of my friends. They probably do not enter a conversation about spiritual matters with the same assumptions I possess.

The implication, therefore, was that I have had to totally rethink what is meaningful to other people. If they do not trust the Bible as a source of truth, what do they deem to be truthful? How can I help them explore the validity of their claims about sources of truth and wisdom other than God and His Word? Are there ways I can show them why the Bible can be considered trustworthy and reliable? If people are searching for meaning in life, are there ways I can approach the purpose of life from a biblical perspective, without exhorting my friends to accept this perspective simply because it originates from the Bible?

Second, since the research showed that most Christians do not believe in absolute truth, it has forced me to redesign the ways I teach and disciple believers. It would be foolish, given the knowledge about Christians' views on truth, to try to build the faith of believers when I know that the foundations of that faith among most believers are weak. Instead, it makes sense to review some of the basic insights, strengthen those fundamental beliefs, then work our way up to deeper perspectives on our faith.

In the same manner, please use the information in this year's volume to discover new ways of seeing the world as other people see it. Use these new insights to create a strategic approach to effective ministry, both in reaching out to those who are not Christians as well as in your relationships with other believers.

THE RESEARCH BASE

The appendix of this book contains a more detailed explanation of how we collected this information and its reliability. Briefly, the information is based on two nationwide surveys we conducted, one during July 1991, and the other during January 1992. Each survey included the answers of more than 1,000 adults from across the nation. When considering the responses of that many people, drawn from a random sample of the aggregate adult population, we can be 95% confident that the responses obtained are accurate to within 4 percentage points of what would have been found if a census of that same population had been conducted.

The appendix also contains the actual data tables from the surveys. If you wish to explore people's answers in greater depth, you may turn to the page with the answers to the question asked of respondents. The data tables are organized topically, in sections, for easy reference. The information is also separated according to the two surveys, July 1991 and January 1992, respectively. We have provided a Data Table Directory to help you find the information of most interest to you (see page 173). Within the various data tables themselves, you will see the information divided into more than 30 different subgroups of the population: men, women, young adults, senior citizens, blacks, whites, Protestants, Catholics and so on. There are often significant differences between these subgroups. You may find it interesting to explore the responses of the types of people to whom you minister most often, as a means of becoming more sensitive to them.

Remember, our responsibility is to be open to serve God in whatever manner He may ask of us. It is His Holy Spirit that converts nonbelievers, not our own clever evangelistic efforts. However, by understanding the world He has placed us in for the purpose of knowing, loving and serving Him, we can be a more useful conduit through which His Spirit can work. May these insights strengthen your ability to be an effective servant for the glory of our risen Savior.

An Overview Of:
The Barna Report
1992-93

Americans today are reminiscent of the Israelites who followed Moses throughout the desert. Their lives were characterized by struggling, searching, complaining, pondering, worrying, seeking adventure and fulfillment. In good faith they expended a considerable amount of energy in an earnest search—but for what? What *was* the Promised Land?

For Americans in the early '90s, the promised land remains just as elusive as it seemed to those who were in the desert more than 2,000 years ago. As our world has changed, so have the perspectives we bring to the search for truth and purpose. But the basic quest remains intact: What is the meaning and purpose of life, and how can we live it to the fullest?

To solve this mystery we are willing to experiment with a wide variety of approaches to maximize life. As a society we engage in bursts of activity intended to explore new dimensions of reality and to arrive at ever more complete conclusions. But try as they might, frustration arises because most people are not quite sure what they are looking for. The prevailing hope is that they will know it when they find it.

In spite of the lack of clarity about the goal, the pace of the search remains almost frenetic. Values and behaviors that used to change every decade or two now shift in just a few short years. With the advent of new technologies, people virtually have instant access to incredible volumes and types of information, from the germane to the arcane. Decisions based on this wealth of data lead to a more jam-packed daily experience. The dreams of the past have become the routine of today; the dreams of today will become realities more quickly than we imagine.

AN UNFOLDING PROCESS

How well do Americans cope with this accelerated world of change and discovery? Like patients with a serious illness, we have our ups and downs. Presently our motion sickness is a bit more under control than it has been in the past decade. But in general we have yet to find the real cure for our disease.

In the '60s, a group of upstarts made it fashionable to question many of the basic assumptions about life. When their probing revealed the ability to radically reshape views and practices related to culture, it was only natural that we then encountered some creative and bold responses to the foundations and traditions regarding attitudes and life-styles.

But the '60s proved to be mostly a time when we were simply testing the possibilities. Deep in the recesses of the minds and hearts of a few hearty souls was the notion that we could redesign this world to truly exploit the untapped opportunities for fulfillment that it possessed. But it would take some time for the masses to catch the vision.

In the '70s, that vision was more completely articulated and pursued. The pace of experimentation exploded. People began to think more critically about the boundaries of their personal reality. The tone changed a bit in the '80s, as the unquenched thirst for experience, adventure, the good life and security in the midst of chaos turned inward.

Beyond being a 10-year span of wanton selfishness, the '80s also set the stage for a new era. The '80s saw people realize they could redesign their world according to their deepest personal desires and fantasies regardless of the societal consequences. The theme of the decade may have been, "It is better to ask for forgiveness than permission: Act now, plead later."

The "Me decade" clearly reflected the utter self-deceit and deep-seated greed and cruelty of humans. But it was a decade that also drove home the reality that all forays into new territory and all attempts to recreate the world come with a price tag. There really is no such thing as a free lunch, but it took Americans the better part of 15 years to reach that simple conclusion.

The '90s, then, are a period in which the pursuit of priorities and socially acceptable goals are returning to vogue. Fatigued by nearly two decades of taking on the world, many adults are admitting they cannot truly mold the entire world in their own image. Pragmatic realists, they are instead scaling back their goals to seek a smaller, more comfortable world in which they can see their imprint on that designer reality.

VALUES ARE SHIFTING

The constantly changing values that Americans embrace continue to be vigorously reassessed and modified. In just the past year, the confluence of major, life-changing world events (collapse of the Soviet Union, the unification of Germany, the war in the Persian Gulf, the deterioration of the national economy, the realization that heterosexuals such as Magic Johnson can contract AIDS) has stimulated a shuffling of our key values.

- Family and personal health remained the most important elements in people's lives. Our time and our friends also hovered near the top of our list of priorities. During the past 12 months, our concern about the meaning of dramatic world events and the enduring search for meaning in life created a significant increase in the value ascribed to religion, the Bible and living comfortably.
- Morally, the foundations continue to take a pounding. Millions of adults believe it is sometimes "necessary" to lie. Millions believe abortion is morally wrong, but should be legally permissible. Although we intellectually dismiss money as a driving value, we acknowledge that it remains the main symbol of success in American life.
- Truth remains a relative concept for Americans. Most adults are convinced that nothing can be known for certain except what they personally experience. These days that must be

quite frightening, since two-thirds of the public contend the world is out of control.

Working Within the Process

As our adult population ages, perhaps it is becoming more comfortable with the notion of working within the system. Most adults are registered to vote, aligned with one of the two major parties, and believe that taking personal action, such as boycotting products or companies, can make a real difference. The desire to make a difference is what drives the behavior of millions of Americans.

Considering the presidential election approaching, people were clear on the issues that would help them decide who they wanted to see in the Oval Office. The compelling issues were those that most precisely related to the voters' personal circumstances: crime, enforcement of drug laws, economics, education and health care. Abortion? A distraction. Separation of church and state? A sideshow.

Actions Speak Louder than Words

Sometimes it seems that we change our attitudes, opinions and values as often as we change our clothing. Why the instant flux? To some degree it is related to our declining ability to arrive at and stick to firm conclusions in light of newer and more alluring personal opportunities. We spend more time thinking about the need to be prepared for the future, but in practical terms we tend to live for the moment.

Yet, we have retained some basic behaviors that assist us in our ambiguous journey through time and space. In a society of such fluidity and transition, the most important indicators of the future are the actions of the day. Despite the growing problem of functional illiteracy, two-thirds of all adults read books (other than the Bible) in any given week. Most adults participate in formal religious activities. Coinciding with our emphasis upon family and friends, we devote considerable sums of our time to strengthen these personal ties.

At the same time, we have abandoned many of the rules regarding proper behavior. When asked to compare our actions against the admonitions of the Ten Commandments, for example, we find that most people engage in practices such as lying and swearing. Millions of Americans admit that they worship gods other than the God of the Bible. A relative handful (6% of the adult population) said they were living in complete harmony with all Ten Commandments. You have to wonder if they are breaking the commandment against telling lies!

WHERE GOD FITS IN

The good news is that most Americans possess perspectives on life and spirituality that conform to an orthodox Christian view of the world. Most Americans claim that the Bible is God's Word and is totally accurate in what it teaches. Most believe that sin is still a relevant concept for today's world. The majority indicate that the Ten Commandments are practical for modern life-styles. The typical adult concurs that Christianity can supply the answers to today's pressing problems. And most adults believe that prayer has the power to change a person's life.

This recital is encouraging. People are more inclined to say that religion and the Bible are very important in their lives today than was true even one year ago. Indeed, for the first time in years, we have seen a significant increase in the proportion of adults who claim they have accepted Christ as their Savior and trust Him for their salvation.

Even the much-maligned mass media seem to offer a ray of hope that people are hearing the truth. This is suggested by data indicating that exposure to religious information through the media remains high. Two-thirds of the public listen to Christian radio or watch religious television in a typical month. Christian books and magazines find large audiences.

But somehow this Christian facade does not demonstrate the spiritual depth that true Christianity, which is based on total commitment and life transformation, reflects in practice. The evidence of an *intense* pursuit of faith is thin. There is no indication of an increase in church attendance, Sunday School attendance, participation in small groups or involvement in other church-related activities. The proportion of adults reading the Bible, or the frequency with which they do so, is unchanged.

Almost one-quarter of all adults now believe in false gods. This is a horrific realization in this latest "age of enlightenment." The major

Christian denominations have images that are no more attractive than those of the Ford Motor Company or the Chrysler Corporation. This explains why church-related activity is not growing, but raises other questions about the Church in America. Not a single people group among the 15 tested believe the church is sensitive. This was also a source of potential despair.

Less than half of all adults surveyed had attempted to share their faith with other people in the past month. This limited focus upon the deepest needs of other people parallels the fact that only 16% believed that Protestant churches are very sensitive to the needs of non-Christians.

So there is clearly some good news and some not-so-good news regarding the moral and spiritual character and pursuits of Americans. The challenge to the Church remains quite formidable.

CHAPTER 1
CLOSE TO THE HEART: AMERICA'S VALUES

CHAPTER HIGHLIGHTS

- The most important elements in life for Americans are family, health, time and friends. Among the least valued elements are money, government and politics.
- During the past 12 months a significant increase in value was ascribed to religion, the Bible and living comfortably.
- A majority of non-Christians now believe that religion and the Bible are very important in their lives.
- More than one out of three adults believe that sometimes it is necessary to lie.
- Three out of five adults said that abortion is morally wrong.
- The majority of Americans maintain that money is still the main symbol of success in life.
- Most adults believe that nothing can be known for certain except what you personally experience in your own life.
- Two-thirds of the public contend that the world is out of control.
- Three-quarters of all adults rejected the notion that men are better leaders than women.

WHAT WE DISCOVERED

People's values change with alarming rapidity these days. Reactions to daily events and opportunities used to be more readily predictable because we knew with greater certainty how adults perceived their world and what they valued. Now we are lucky if we can determine what factors to study to understand their present value system.

Of the 10 values we examined in the 1991 study and then again in this year's study, half underwent a significant change in importance in just a 12-month period. This shift conforms to the belief held by many researchers that Americans are still in a period of emotional flux.

Struggling with emotional discomfort and intellectual uncertainty regarding such key matters as purpose, faith and success, millions of adults continue to tinker with their respective worlds. They are seeking just the right balance of ideas, experiences, values and tangible goods to arrive at a pleasing harmony of their internal and external realities.

If You've Got Your Family and Your Health...

A year ago, the aspects most valued by adults were family and health. This year, those same two elements top the charts again, having minor increases in the level of importance ascribed to each. Overall, 96% of all adults said family was very important to them. Ninety percent stated that health was very important. (See data tables 60,63.)

The next most valued aspects were time and friends. Over three-fourths of all respondents (78%) described their time as very important; a similar proportion (76%) said their friends were very important. This latter statistic reflects a significant increase from the 1991 level. A year ago, friends were deemed very important to 67% of the adult population. A nine-point jump in one year is very noteworthy. (See data tables 57,59.)

The next highest echelon of values included religion (very important to 69%), the Bible (67%), free time (64%) and living comfortably (60%). The most significant matter in this is the large increase in value placed upon the pair of religious elements. The perceived importance of religion rose 10 points from a year earlier; the Bible leaped 12 points from its 1991 level. (See data tables 54,55,58,61.)

The importance of a person's career remained stable compared to 1991 (54%). That was the same level of importance related to a person's community (52%). The lowest ranked items were money (40%)

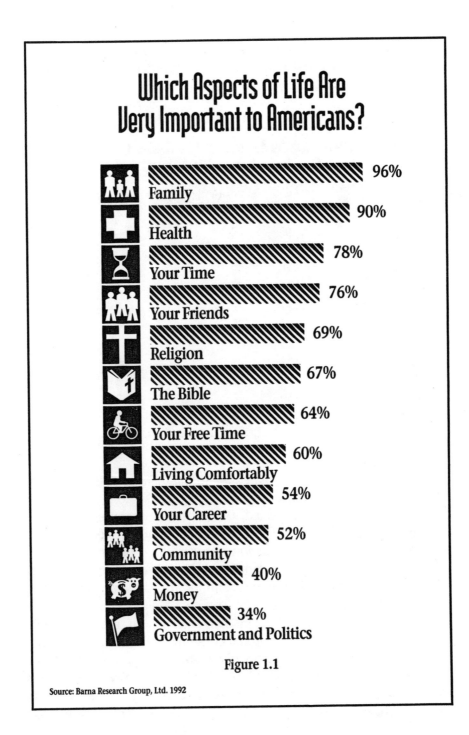

Which Aspects of Life Are Very Important to Americans?

Family	96%
Health	90%
Your Time	78%
Your Friends	76%
Religion	69%
The Bible	67%
Your Free Time	64%
Living Comfortably	60%
Your Career	54%
Community	52%
Money	40%
Government and Politics	34%

Figure 1.1

Source: Barna Research Group, Ltd. 1992

and government and politics (34%). Although money remained low on the list, it also experienced a substantial increase from its 1991 level (33%). (See data tables 56,62,64,65.)

Importance of Various Aspects of Life (Base: 1,013 adults)
How Important Is this Aspect?

Aspect	Very	Somewhat	Not too	Not at all	Don't know
family	96%	3%	—	—	—
health	90	9	—	—	—
your time	78	18	2	1	1
your friends	76	19	3	1	1
religion	69	23	5	3	—
the Bible	67	22	8	3	1
your free time	64	29	4	—	2
living comfortably	60	35	3	1	1
your career	54	26	4	5	11
your community	52	39	4	3	1
money	40	46	10	3	1
government and politics	34	42	13	9	2

When it comes to the differences and similarities between born-again Christians and non-Christians, five aspects had significant distinctions. As would be expected, the largest gap between these two people groups pertained to the two religious factors tested. Although 87% of the Christians said religion was very important in their lives, 57% of the non-Christians concurred. Nine out of ten Christians (89%) stated that the Bible was very important to them, compared to just half of the nonbelievers (51%). (See data tables 54,55.)

NOTE: The term born-again Christian, or Christian, refers to people who said they had made a personal commitment to Jesus Christ that was still important in their lives today. *And* when asked to indicate their beliefs about life after death they chose one of seven statements posed: "When I die I will go to heaven because I have confessed my sins and have accepted Jesus Christ as my Savior." This classification method found 40% of the adult population fitting the "born again" designation. The term "born again" was not used in the survey.

In spite of these gaping differences, a majority of nonbelievers said that both religion and the Bible were very important in their lives today. This is not exactly evidence of a spiritual revival. But it suggests an environment in which a reasonable discussion of religious thought and a rational display of religious practice is wholly acceptable, if not desirable. As Americans search for meaning, religion remains one possible source from which people believe they might glean some insight or guidance.

A higher proportion of Christians rated friends very important than was true among non-Christians (80% versus 73%, respectively). Christians were also slightly more likely to describe their community as very important than were non-Christians (56% vs. 50%). Money was a higher priority to non-Christians (44%, compared to 32% among Christians). (See data tables 56,59,64.)

Age made an even greater difference than spiritual perspective regarding values and priorities. The top two priorities were consistent across all age groups: Family and health topped the list for the four generations studied, although the levels of importance did vary somewhat. Young adults (i.e. those 18 to 26 years old, known to many people as the baby busters) attached much greater significance to career and to living comfortably, and less importance to religion and free time. This is a fairly common focus of people at this stage in their lives. Getting established in the marketplace consumes much of the busters' thoughts and energy. It is disturbing, though, to discover that their efforts to make inroads into the world are happening without much value placed on religion. (See data tables 54,58,60-63.)

Baby boomers (i.e. adults 27 to 45 years old) placed a greater premium upon their free time and a growing emphasis upon living comfortably. This latter finding reflects the confusion of boomers regarding the importance of possessions and the good life. After years of striving to satisfy their perceived material needs, most boomers have sufficiently achieved that goal to realize it has not truly satisfied their deepest yearnings. (See data tables 58,61.)

Much to their own frustration, most boomers have not yet found other worthy goals to replace their materialistic urges. Statistically, their quest for the comfortable life appears less dominating than is true among other generations. Notice, though, the value placed upon liv-

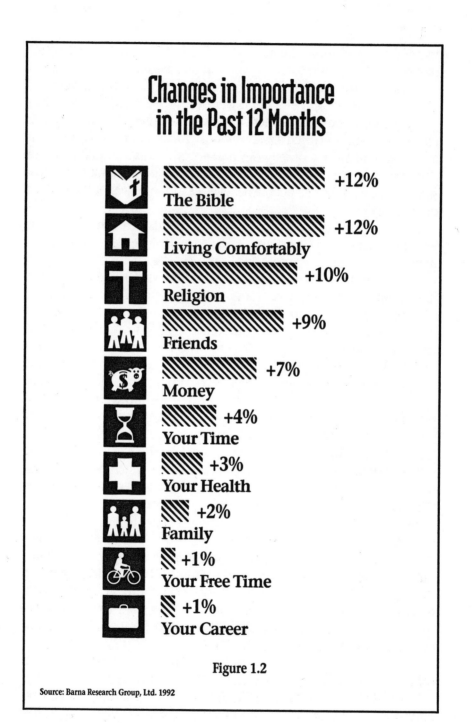

Changes in Importance in the Past 12 Months

The Bible +12%

Living Comfortably +12%

Religion +10%

Friends +9%

Money +7%

Your Time +4%

Your Health +3%

Family +2%

Your Free Time +1%

Your Career +1%

Figure 1.2

Source: Barna Research Group, Ltd. 1992

ing comfortably increased by 11 percentage points from 1991 to 1992, keeping pace with the growing interest demonstrated by the other 3 generations tracked. This is further evidence of the transition in which millions of boomers find themselves. (See data table 58.)

Older adults reflect the emotional distancing from the workplace to a desire for lasting relationships and a good environment in which to live. The pre-boomers (46 to 64 years of age) were relatively more concerned than other people about their friends, leisure pursuits and their community. Senior citizens placed a heightened degree of importance on living comfortably, their community, and government and politics. Given their circumstances, it is not unexpected to find that they ascribed comparatively limited importance to their time, their free time and career. (See data tables 57-62,64,65.)

Substantial differences were apparent between whites, blacks and Hispanics. Whites were much more likely to describe their friends as very important. Compared to the two ethnic groups they were less likely to see their time, their free time, living comfortably, their careers, and government and politics as very important. Blacks, in comparison to both whites and Hispanics, rated religion, the Bible, community, money, and government and politics as more important. Hispanics responded almost identically to whites on 5 of the 12 items evaluated; similar to blacks on 6 items; and were in between the response levels of whites and blacks on 2 items (the Bible, and government and politics).

IS A NEW DAY DAWNING?

What does this repositioning of values by Americans mean? For one thing, it suggests that the search for meaning and fulfillment is still on. The drive that baby boomers initiated back in the late '60s to discover the ultimate purpose of life and to restructure the universe around their discoveries remains active today. Not satisfied with the answers they have received from two decades of exploration, boomers (and other generations now dragged along by force of the boomers' aggressive effort to find significance) are continuing their quest for the perfect perspective.

The turn to religion in the past year is worth examining more deeply. The impetus for this broader attachment to religious elements may well have been the cataclysmic changes happening lately. Reflect on some of the tumultuous and world-changing events that transpired in the 12 months preceding the survey.

- After several months of tension awaiting decisive action by one side or the other, the Gulf War exploded in January 1991. The United States military, its image severely tarnished by recent gaffes in Viet Nam, South America and the Middle East, led a devastating strike against hapless Iraq. This victory restored Americans' confidence in the military while changing the balance of power in the Middle East.
- Our long-time archenemy, the Soviet Union, finally gave up on communism and converted to democracy. But the infrastructure of the nation was weak, at best. The nation dissolved into a patchwork of confederated states desperately struggling for social, economic and political stability. Meanwhile the nations of Eastern Europe experienced a similar economic and political collapse and began a long-term rebuilding process.
- Magic Johnson, a major sports star and the epitome of health and the good life, contracted the HIV virus. In the wake of his heavily publicized and swift retirement from the game he had mastered, Johnson exchanged his basketball uniform for the suits he now wears as a spokesman about AIDS and an advocate for "safe sex."
- George Bush's denials notwithstanding, the American economy went into a tailspin. Unemployment hit record levels for the past decade, consumer confidence plummeted, and even Bush ultimately had to admit we were immersed in a full-out recession. High profile but unsuccessful attempts at muscling Japan into changing their trade policies led to nationwide instances of Japan bashing, which only served to draw greater attention to the sagging economy.

These major shifts in our world challenged several of the values we hold dearest. Family and health were threatened by the deadly AIDS disease, now afflicting heterosexuals as well as homosexuals. The decline of Eastern Europe and Russia, and the tense moments preceding the attack on Iraq, served to challenge the world stability that had previously allowed us to focus on backyard issues. Our recession has reminded us that a comfortable life-style is not constitutionally guaranteed.

In the face of these transitions, many people are turning to old standbys for solace and insight. Family is certainly one source of such support. Religion and the Bible are among the elements from which many people are seeking comfort and wisdom.

How long will this openness to the value of religion and the helpfulness of the Bible last? If past behavior is any indication (and it is usually the most reliable indicator of future behavior), this attentiveness will last as long as people receive practical value from the religious world. Once adults sense that their time and energy are being wasted or are not sufficiently productive, they will move on to the next source of high potential value.

The research uncovered another important body of insights related to values. Although there were significant increases in the perceived importance of several aspects of life, each generation studied displayed a different emphasis in the reorganized ranking of priorities in life. The data in the accompanying table demonstrate the following patterns:

- The priorities that received the largest increases in perceived importance among baby busters were time, religion and living comfortably.
- The priorities experiencing the greatest jump in importance among baby boomers were time, the Bible and friends.
- Among the pre-boomers, friends, religion, the Bible and money were the aspects to receive substantially higher ratings of importance this year than last year.
- Senior citizens focused on the tangible quality of life issues. Seniors committed the greatest increase in importance to living comfortably, money and their career.

Notice yet another pattern. For boomers and pre-boomers, not a single aspect was deemed less important than was true in 1991. Both population segments assigned equal or higher value to every one of the 10 aspects assessed in both years. This may be evidence of a pair of generations who are not so much struggling with a restructuring of their basic values, as much as they are fearful of having anything deemed important or valuable to them taken away or diminished in importance by their circumstances.

The Percentage-point Change in the Proportion of Selected People Groups Who Said a Life Aspect Was Very Important, from 1991 to 1992

Aspect of life	Busters	Boomers	46-64	65 or older
family	—	+2	+2	+3
health	-3	+3	+5	+3
your time	+11	+8	+1	-8
your friends	-7	+9	+14	-2
religion	+12	+8	+13	-1
the Bible	+8	+10	+17	-2
your free time	-2	+5	—	-8
living comfortably	+10	+11	+9	+16
your career	-3	—	+9	+8
money	-3	+5	+14	+18
respondents	171	402	254	157

JOURNEY TO THE CENTER OF THE MIND

In the midst of this time of transition and exploration, many church leaders are criticizing the public for the apparent bankruptcy of people's morals, ethics and convictions. Understanding the morals and ethics of adults and the convictions that lead to these stands is no simple task. The research does provide some clues, though, as to how Americans think.

Moral behavior. Although almost two-thirds of the population disagree that "lying is sometimes necessary," 36% agree with this notion. Amazingly, over half of the baby busters (51%) agree that lying is sometimes necessary. Other groups more likely than average to assent were Hispanics (47%), adults who had never been married (49%), suburbanites (42%), residents of the Northeast (44%) and Pacific states (45%), non-Christians (42%), Catholics (44%), Lutherans (48%), and adults who had not read the Bible in the past week (45%). (See data tables 69.)

Another insight into the moral character of Americans relates to views on abortion. The majority of the nation's adults (57%) agreed that "abortion is morally wrong." This stance was more likely among

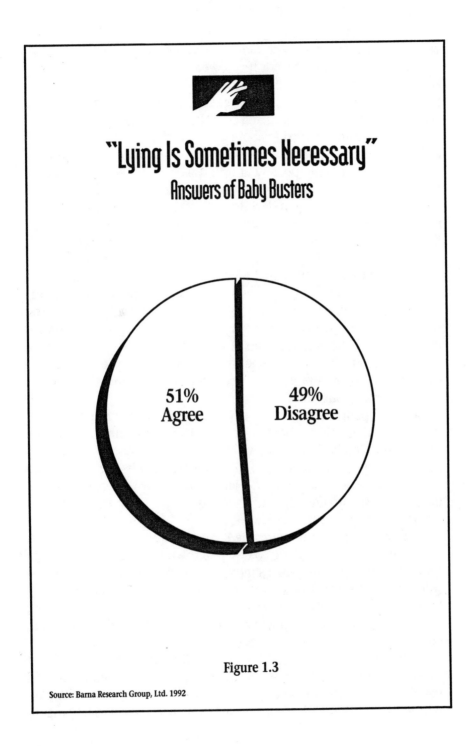

"Lying Is Sometimes Necessary"
Answers of Baby Busters

51%
Agree

49%
Disagree

Figure 1.3

Source: Barna Research Group, Ltd. 1992

women than men. It was also most prolific among adults with less formal education, married adults, lower-income adults, blue-collar employees, people living in rural areas and in the South, among people not registered to vote, born-again Christians, and people who attend charismatic or Pentecostal churches. (See data table 68.)

What is most remarkable about this belief is it apparently fails to influence people's response to the widespread practice of abortion. Although most people portray abortion as a moral error, they allow that it is a person's right to commit such a moral offense. The abortion issue would not be a key in deciding who should lead the policy-making and government of America. Most Americans make a clear distinction between how they would handle the abortion issue in their own lives and how they believe others should handle the issue.

Consider two possible conclusions we can draw from the abortion situation. First, most adults believe it would be improper to enact legislation and policies based on a defined notion of morality. The expression "you cannot legislate morality" is likely an accepted creed for most people. Unfortunately, this is superficial thinking since all laws and policies are based on some underlying moral system. The real question is which moral code is serving as the foundation for the development of our rules.

Second, people's views on abortion and other "moral issues" describe a population whose rejection of absolute truth and acceptance of moral relativism has resulted in a political system plagued by inconsistency and confusion. Is it feasible that adults are straining to make sense of our laws and life-styles because our leaders have abandoned the worldview that formerly directed their thoughts and actions?

Success. Americans remain glued to the notion of visible success. A minority of them are willing to describe the pursuit of money as very important in their lives, but a slight majority maintain that money "is still the main symbol of success in life" (52% agree, 47% disagree). Money is seen in this light by an above-average proportion of men, ethnic minorities, singles, downscale adults, Southerners, Baptists, and charismatics and Pentecostals. (See data table 72.)

In the same vein, 6 out of 10 adults believe they have to look out for number one. Fifty-nine percent concurred with the statement, "If you don't look out for your own best interests, you can be sure that no one else will, either." The people groups who showed a special propen-

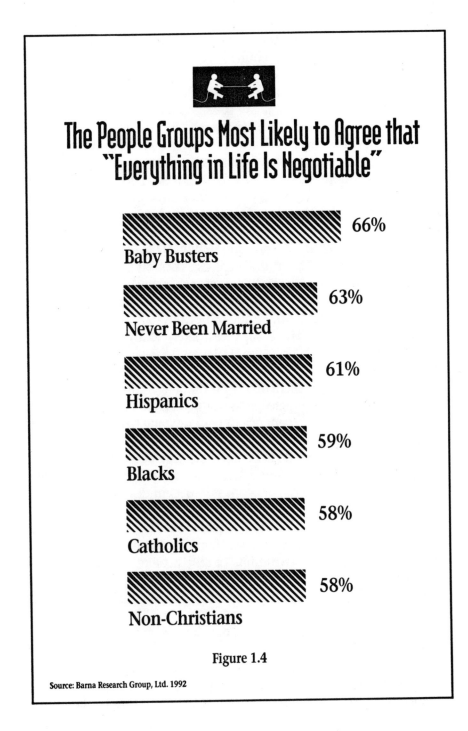

The People Groups Most Likely to Agree that "Everything in Life Is Negotiable"

Baby Busters	66%
Never Been Married	63%
Hispanics	61%
Blacks	59%
Catholics	58%
Non-Christians	58%

Figure 1.4

Source: Barna Research Group, Ltd. 1992

sity to support this perspective were ethnic minorities, non-Christians, people who do not attend church, and those who do not read the Bible. (See data table 45.)

Why then are there poor people? Relatively few adults (19%) admitted they believe people are poor because of laziness. Of special interest was the finding that blacks were twice as likely as other adults to strongly ascribe poverty to laziness, but were also considerably more likely than others to strongly reject that sentiment. In other words, most blacks had intense opinions about poverty perhaps because it is such a core issue among blacks. (See data table 43.)

Perspective. Last year our research showed that most people dismissed the notion of the existence of absolute truth. This year's research shows that half of the adult public (50%) believe "everything in life is negotiable." This attitude coexists comfortably with the rejection of absolute truth. The people groups that most ardently supported the negotiability of all matters included the baby busters (66% agreed with the statement), ethnic minorities (60%) and never-been-married adults (63%). The groups least likely to accept this thinking were the elderly (37%), Christians (39%) and Bible readers (39%). (See data table 42.)

The self-centered, experiential view of life was further supported: 6 out of 10 adults (60%) agreed, "Nothing can be known for certain except the things you experience in your own life." Baby busters were especially prone to this view (71%), along with blacks (75%), and people who attend charismatic or Pentecostal churches (68%). The people groups most likely to challenge such thinking were college graduates (54% disagreed), white-collar workers (50%) and Methodists (46%). (See data table 70.)

Control. The issue of control remains a critical consideration for most Americans today. Beside the widespread desire to possess control over life circumstances, two-thirds of all adults believe "the world is out of control these days" (64%). This perceived loss or lack of control has made the enjoyment of life even tougher for millions of adults. (See data table 44.)

Those who were particularly likely to view the world as running amuck were baby busters and senior citizens (69%), people with a high school or less advanced education (71%), blacks (79%), women (71%), and people from low-income households (71%). Notice that these are the people commonly deemed to be "disenfranchised"—i.e.

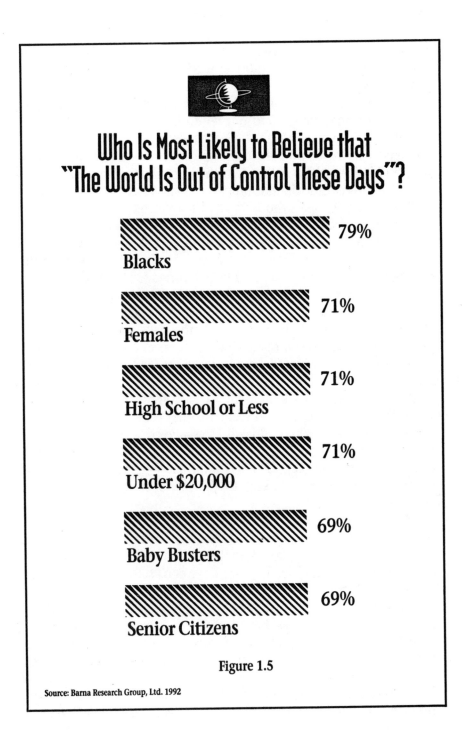

Who Is Most Likely to Believe that "The World Is Out of Control These Days"?

Blacks — 79%

Females — 71%

High School or Less — 71%

Under $20,000 — 71%

Baby Busters — 69%

Senior Citizens — 69%

Figure 1.5

Source: Barna Research Group, Ltd. 1992

people who are typically isolated from the societal decision-making process and who have the most limited access to political and economic power.

Despite the concern that things are constantly changing, are unpredictable, and may be beyond our control, almost three out of four Americans (72%) maintain the belief that "one person can really make a difference in the world these days." Perhaps one person cannot actually *control* the world, but we retain the hope that our best efforts can at least *influence* some dimension of our reality. (See data table 71.)

The types of people who were most convinced of the potential to impact the world were college graduates (80%), upper-income adults (81%) and Baptists (81%). The people who held the least hope of a person impacting the world were baby busters (33% disagreed with the statement), adults who had never been married (32%), Midwesterners (31%), Catholics (30%), and charismatics and Pentecostals (31%).

A different slant on views about the world regards perceptions of leadership capabilities. Long gone are the days when most people assumed a "leader" was a man. Three-quarters of all adults (76%) disagreed with the statement "men are better leaders than women." Although men found it a harder concept to swallow, even a majority of them dismissed the statement (69% compared to 82% among women). The only population segments that were close to embracing this sentiment were senior citizens (35% agreed with the statement). For some people, though, the prospect of women assuming key leadership positions may represent yet another element of stability and control that has been shattered by the march of time and progress. (See data table 41.)

Music. For many adults, the popular music of the day is one of the thorns that sticks in their sides. Through the years, from Elvis to the Beatles to Jimi Hendrix through to the current megastars such as Guns N' Roses, Skid Row and Ice T, adults have consistently questioned the value and values represented by the chart-topping musical acts.

Attitudes in 1992 are no different. A majority of adults (52%) agreed that "today's popular music has a negative influence on most people." Women, the elderly, blacks, Southerners, born-again Christians, Baptists, charismatics and Pentecostals, church attenders, and Bible readers were most likely to espouse this view. The groups most likely to reject the perspective were baby busters (62%), adults who had never been married (58%) and upper-income adults (57%). (See data table 66.)

Not only is the prevailing mood about today's sounds negative, but so is the view of the accompanying visuals. The majority (56%) rejected the notion that the "values and life-styles shown in music videos generally reflect the ways most people think and live these days." No segment of the population believed this statement to be accurate, although blacks, Hispanics, low-income adults, charismatics and Pentecostals, and people not registered to vote came close (all exceeded 40% in agreement with the statement). (See data table 67.)

ACTION STEPS

Strategically, leaders know that the most effective approach to achieve one's goals is to capitalize on areas of strength and operate around areas of weakness. For the Church, in this time of flux and confusion, how might we make the most of the myriad opportunities that surround us?

Follow the heart. Today, adults are focused on matters such as family and health. What is your church doing to encourage strong family systems? Other research we have conducted indicates that churches talk a better game of family ministry than they deliver.

Scrutinize the teaching, the programs and the alternatives you are offering to people who are interested in enhancing their family situations. Model the desired behaviors. Provide training that prepares people for the difficult situations they will encounter as parents, as siblings, as grandparents. Offer chances for families to engage in family activities: not activities *about* the family, but activities in which entire families interact in significant ways.

Respect people's time. Time remains a central issue in the lives of most young and middle-aged adults. If you wish to retain the allegiance of these people, design your ministry in ways that respect their precious time. Meetings that run long, programs that start late and services that meander are signals to adults that their time is not deemed important by the Church. Many adults will respond by shifting their attention and resources elsewhere.

Encourage relationships. Most churches claim they are "friendly." But that may not be enough these days. In a culture where time is always lacking and communication skills are minimal, people may not even know how to go about establishing meaningful relationships

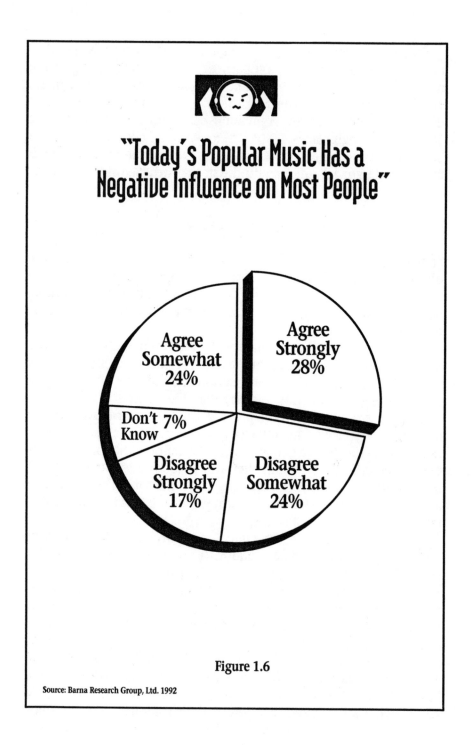

"Today's Popular Music Has a Negative Influence on Most People"

Agree Somewhat 24%

Agree Strongly 28%

Don't Know 7%

Disagree Strongly 17%

Disagree Somewhat 24%

Figure 1.6

Source: Barna Research Group, Ltd. 1992

with friendly people. The Church has the chance to establish community by offering outlets that create and nurture real relationships. Small group systems, social events, relational teaching and modeling relational development are effective methods of providing adults with both the emotional and tangible security they are searching for through relational means.

Use the Bible. Americans are ready to embrace the Bible as a valuable resource, if you can prove to them that it contains true wisdom and insight. They are not interested in theology for its own sake. They are interested in practical answers to tough questions about the meaning of life, the best strategies for achieving success in life and how to experience the best that God has to offer on earth. Assume that people have been exposed to the Bible but have little understanding of its contents, how to read it, how to study it and how to apply it. Provide them with bite-size pieces of truth and value and they will continue to explore His Word.

This is especially critical in a period when people are rewriting the rules of morality and ethics due to a philosophic void. Americans accept deceit and legalized immorality as viable alternatives because they lack a worldview that persuasively explains why they should not. If we can demonstrate that the Bible is more than just a historical document, or a book of religious do's and don'ts, our culture could be radically transformed for the better.

Experience God's presence. Americans want the real thing. They prefer to experience a condition than to hear about that condition. In the same way, the Church has missed the mark with millions of seekers because these spiritual pilgrims were subjected to teaching *about God* instead of an experience *with God.* Many have sought to understand the Bible but emerged with information about the Bible. Countless Americans have rejected Christianity because they wanted to grow in spirituality but were taught about spirituality.

Study the spiritual life cycle and development process of people. Create a path for spiritual challenge and growth that will take people from their current state to a more advanced state of insight and experience. Encourage personal encounters with God through prayer, through worship, through understanding who He really is as explained in Scripture. Help every person you encounter have a "breakthrough" experience with God by personalizing ministry to meet their needs in light of God's provision and reality.

Exploit people's hope. Considering our current world circumstances, it is incredible that most Americans believe any person can make a difference in the world. We remain a people of hope. The Church can build on that hope by more effectively giving a solid reason for the hope that sustains us. Identify viable goals for ministry and assist people in the quest to reach those goals, through God's blessing and the power of the Holy Spirit. People want their lives to count for something significant. Through your ministry, enable them to make that goal a reality.

DIMENSIONS OF OUR FAITH

CHAPTER HIGHLIGHTS

- Three-quarters of all adults believed that the Bible is God's written Word and is totally accurate in all it teaches.
- A large majority believed that the Ten Commandments are relevant to today's world.
- Three out of four adults disagreed that sin is an outdated concept.
- A small amount of adults rejected the notion that good people will live in heaven even if they have not accepted Christ as their Savior. In total, 4 out of 10 adults believed leading a good life can earn them a place in heaven, apart from a relationship with Christ.
- Two-thirds of American adults agreed that the Christian faith has all the answers to how to lead a successful life.
- Most people believed that prayer has the power to change people's life circumstances.
- There was widespread confusion whether church attendance is a biblical mandate.
- Few people believed that astrology and horoscopes are accurate predictors of the future.

WHAT WE DISCOVERED

The Bible is clear in stating that people are saved by the grace of God, not by their own efforts to achieve righteousness. The key to our salvation, then, is the nature of our faith: in whom we put our faith, and the intensity of that belief.

In studying the spiritual perspectives of Americans, confusing or contradictory findings sometimes emerge. Although millions of Americans can describe or affirm various religious beliefs, they do not take these perspectives so seriously as to integrate them into the fabric of their lives. Consequently, their beliefs change with surprising frequency.

Most Americans have little depth to their religious reflections. Many people are able to parrot a few religious themes they learned when they were young, and some have added new concepts to that religious vocabulary based on a variety of personal revelations and trials experienced as adults. The average American, though, is neither a deep theological thinker nor worries about the importance of developing life-shaping religious convictions.

The Role of the Bible

Most Americans own at least one Bible. Relatively few read it. Yet, the vast majority of Americans state that the Bible is "the written Word of God and is totally accurate in all that it teaches." Overall, 56% of all adults strongly agree with this perspective, and an additional 18% agree somewhat. That represents three out of four adults who agree with this viewpoint. (See data table 73.)

Not every people group held similar views on the matter, though. For instance, although nearly two-thirds of adult women strongly agreed with the statement (64%), less than half of America's men concurred (48%). Age was also related to views on the Bible: the older a person was, the more likely they were to strongly agree that the Bible is God's Word and is totally accurate. Forty-four percent of the baby busters said this, half of the boomers did (52%), two-thirds of the 46- to 64-year-olds strongly agreed (63%), and three out of four senior citizens expressed the same view (75%).

Education seems to be a barrier to people believing in the Bible. Among people with a high school or less education, 67% strongly agreed with the statement. Half of the adults who attended but did not

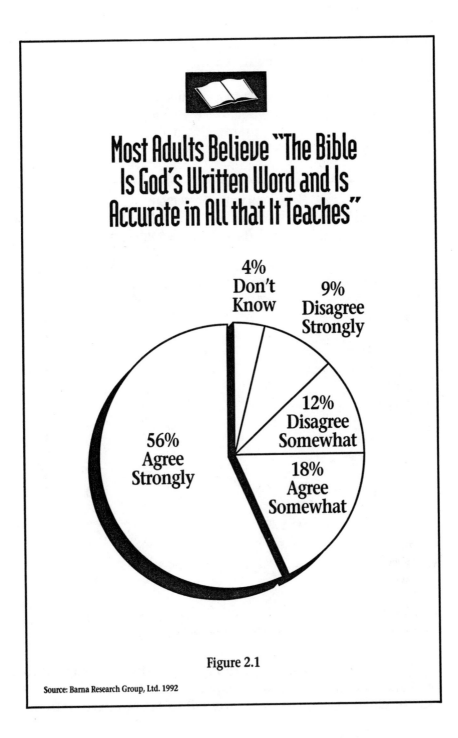

Most Adults Believe "The Bible Is God's Written Word and Is Accurate in All that It Teaches"

4%
Don't
Know

9%
Disagree
Strongly

12%
Disagree
Somewhat

56%
Agree
Strongly

18%
Agree
Somewhat

Figure 2.1

Source: Barna Research Group, Ltd. 1992

graduate from college concurred (48%). But just one-quarter of the college graduates (28%) strongly agreed. In fact, nearly half of the college graduates (46%) disagreed with the statement.

Because educational achievement and household income are closely related, it is not surprising that the higher a person's income level was, the less likely they were to strongly agree with the validity of the Bible's source and teaching.

Reactions to the Statement:
"The Bible is the written Word of God and is totally accurate in all that it teaches." (Base: 1,013 Respondents)

People Group	Agree		Disagree		Don't
	Strongly	Somewhat	Somewhat	Strongly	Know
all adults	56%	18%	12%	9%	4%
men	48	20	14	12	6
women	64	17	11	6	2
baby busters	44	21	16	11	8
baby boomers	52	21	15	10	3
46-64 years old	63	17	6	9	3
senior citizens	75	7	9	4	4
high school or less	67	17	8	5	4
some college	48	22	16	8	6
college graduate	28	22	24	22	5
Northeast	43	24	17	11	5
Midwest	50	24	13	10	4
South	74	8	8	5	5
Mountain	45	14	8	23	9
Pacific	49	26	16	8	0
married	60	17	12	8	3
never married	43	21	16	13	7
divorced	52	28	9	8	3
widowed	76	10	8	3	3

Marital status was also related to views on the Bible. Note that married and widowed people were considerably more likely than single adults (either never married or divorced) to strongly agree with the statement about the Bible. Singles who had never been married had the least favorable view of the Bible.

Interestingly, geographic location was also strongly associated with views on Scripture. Only half of the residents of urban and suburban communities strongly affirmed the statement. Two-thirds of the people living in rural settings strongly agreed. Regionally, three-quarters of the adults in the South strongly agreed, compared to half of the residents of the Midwest and Pacific states. Belief in the Bible was lowest in the Northeast and Mountain areas.

Eight out of ten born-again Christians (80%) affirmed the statement strongly, which was twice the level among non-Christians (40%). Denominationally, there were major distinctions. The charge was led by those attending charismatic or Pentecostal churches, 88% of whom strongly agreed with the statement, and by Baptists (79%). Yet, fewer than half of those who attend Catholic (46%) and Lutheran (44%) churches strongly agreed, and exactly half of the Methodists lodged such affirmation.

As you might expect, people who had read the Bible in the past week were twice as likely as those who had not done so to strongly agree with the statement (77% versus 38%, respectively). In total, one-third of those who did not read from the pages of Scripture in the past week actually disagreed with the statement. Perhaps most amazingly, 1 out of every 12 people who had read the Bible in the prior 7 day period also disagreed with the statement. (See data table 49.)

Overall, most adults believe the Bible is just what the Church claims it to be: the authoritative Word of God, reliable and accurate as a guide for life. Most people choose not to read it for reasons other than doubts about its authenticity or accuracy.

The statistics also raise some questions about what types of teaching from and about the Bible people receive in some of the "Christian" churches in this nation. For a majority of people attending Catholic, Lutheran and Methodist churches (among others) to disavow the validity of the statement calls into question the meaning of the term "Christian" as well as the basis of the person's faith.

The Ten Commandments

As Americans continue their prolonged search for meaning and purpose in life, the survey revealed an interesting insight. Most people believe that the ancient biblical standard for holy living, the Ten Commandments, is still relevant for people today. Overall, just one out of five adults (18%) agreed that "the Ten Commandments are *not* relevant for people living today." The remaining respondents either disagreed somewhat (15%), disagreed strongly (64%), or were not sure (3%). (See data table 77.)

Perhaps you would expect to find that baby busters, the youngest adults, were most likely to doubt the value of the commandments. But did you expect senior citizens to be nearly as likely to hold that same view? Although 29% of the busters agreed with the statement posed, 23% of the seniors concurred. In fact, the largest proportion of adults to strongly agree with this negative sentiment was among the elderly (17%)!

Other population groups that were well above average in their penchant for agreeing with this statement were people with the lowest levels of education: blacks, adults who had never been married (the highest of all, 30%), low-income adults, residents of the Midwest and non-Christians.

Once again, it is surprising to find that more than one out of every seven people who had read the Bible in the past week (15%) agreed with a statement suggesting that such a key portion of God's Word is not pertinent to today's people. (See data table 49.)

Is Sin for Real?

Sometimes you may observe Americans' behavior and conclude that people dismiss the notion of sin altogether. Conceptually, though, most people disagreed with the statement, "the whole idea of sin is outdated." In total, 57% strongly disagreed with the statement, and another 19% disagreed somewhat. That's three out of four adults. Ten percent agreed somewhat with the sentiment, another 10% agreed strongly, and 6% did not know what to think. (See data table 78.)

The demographics of respondents who agreed that sin is an outdated notion break with some of the expectations. Baby boomers, the generation of adults renowned for their self-centered, selfish, no-rules behavior, were the *least* likely to agree that sin is an outdated concept. Hispanics were three times more likely than any other ethnic group to strongly agree that sin is outdated. Catholics, who attend a church that teaches the importance of works in earning salvation, were nearly twice as likely as Protestants to agree that the concept of sin is antiquated.

At the same time, there were some expected response patterns.

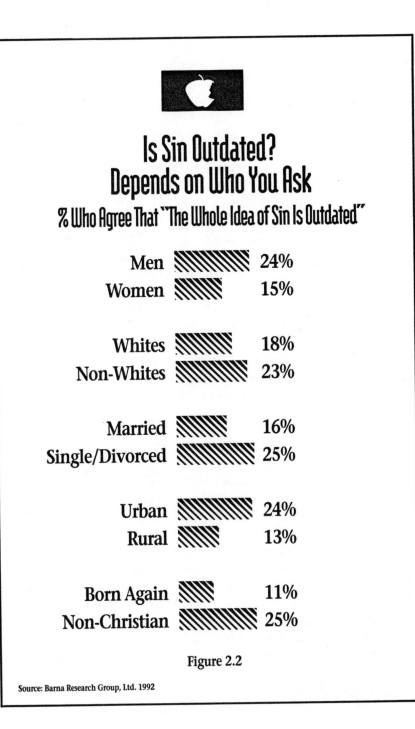

Is Sin Outdated?
Depends on Who You Ask
% Who Agree That "The Whole Idea of Sin Is Outdated"

Men		24%
Women		15%
Whites		18%
Non-Whites		23%
Married		16%
Single/Divorced		25%
Urban		24%
Rural		13%
Born Again		11%
Non-Christian		25%

Figure 2.2

Source: Barna Research Group, Ltd. 1992

Men were much more likely than women to concur that sin is an outdated notion. Single adults were three times more likely than married adults to strongly agree with the statement. Agreement was more common among the wealthiest than among those who are at the lower end of the income scale. People residing in rural areas were only about half as likely to view sin as outdated as were people in more densely populated communities.

About 1 out of 10 born-again Christians agreed that sin is outdated (11%). Although this is substantially less than was true among non-Christians (25%), it represents a significant proportion of believers.

Last year's study discovered that the vast majority of Americans do not believe in absolute truth. If you combine that insight with the prevailing perceptions about sin, you might conclude that although Americans believe in the idea of sin, they reject the notion of an absolute definition of sin. Thus, an act that is a sin in my eyes may not be something you would consider sinful. To most adults, this conflict in perspective is perfectly permissible. When all truth is deemed relative, so is the evaluation of our actions.

This is especially important to understand considering such a large percentage of the non-Christian population (25%) agreed with the statement that sin is an idea whose time has passed.

The Significance of Jesus Christ

In general, research indicates that Americans increasingly love the easy way out. In our fast-paced, stress-filled culture, we are more likely to consider it foolish than virtuous for a person to ignore shortcuts in favor of pursuing a complete and authentic experience. Gone are the days when people embraced the work ethic, accepted the importance of sacrifice in life, and believed that it was better to be honest than rich.

In much the same way, many people's views about life after death reflect a penchant for the easy solution. Survey respondents were read the statement, "all good people, whether they consider Jesus Christ to be their Savior or not, will live in heaven after they die on earth." Two-fifths of the population agreed with that statement (25% strongly, 15% somewhat), and not quite half of the public disagreed (16% somewhat, 33% strongly). The other 11% did not have an opinion. (See data table 80.)

Demographically, the responses were consistent across almost all of the categories examined. One exception related to geography. People

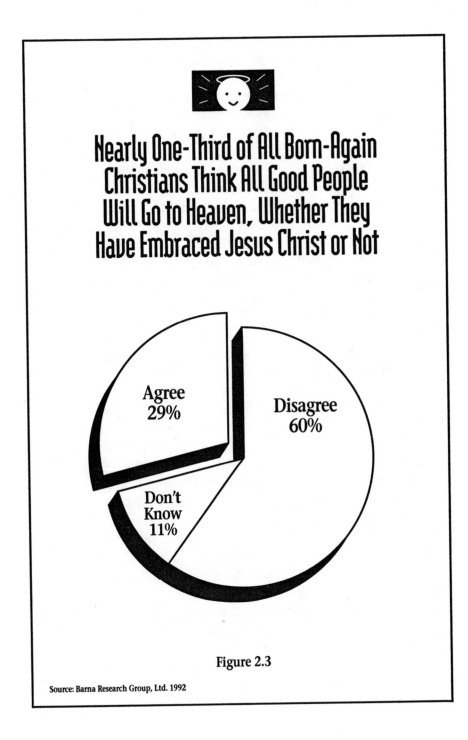

Nearly One-Third of All Born-Again Christians Think All Good People Will Go to Heaven, Whether They Have Embraced Jesus Christ or Not

Agree
29%

Disagree
60%

Don't
Know
11%

Figure 2.3

Source: Barna Research Group, Ltd. 1992

in the Northeast were most likely to agree with this statement (54%); those living in the South were least likely to accept this idea (32%). The other exception was party affiliation among registered voters. Those who were independent of a party attachment were substantially more likely to accept this viewpoint (57%) than were adults aligned with either the Democratic (35%) or Republican (36%) parties.

What may be most disheartening for church leaders is to discover that 3 out of 10 born-again Christians agree that all good people will go to heaven regardless of the nature of their relationship with Jesus Christ. This is notably less than the 48% among non-Christians, but it betrays a gross misunderstanding of what the Bible teaches regarding entrance into God's presence. Consider what may be happening evangelistically as these well-intentioned but misguided people share their views on faith and eternity with their uninformed, unsaved friends.

It is not possible to determine from this question how this perception influences people's views of their own salvation. Realize that it is possible to believe good people will live eternally without Christ, but their own salvation has been sealed by their relationship with Him. In other words, many people currently classified as born-again Christians, by nature of their personal faith in Christ, may concurrently believe that other people who live good lives, apart from a true relationship with and dependence upon Christ, will join them in heaven.

Sadly, the vast majority of Catholics (65%) agree with the good-behavior-opens-the-gates philosophy. A majority of Methodists believed this, too (51%). Even one-third of all Lutherans (35%) and one-quarter of all Baptists (26%) accepted this thinking.

Surprisingly little difference on this matter surfaced in the views of those who attend church services and those who do not. What is being taught in our churches about the nature of salvation? The importance of clear and accurate teaching on such a critical matter is underscored by the fact that one-third of those adults who read the Bible during the past week concluded that good people get to heaven, with or without Christ as their Savior. In other words, they may be reading the words on the pages of the Bible, but without someone to help them accurately interpret their meaning in context, they appear to be arriving at erroneous—and life-threatening—conclusions. (See data table 49.)

There Is Hope in Christianity

Fortunately, most American adults believed that "the Christian faith has all the answers to leading a successful life." Two-thirds of adults agreed with this viewpoint (41% strongly, 27% somewhat), 29% rejected it (17% somewhat, 12% strongly), and just 3% had no opinion. (See data table 74.)

The influence of self-sufficiency in the world is evident in these views. The higher a person's income and the more advanced their education, the less likely they were to agree with the statement. Other hard-to-convince segments of the population included singles who had never been married (56%) and residents of the Pacific states (57%).

A note of encouragement is found in the majority of non-Christians (55%) who agreed with the statement. A stumbling block may be the definition of success, but the figures suggest that millions of non-believers possess the attitude that Christianity has something of true value to offer.

The Power of Prayer

People believe that prayer has power. Seven out of ten adults disagreed with the statement, "people's prayers do not have the power to change their circumstances." Almost half of the people surveyed strongly disagreed (49%), and one-quarter disagreed somewhat (22%). Those who agreed were evenly divided between moderate (13%) and strong (12%) disagreement. (See data table 75.)

Who was least likely to strongly affirm the power of prayer? Men, baby busters, never married and divorced people, non-Christians, Catholics, Methodists, those who do not attend church, and those who do not read the Bible.

What Americans Believe 1991 found that the majority of Americans believe it does not matter to whom you pray; we are all praying to the same deity regardless of the name ascribed to that power. It is encouraging to see that most people believe in the power of prayer, but we must also discern to whom people are praying before we get truly excited about people's reliance upon prayer as an authentic spiritual resource.

Attending Church

There is much confusion about the importance of attending church services. A small amount of adults (47%) agreed that "the Bible does not command people to attend a church; that is a man-made requirement." Nearly as many (44%) disagreed, and 9% did not express an opinion on this statement. (See data table 79.)

The people groups most likely to agree that church attendance is not a biblical mandate were baby busters (59%), divorced people (59%), independents (60%), Catholics (61%), those who did not attend church in the past week (57%) and those who did not read the Bible in the preceding week (58%).

The people most likely to disagree with this statement were blacks (51%), adults from households earning under $20,000 (50%), blue-collar workers (52%), Southerners (50%), Republicans (50%), born-again Christians (58%), Lutherans (58%), people attending charismatic or Pentecostal churches (63%), those who had read the Bible in the prior week (57%) and those who had attended a church service within the last seven days (56%).

Reading the Stars

How entrenched in our life-styles are elements of the "new age" religious perspectives? Experts have widely divergent opinions on this matter, partly because it is difficult to identify exactly the details of the new age faith view. Most experts concur that part of the new age thinking is the ability to rely on spiritual forces, other than God, to guide or foretell the future through practices such as astrology and the use of horoscopes.

Relatively few American adults believe that "horoscopes and astrology usually provide an accurate prediction of the future." Just 2% strongly affirmed that statement, and 12% agreed somewhat. Most people either disagreed somewhat (20%) or disagreed strongly (62%). (See data table 76.)

Breaking with the expectation, not a single one of the baby busters we interviewed strongly agreed in the reliability of horoscopes, but 5% of the elderly did. And among the six denominational groups we were able to study, the group most likely to strongly agree with the statement was the group that was least expected to do so—Baptists (5%).

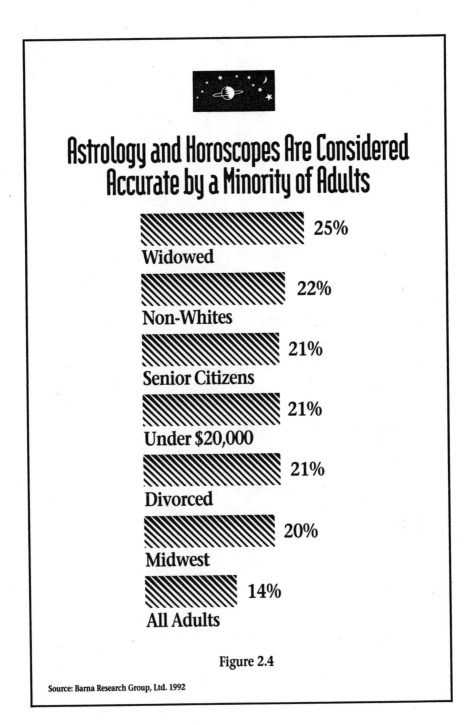

Astrology and Horoscopes Are Considered Accurate by a Minority of Adults

25%
Widowed

22%
Non-Whites

21%
Senior Citizens

21%
Under $20,000

21%
Divorced

20%
Midwest

14%
All Adults

Figure 2.4

Source: Barna Research Group, Ltd. 1992

PUTTING IT ALL TOGETHER

Not many adults would provide a firm answer to all eight of these statements that would reflect a consistent, orthodox Christian view of the world. In total, only 8% of the population gave a response to all eight statements that might be described as a consistently biblical perspective. Among those people, more than 9 out of 10 (93%) were born-again Christians. Overall, 17% of all the born-again Christians interviewed gave the orthodox view for all eight statements, compared to less than 1% among the non-Christians with whom we spoke.

Taking a Biblical Stand

Statement	Biblical View*	All Adults	Born Again? Yes	No
The Bible is the written Word of God and is totally accurate in all that it teaches.	agree	56%	80%	40%
The Ten Commandments are not relevant for people living today.	disagree	64%	77%	55%
The whole idea of sin is outdated.	disagree	57%	72%	46%
All good people, whether they consider Jesus Christ to be their Savior or not, will live in heaven after they die on earth.	disagree	32%	51%	21%
The Christian faith has all the answers to leading a successful life.	agree	41%	58%	30%
People's prayers do not have the power to change their circumstances.	disagree	49%	68%	36%
The Bible does not command people to attend a church; that is a man-made requirement.	agree	27%	41%	17%
Horoscopes and astrology usually provide an accurate prediction of the future.	disagree	65%	71%	56%
Biblical view on all eight statements		8%	17%	1%

*NOTE: All of these responses are assumed to be in the "strong" category of either agreement or disagreement with the statement.

ACTION STEPS

For Christians, some of these statistics provide alarming insights into the minds and hearts of the American people. Clearly, a large degree of misunderstanding exists about true Christianity. Those believers who are committed to championing the truth of the faith face a significant challenge.

What strategies might you embrace toward clarifying the truth of Christianity?

Clarify the role of the Bible. Intuitively, perhaps, people accept the Bible for what the Church claims it to be. In practical terms, though, relatively few people utilize it as the invaluable resource it is. If people accept it as an accurate source of insight and wisdom, why don't they turn to it for guidance more often?

Increasing numbers of Americans are functionally illiterate. This means that millions of adults cannot read certain versions of the Bible. Perhaps providing people with versions that are simpler to comprehend would encourage them to read it and take the admonitions to heart.

Fewer and fewer people leave our schools with adequate study skills. Giving people a Bible and asking them to decipher its meaning is, for millions of adults, like handing them a dictionary written in a foreign language. All the words are there, but they just don't seem to form a meaningful perspective. Help people navigate through the Bible, in much the same way Philip came alongside the Ethiopian official with study assistance and interpretation (Acts 8).

Provide people with a realistic perspective on the value of the Bible. Millions of adults presently think of Scripture as an oppressive rule book, the guidelines of how not to live and the penalties for bad behavior. Instead, open their eyes to the freedom described for living the Christian life. By portraying the Bible as a valuable resource rather than the dreaded rule book, more people might willingly pursue its wisdom.

Define truth. In an age where we tend to view ourselves as the place of truth and authenticity, the Church has a responsibility to teach a biblical view of truth. Indeed, for people who define sin as acts that offend them or do not meet their personal standards of goodness, we can help them see a more realistic view of the world by exploring the Bible with them. Since most people accept the Ten Commandments as valid and relevant, using that well-known but largely misunderstood section of the Bible as a launching pad for a discussion of truth and success might be productive.

Clarify the means to salvation. Forgive me for including this seemingly simple exhortation. Certainly, any Christian person or church would blanch at the thought of teaching that salvation by any means other than God's grace through Christ is plausible. Yet, when we see the numbers of church-going, confirmed church members who are relying on their own best efforts rather than Christ's work on the cross for their personal salvation, we must stop to reexamine what is happening.

Many Christian churches exhort their people to go to their friends and share their faith with those acquaintances. But what nature of faith are they sharing? The fact that so many people, believers included, adhere to the philosophy that "God will save all good people, regardless of their relationship with Christ" must cause us to assess the evangelistic notions being expounded in the world by the people whom we deem to be believers. As a Christian, and especially if you hold a position of leadership within the church, you have a serious responsibility to explore the nature of the evangelism that is taking place in our Lord's name.

Further, while witch hunts are unjustifiable, we must be wise regarding our assumptions about who truly understands the gospel. Many who call themselves Christians have no clue as to the truth about sin and salvation, about the Resurrection and redemption. Look beyond people's words to the spiritual fruit of their lives. Lovingly explore the depth of people's Christian understanding and commitment and accept the privilege of aiding them in growing more authentically and fully in His love and acceptance.

The benefits of faith. The Christian faith has many answers for people's daily struggles. Interestingly, most people agree that Christianity holds the keys to understanding success, yet so few truly pursue such wisdom.

In this benefit-driven society, can you help the people with whom you come in contact to grasp the benefits that Christianity has to offer? If commitment and diligence are necessary to grasp the deepest insights of the Christian faith, can you lead people to that faith in a way that makes it both accessible and life-changing?

THE IMAGE OF THE CHURCH

CHAPTER HIGHLIGHTS

- Of the four major Christian denominations whose images were evaluated, none were seen as "very favorable" by even one-third of the population.
- When people were asked how sensitive Protestant churches are to the needs of each of 15 different people groups, there was not one such group for which at least half of the respondents felt churches were very sensitive.
- Just three population groups stood out as segments to which churches were viewed as having a stronger-than-average ministry: families, young children and the elderly.
- Only 16% believed that Protestant churches are very sensitive to the needs of non-Christians. Sadly, although only 9% of the non-Christians claim that Protestant churches are very sensitive to their needs, three times as many Christians claim the churches meet the challenge (26%).
- For 11 of the 15 people groups researched, born-again Christians were at least twice as likely as non-Christians to believe that Christian churches are very sensitive to the needs of that people group.
- About half of all adults believed "most Christian churches provide meaningful opportunities for women to serve in areas of ministry in which they have special talents and abilities." One-third of adults (36%) did not believe such opportunities exist in most Christian congregations, and 15% were uncertain.

WHAT WE DISCOVERED

Many years ago the expression "image is reality" gained prominence. In our frenetic, information-laden culture, vague images of people, programs and organizations are often all that our judgments are based upon. As superficial as such images may be, they form the basis of numerous significant decisions and actions in our lives. For this reason, many people in leadership positions are very sensitive about the image their organizations have among the people they hope to reach.

Judging by the comparative image of the leading church denominations in America, the image of the Christian Body needs some serious enhancements. When compared with the image of other organizations, the perception of most adults regarding the leading denominations is far from enviable.

Unflattering Company

Overall, the survey examined people's impressions of 12 national organizations. Seven of those were religious organizations, two were political, one was a nonprofit charitable group, and two were for-profit businesses. As the figures in the accompanying chart show, there was a wide range of feelings about these organizations.

By far the most positive images were ascribed to the two organizations most closely associated with helping people in need: the American Cancer Society (63% very favorable image) and the Salvation Army (57% very favorable image). Besides having established themselves as organizations approved by the vast majority of Americans, they were also well-known to most people. Fewer than 1 out of every 10 adults failed to have an impression of either group. (See data tables 19,20.)

Although the Salvation Army is a religious denomination and has hundreds of churches across the nation, most people are unaware of those churches and instead perceive the Army to be a social-concern ministry.

After these two paragons of virtue, however, the next closest organization tested had just half as many adults who held a "very favorable" impression. Twenty-nine percent of the adults interviewed said they had a very favorable impression of the Baptist Church, the highest ranking achieved by any of the major denominations evaluated. (See data table 11.)

The Baptist Church was trailed by a series of organizations that

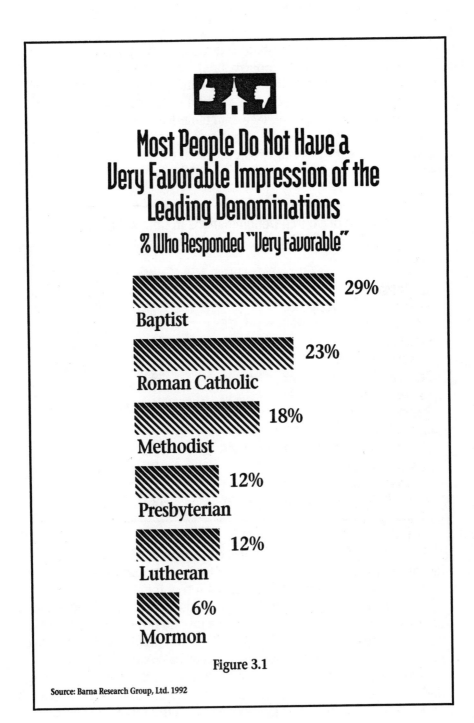

Most People Do Not Have a Very Favorable Impression of the Leading Denominations

% Who Responded "Very Favorable"

29% Baptist

23% Roman Catholic

18% Methodist

12% Presbyterian

12% Lutheran

6% Mormon

Figure 3.1

Source: Barna Research Group, Ltd. 1992

received virtually indistinguishable ratings from the public. These entities included the Roman Catholic Church (23% very favorable image), the Democratic Party (also 23%), the Ford Motor Company (20%), the Republican Party (20%), the Methodist Church (18%) and the Chrysler Corporation (16%). (See data table 13-18.)

Bringing up the rear in the image standings were the Presbyterian Church (12% very favorable), the Lutheran Church (12%) and the Mormon Church (6%). (See data tables 10,12,21.)

Images of Church Denominations in Comparison to Other Major Organizations (Base: 1,060 adults)

Organization	—Favorable—		—Unfavorable—		Don't Know
	Very	Somewhat	Somewhat	Very	
American Cancer Society	63%	27%	1%	2%	7%
Salvation Army	57	35	2	1	5
Baptist Church	29	36	10	5	20
Roman Catholic Church	23	36	16	7	18
Democratic Party	23	39	19	19	9
Ford Motor Company	20	46	11	6	18
Republican Party	20	38	18	14	10
Methodist Church	18	42	8	4	29
Chrysler Corporation	16	44	9	5	25
Presbyterian Church	12	38	8	4	38
Lutheran Church	12	35	8	5	40
Mormon Church	6	21	18	19	35

Notice the considerable proportions of people who indicated they did not know enough about some of these organizations—primarily the religious groups—to have an impression of them. Such a high percentage of "don't know" response often indicates that even those people who offered an opinion of such an entity do not hold that opinion with much intensity. In other words, their judgment could be swayed rather easily, either to the positive or negative side of the ledger.

If the proportions are calculated solely among those people who had an impression of each of these organizations, the picture that emerges is a bit different. (They are shown in the following chart.)

Images of Church Denominations in Comparison to Other Major Organizations, Among Adults Who Had a Substantive Impression of the Organization

	—Favorable—		—Unfavorable—		
Organization	Very	Somewhat	Somewhat	Very	Base
American Cancer Society	68%	29%	1%	2%	986
Salvation Army	60	37	2	1	1,007
Baptist Church	36	45	13	6	848
Roman Catholic Church	28	44	20	8	869
Democratic Party	25	43	21	11	965
Methodist Church	25	59	11	6	753
Ford Motor Company	24	56	13	7	869
Republican Party	22	42	20	16	954
Chrysler Corporation	21	59	12	7	795
Lutheran Church	20	58	13	8	636
Presbyterian Church	19	61	13	6	658
Mormon Church	9	33	28	29	689

Although the percentages of positive impressions increase a bit through such recalculations, notice that even when the figures are revised the ranking remains virtually the same and the aggregate percentages of adults who have very favorable impressions of the major denominations changes only a little.

A Variety of Images

The data identify those segments of the population who maintain the most and least favorable views of these groups. By denomination, consider who has the most intensely-held perspectives about that group.

Presbyterian Church. The most favorable outlook was held by senior citizens (29% very favorable) and widowed adults (28%). Hispanics were nearly three times more likely than others to have a very unfavorable view of Presbyterian churches (11%). (See data table 10.)

Baptist Church. Positive perceptions were most common among the senior citizens (40%), blacks (68%), widowed adults (46%), people from households earning under $20,000 (40%), residents of the South (45%), born-again Christians (46%) and Bible readers (43%). The least favorable impressions were maintained by Hispanics (14%). (See data table 11.)

Lutheran Church. The most favorable views were found among residents of the Midwest (21%); the least positive image was held by blacks (14%). (See data table 12.)

Methodist Church. Women were twice as likely as men to have a very favorable impression of Methodist churches. The elderly were twice as likely as all other adults to hold such a favorable view. No population segments seemed especially hostile toward the Methodist church. (See data table 13.)

Roman Catholic Church. This church was most appreciated by Hispanics (55%) and least favored by blacks (12%). (See data table 14.)

Mormon Church. The only non-Christian denomination evaluated reaped its greatest support from among divorced adults (10%). It was least favored by upper-income adults (27% very unfavorable), born-again Christians (28%) and Bible readers (27%). (See data table 15.)

Sensitivity to Needs

Research has shown that one of the keys to an effective ministry is to understand and effectively address people's felt needs. Surprisingly few Christian churches consciously and consistently minister in light of knowledge about people's needs. Those that do are frequently among the fastest-growing and most studied churches in an area.

Contemporary Americans are attracted to churches that clearly communicate a passion for helping people cope with life by providing realistic, practical solutions. Although many church leaders believe that churches are doing a good job at addressing people's needs, the research indicates that most adults are considerably less impressed with the efforts of Protestant churches.

When asked to rate how sensitive Protestant churches are, as a group, in addressing the real needs of each of 15 different people groups, the results are revealing. As you examine the figures in the accompanying table, you may notice these realities:

- Of the 15 people groups evaluated, there was not a single group for which at least half of the respondents claimed that Christian churches are very sensitive to their needs.
- An average of more than one-third of all adults had no idea whether or not churches are sensitive to the needs of such peo-

The Image of Denominations
Varies by the Faith Commitment of Adults
% Who Responded "Very Favorable"

Mormon
- 5%
- 7%

Lutheran
- 16%
- 9%

Presbyterian
- 16%
- 9%

Methodist
- 25%
- 14%

Catholic
- 20%
- 25%

Baptist
- 46%
- 18%

Figure 3.2

Born-Again Christians
Non-Christians

Source: Barna Research Group, Ltd. 1992

ple groups. For some respondents this was because they were not acquainted with the work of Protestant churches (i.e. they were Catholic, non-Christian, or unchurched). For a substantial number of others, however, their inability to judge was because they did not view Protestant churches in light of caring about the specific needs of various people groups. Their experience was characterized by the remark, "A church does what a church does; it doesn't matter who attends the church or what their needs are, the church just does what it has always done."

- Very few people claimed that churches were "not at all sensitive" to people's needs. However, many people have a difficult time describing specific ways churches demonstrate their sensitivity to the unique needs of a given audience.
- Just three population groups stood out as segments to which churches are seen as having a stronger-than-average ministry: families, young children and the elderly.

How Sensitive Do People Perceive Protestant Churches to Be to the Needs of People Groups? (Base: 1,060 adults)

	How sensitive to the group's needs?				
People Group	Very	Somewhat	Not too	Not at all	Don't know
families	46%	23%	2%	1%	28%
the elderly	39	26	4	2	28
children under 13	37	25	5	3	30
the poor	28	32	9	3	29
teenagers	28	31	9	4	29
women 35 or older	22	38	5	2	34
men 35 or older	19	36	7	2	35
women under 35	17	39	7	3	34
single parents	17	37	10	3	33
single adults	16	36	12	3	32
non-Christians	16	31	13	7	33
blacks	14	35	10	3	38
men under 35	12	38	9	4	36
Hispanics	12	30	11	4	43
Asians	10	29	11	4	45

In most instances, our assumptions about the sensitivity of Protestant churches to the needs of specific people groups appear to be on the mark. When we compare the sensitivity levels accorded to churches by all adults with those awarded by people within the people group in question, in all but four cases there were no significant differences.

In three cases the data showed that people were apt to assume Protestant churches are less sensitive to a particular group's needs than was reported by the people from that group. For instance, only 14% said that Protestant churches are very sensitive to the needs of black adults. However, more than twice as many blacks (31%) said they perceive these churches to be very sensitive to their needs. Similarly, churches apparently are more sensitive to the needs of older women and Hispanics than most people imagined. (See data tables 26,30,31.)

White respondents were substantially more likely to express the view that Christian churches are not sensitive to the needs of ethnic groups than was perceived to be the case by the people from those ethnic populations. This is probably because most white Americans attend churches dominated by whites. Given this as their frame of reference, they may think about the ethnic minorities who attend their church and conclude the needs of ethnic minorities are not met as effectively as if those people attended a church that focused on that ethnic group.

Many whites are unaware that the majority of ethnic minorities attend churches dominated by people from their own ethnic background. The awareness of the inability of a white church to minister sensitively to people of different backgrounds, though, may be cause for consideration of the value of gaining interaction between churches of different racial and ethnic dominance.

Misreading the Situation

One of the more disappointing and challenging findings is how few people (16%) believe Protestant churches to be sensitive to the needs of non-Christians. Worse, *an even smaller proportion of the non-Christians themselves claim that Protestant churches are very sensitive to their needs (9%)*. In a world in which Christians are called to be the change agents influencing the lives of people who do not know Jesus Christ personally, little can be more heart-piercing than to learn that our target audience does not perceive us to be in touch with their needs. (See data table 36.)

Part of the difficulty is that *Christians are more comfortable with their level of sensitivity to nonbelievers than reality justifies.* Only 9% of the non-Christians claim that Protestant churches are very sensitive to their needs; three times as many Christians claim the churches meet the challenge (26%).

A closer study of the findings shows that for 11 of the 15 people groups researched, born-again Christians were at least twice as likely as non-Christians to believe that Protestant churches are very sensitive to the needs of that people group. This study cannot determine whether the Church in America is or is not truly sensitive to the needs of these different population segments. However, whenever believers are comfortable in their perception that they are consistently and meaningfully touching people's lives, especially the lives of nonbelievers, the chances of improving the quality of their sensitivity and influence are remote.

Can Women Minister?

One other factor tested in relation to the image of the Church pertained to the opportunities provided for women to minister to other people. In some churches, the issue of the role and authority of women in ministry has become a major battleground. As women have assumed increasingly prominent leadership roles in government and business, many people are seeking for similar opportunities to be available to women in the Church, as well.

About half of all adults believe that "most Christian churches provide meaningful opportunities for women to serve in areas of ministry in which they have special talents and abilities." One-third of adults (36%) do not believe such opportunities exist in most Christian congregations; 15% are uncertain. (See data table 40.)

Here again is a case where the target audience in question holds a more positive view on the situation than do other people. Fifty-five percent of all women agree that significant ministry opportunities exist in most Christian churches. In contrast, only 43% of the men in America concur.

There are some important distinctions, though. Younger adults are less likely to accept the proposition, perhaps because they have a different level of expectations regarding ministry and authority for women than do their elders. Blacks were significantly less likely than whites to perceive such ministry options to be available. Born-again

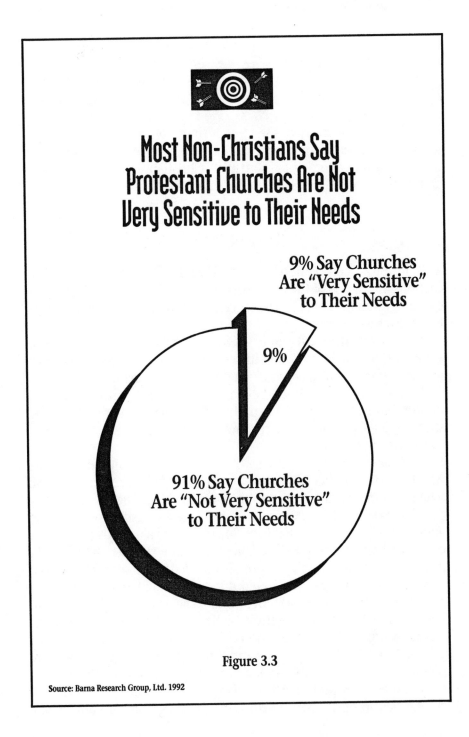

Most Non-Christians Say Protestant Churches Are Not Very Sensitive to Their Needs

9% Say Churches Are "Very Sensitive" to Their Needs

9%

91% Say Churches Are "Not Very Sensitive" to Their Needs

Figure 3.3

Source: Barna Research Group, Ltd. 1992

Christians were substantially more likely than non-Christians to hold this view (61% among Christians, 42% among non-Christians).

We also found that people who read the Bible and those who attend church are much more likely than people who do not engage in these activities to view the Church as offering ministry alternatives to women. Whether the decreased involvement of these people in Bible reading and church attendance is a consequence of their views about the limited role afforded to women in Christian churches cannot be determined from these figures, but remains a distinct possibility.

ACTION STEPS

As in for-profit corporations, churches need to be attuned to the perceptions and needs of the audiences they hope to reach. This requires constant awareness of the experiences, assumptions and opportunities to minister to the target groups of the Church.

Aggressively study and hone your church's image. Do people know your church exists? If so, when they hear the name, what images come to mind? If your church name includes the denominational affiliation of the congregation, is that viewed in a positive or negative light? It is important to continually be exploring your image. Intentionally and strategically act to build positive awareness of your ministry. Do not leave this to chance.

Address people's felt needs. Are church leaders the only people who fail to realize that Christian churches are not hitting the bull's-eye when it comes to meeting the unique and critical needs of the key people groups within the community? Take a constant pulse of the audiences you have targeted for ministry and evaluate your outreach efforts in light of those needs. Offering a "one size fits all" brand of ministry does not cut it anymore. Acknowledge the distinct needs of various people groups and reach out in ways designed to satisfy those specific needs. When you discover what types of ministry satisfy people's needs without compromising biblical values or your church's reason for being, pursue those opportunities with a vengeance.

Reaching ethnic groups. We cannot hope to reach ethnic groups by providing a ministry for them identical to that offered to whites.

If you are seeking to reach the Hispanic community, a Protestant church has an uphill struggle ahead. Many Hispanics are not predis-

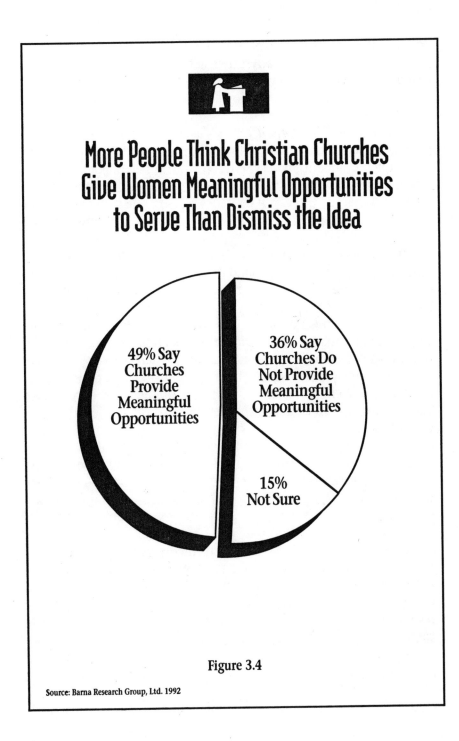

More People Think Christian Churches Give Women Meaningful Opportunities to Serve Than Dismiss the Idea

49% Say Churches Provide Meaningful Opportunities

36% Say Churches Do Not Provide Meaningful Opportunities

15% Not Sure

Figure 3.4

Source: Barna Research Group, Ltd. 1992

posed to the Catholic church, but the majority lean toward Catholicism and are skeptical of any other faith. Plan a strategic outreach that goes beyond simply speaking their language and acknowledging their customs and culture. Develop an outreach that truly responds to their family and personal needs.

Focus on non-Christians. Can the data be any more clear and compelling? Fewer than 1 out of 10 non-Christians stated that the Protestant church in America is very sensitive to their needs. For three-quarters of the people groups studied, non-Christians were less than half as convinced that the Protestant churches are very sensitive to the needs of people in those groups. Given these perceptions, how attractive can the Church be to these nonbelievers?

The obstacle is not ignorance. Given the plethora of technologies and information resources at hand these days, what can be the excuse for not knowing and addressing the needs of the very people Jesus Himself identified as our primary ministry target?

Get to know the non-Christians in your area by spending time with them personally. From a professional standpoint, you may wish to conduct occasional focus groups among the target groups you wish to reach. Listen to their fears, their anger, their anxieties, their assumptions related to churches. Accept their feelings and experiences at face value and create an outreach that responds to the barriers they perceive to exist.

Personally, take the time to build long-term relationships with nonbelievers. Listen to and share in their joys and frustrations. Model "friendship evangelism" for other people in your church so that they, too, can have a fruitful ministry among the people we must jointly reach. Make the development of true, nonmanipulative friendships with nonbelievers an intentional goal of your life.

Equip the believers in your church for the task of loving nonbelievers into God's Kingdom. This requires more than simply exhorting your people to invite their friends to a few worship services or an evangelistic event. Prepare them for the task of relating on a deep level with other people who have different views of the world. Prepare them for nonconfrontational evangelism.

ACKNOWLEDGING THE SAINTS

- Seventy-three percent believe in the God described in the Bible; the other one-quarter of America is seeking a different deity.
- Among non-Christian adults, 40% do not believe in the God worshiped by the Christian church.
- Nine out of ten adults consider themselves Christians.
- During 1991, there was a five point increase in the proportion of adults who might be considered born-again Christian; they now represent 40% of the adult population.
- Just one out of every eight adults can be considered an evangelical. Less than 1% of all evangelicals live in New England; the majority reside in the South.
- Evangelicals are most common within charismatic and Pentecostal churches. They are twice as likely as other adults to take an active part in a wide range of religious activities.
- Evangelicals are more likely registered voters than are other adults, and are as likely Democrats as Republicans. They place a higher priority on abortion and welfare/unemployment policies than do other adults.

WHAT WE DISCOVERED

Language can be very imprecise. Take the word "success," for example. People might interpret the word in different ways. Depending on one's perspective, success might allude to wealth, power, respect, a nice home and loving family, fame, good health, a satisfying career or even harmony with God.

Similarly, terms such as "Christian" and "God" have a vast array of meanings in our culture. This helps to explain why so many people call themselves "Christian," but so few have a relationship with Jesus Christ or give any evidence of a life transformed by God's grace.

Beliefs About God

More than 9 out of 10 American adults say they believe in God. But who is the god they believe in? (See data table 91.)

Not quite three-quarters of the population (73%) contend that "God is an all-powerful, all-knowing and perfect creator of the universe, who rules the world today." (See data table 91.)

There are other, less traditional (and certainly not Christian-based) beliefs about God. Ten percent of the public believe that "God is the total realization of personal, human potential." Another 6% claim that "God represents a state of higher consciousness that a person may reach." Smaller proportions of the public ascribe to the following definitions of God: "everyone is God" (2%); "there are many gods, each with different power and authority" (2%). One percent said "there is no such thing as God." Another 6% did not know how to describe God. (See data table 91.)

Shirley MacLaine and other prophets of the New Age are spinning their yarns about spiritual matters. As a result many adults have bought into non-Christian perspectives about the spiritual realm. Indeed, it is today's youngest adults (busters and boomers) who are most prone to perceive God in nonorthodox ways. Although 82% of adults 46 or older concurred that God is the all-powerful and ruling creator of the world, only 67% of the younger adults championed the same view.

Interestingly, 7% of the people classified as born-again Christians assumed a nonorthodox view of God. Most of these adults claimed that God is the full realization of human potential (5%); 2% described Him as a state of higher consciousness than we can reach. Let us pray

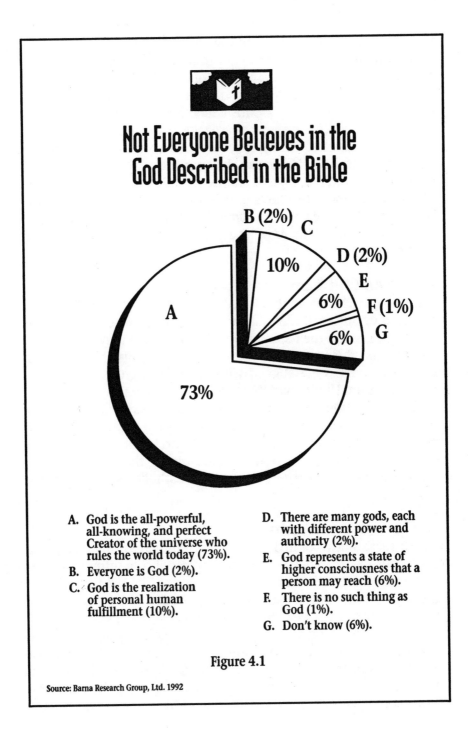

Not Everyone Believes in the God Described in the Bible

B (2%) C

10%

D (2%)

E

6% F (1%)

A

6% G

73%

A. God is the all-powerful, all-knowing, and perfect Creator of the universe who rules the world today (73%).

B. Everyone is God (2%).

C. God is the realization of personal human fulfillment (10%).

D. There are many gods, each with different power and authority (2%).

E. God represents a state of higher consciousness that a person may reach (6%).

F. There is no such thing as God (1%).

G. Don't know (6%).

Figure 4.1

Source: Barna Research Group, Ltd. 1992

that these people misinterpreted the meaning of the question posed.

Among the adults who were not in the born-again category, 40% sided with a nonorthodox description of God. This poses some serious questions regarding evangelistic strategy. Realizing that 4 out of 10 adults we meet who are not Christian do not accept our definition of God must influence the approach we take in sharing the gospel.

Some serious concerns are raised by the responses of adults associated with a few of our Christian denominations, too. For instance, 3 out of 10 Catholics (27%) rejected the orthodox view of God in favor of one of the New Age-influenced perspectives. A similar percentage of Methodists (26%) rejected the orthodox view of God and selected a nonorthodox definition. Another 6% were unable to choose any of the definitions.

We Are All Christians...

Many people who live in the United States, because they are American, believe they automatically qualify as Christians. When people were asked to designate their spiritual identity, 88% said they were Christian; 5% said they were atheists or had no religious affiliations; 2% were Jewish; 5% were aligned with other faith groups (Unitarian, Baha'i, Muslim, Hindu, Buddhist). (See data table 92.)

The people most likely to describe themselves as Christian were women (93%); people over 45 years old (94%); Southerners (93%); born-again Christians (97%); and people who had attended a church service in the past week, read the Bible during that period, or who aligned themselves with a Protestant or Catholic church. (See data table 92.)

You Must Be Born Again

As last year's study pointed out, it is not unusual for the majority of Americans to claim they have made a personal commitment to Jesus Christ that is still important in their lives today. The 1992 study found the same pattern intact. Two-thirds of the nation's adults (65%) made that claim this year. (See data table 110.)

Among those people, though, 4 out of 10 were relying upon something other than God's grace through Christ's death and resurrection as the basis of their salvation. In total, among the people who said they had a personal commitment to Christ, here is what they expect to experience after they die. (See data table 111.)

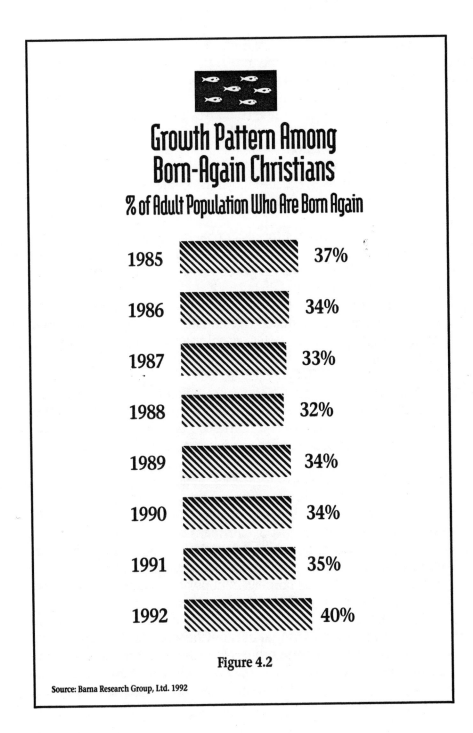

Growth Pattern Among Born-Again Christians

% of Adult Population Who Are Born Again

Year	%
1985	37%
1986	34%
1987	33%
1988	32%
1989	34%
1990	34%
1991	35%
1992	40%

Figure 4.2

Source: Barna Research Group, Ltd. 1992

Will go to heaven because they have tried to obey the Ten Commandments	6%
Will go to heaven because they are basically a good person	9%
Will go to heaven because God loves all His people and will not let them perish	6%
Will not go to heaven	2%
Don't know what will happen after they die	14%
Will go to heaven because they have confessed their sins and accepted Jesus Christ as their Savior	62%

Overall, this translates to 40% of the adult population claiming they have made a personal commitment to Jesus Christ and believe they will go to heaven after they die because they have confessed their sins and accepted Christ as their Savior.

The 40% figure is the highest statistic we have yet measured since we began using this approach to estimate the number of the born-again population in 1984. After several years of stagnation, in which there was no real growth, this year's figure represents a five percentage-point jump over 1991's figure (35%).

What might have caused this sudden spurt of spiritual wisdom? Scholars suggest that times of great turmoil and social upheaval turn people back to basics. The tumultuous national and international events of 1991, described in the earlier chapter in the context of our changing values, may well have been the motivation for many people's decision to trust Christ for their salvation.

Several people groups experienced an above-average increase in Christians compared to last year's figures. The groups witnessing the fastest growth in the number of Christians were busters and boomers; adults who attended, but did not complete, a college education; and residents of the Midwest and South. (See data table 111.)

Demographically, the born-again population is not the down-and-out, aged group of "losers" portrayed by some journalists. The statistics indicate that the median household income among born-again adults was somewhat lower than that of non-Christians (about $26,000 versus $28,400). However, the profiles also show that millions of born-again believers have a college education and that baby boomers are every bit as likely to be Christian as are adults from any other age group. (See data table 111.)

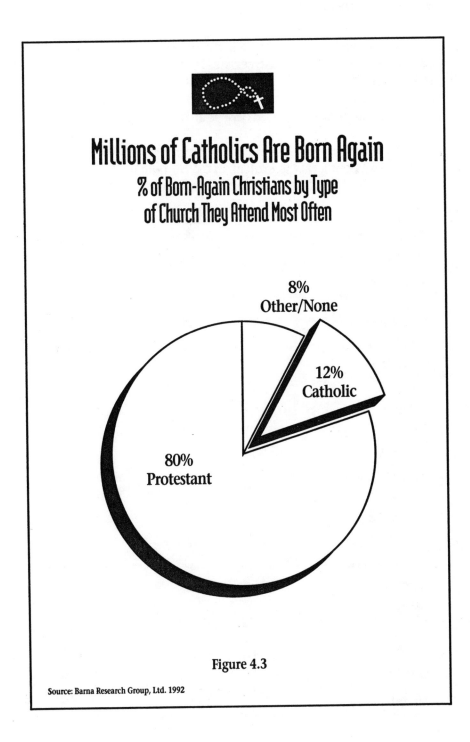

Millions of Catholics Are Born Again

% of Born-Again Christians by Type of Church They Attend Most Often

8%
Other/None

12%
Catholic

80%
Protestant

Figure 4.3

Source: Barna Research Group, Ltd. 1992

We observed a discernible increase of Christians within the Catholic Church in the past decade. In 1985, we noted that about 16% of the Catholics in this country were born-again Christians. The figure has risen to 22% today. It is considerably less than the 57% among Protestants, but the increase is encouraging.

Demographic Profiles of the Born-again and Non-born-again Populations

Characteristic	Born-again	Not born-again
men	36%	64%
women	44	56
baby busters (18-26)	30	70
baby boomers (27-45)	44	56
pre-boomers (46-64)	46	54
senior citizens (65+)	38	62
whites	43	57
blacks	40	60
Hispanics	26	74
high school or less	39	61
some college	55	45
college graduates	35	65
under $20,000	43	57
$20,000-$39,999	43	57
$40,000-$59,999	35	65
$60,000 or more	34	66
Northeast	29	71
Midwest	39	61
South	54	46
Mountain/Pacific	32	68
Catholic	22	78
Protestant	57	43

The Elusive Evangelicals

During 1991 we conducted a study funded by the Pew Trust, for Evangelicals for Social Action. One of the key findings from the study was that almost nobody—including the people you might classify as evangelicals on the basis of their beliefs and practices—knows what the term "evangelical" means.

Various researchers have conducted studies purporting to identify the number of evangelicals in America and to describe their nature. Before you accept those findings be sure you know how the people fitting the label were defined.

In our 1992 survey, we asked a series of questions which, when combined, can be used as one means of identifying people who might be considered evangelicals. The items used to classify a person this way were:

- Said the Bible is very important to them;
- Strongly agree that the Bible is the written Word of God and is totally accurate in all that it teaches;
- Believe that God is the all-powerful, all-knowing, perfect creator of the universe who rules the world today;
- Believe that people's prayers have the power to change their circumstances;
- Consider themselves to be Christian;
- Read the Bible at least once a week, outside of church;
- Shared their religious beliefs with someone who had different beliefs, within the last month;
- Have made a personal commitment to Jesus Christ that is still important in their lives today;
- Believe that when they die they will go to heaven because they have confessed their sins and have accepted Christ as their Savior.

A very select segment of the population—just 12%—satisfy all nine of these criteria. This group receives an enormous amount of media coverage given their relatively slim incidence within the population. Projected to the aggregate adult population, we would estimate slightly less than 23 million evangelicals are running loose across the land.

Let me hasten to add that this multi-question definition is not meant to be the last word on who is and who is not an evangelical. Only God knows the true answer. In time perhaps He will reveal that answer to us. In the meantime, we can use this approach to estimate the size and characteristics of the evangelical population.

Evangelicals are distinct in belief and behavior from both non-Christians and even born-again Christians. The research informs us about evangelicals in the following manner.

- In the past week, 78% of all evangelicals attended a church worship service; 52% attended a Sunday School class; 50% had volunteered their time for a church.
- Ninety-three percent called religion very important to them. They were more likely than other adults to classify their friends and their community as very important; they were less likely to view money as very important.
- They were substantially more likely than others to see today's music and music videos as a corrupting influence; to consider abortion morally wrong (77%); and to believe that one person can make a real difference in the world.
- Among the evangelicals, 26% were Baptist; 13% were from nondenominational churches; 11% from Pentecostal and Foursquare churches; 7% from Assemblies of God congregations; 7% from Methodist churches; 6% associated with the Church of Christ; and 4% were Catholic. The remaining 26% were distributed among several dozen other denominations.
- Looking within specific denominations, we found that 15% of the Baptists could be classified as evangelicals; 2% of the Catholics; 4% of the Lutherans; 13% of the Methodists; 11% of the people attending mainline Protestant churches; and 37% of the people involved in charismatic or Pentecostal churches.
- Fifty-eight percent always attend the same church; 31% usually attend the same church but sometimes visit others; and 11% divide their attendance between two or more churches.
- They were at least twice as likely as others to regularly teach a Sunday School class (16%), participate in a small group (63%) and serve as a church leader (23%).
- They were 45% more likely than others to watch religious TV. They were twice as likely to listen to Christian radio, to read Christian books, to donate to ministries other than a church,

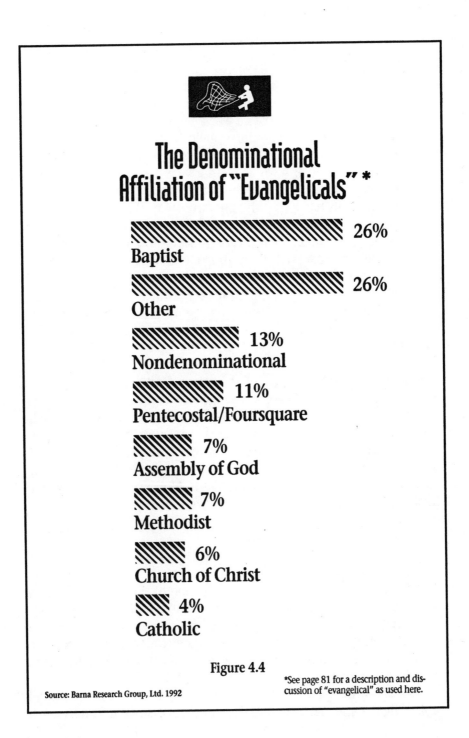

The Denominational Affiliation of "Evangelicals" *

26%
Baptist

26%
Other

13%
Nondenominational

11%
Pentecostal/Foursquare

7%
Assembly of God

7%
Methodist

6%
Church of Christ

4%
Catholic

Figure 4.4

*See page 81 for a description and discussion of "evangelical" as used here.

Source: Barna Research Group, Ltd. 1992

to share their faith with nonbelievers, and to read a Christian magazine.

- One-third of the evangelicals said they read their Bible every day in a typical week. The average number of days this group reads the Bible is five days a week. By comparison, the national average among all adults is one day a week.
- Eighty percent are registered to vote (compared to 70% among nonevangelicals): 43% as Democrats, 40% as Republicans, 14% as independents, and 3% could not recall their affiliation.
- Evangelicals had a slightly different political agenda than did other Americans. The most important issues to them were crime (72% cited this as a very important issue in their presidential candidate selection), drug law enforcement (71%), the economy (65%), public education (62%), abortion (60%) and health care (60%). Comparatively, education was a lower ranking priority and abortion a higher priority. Welfare and unemployment policy was also a more volatile issue to the evangelicals.

The demographic profile of the evangelical segment reflected a slightly different type of people. Evangelicals tended to be several years older than the national average (44 years of age), were less well educated, had lower annual incomes and more than half of them were located in the South. Less than 1% of the evangelical base resided in New England; just 2% of New Englanders qualified as evangelicals. Only 8% of the population in the entire Northeast was evangelical. Only 7% of the Pacific states residents were evangelicals.

ACTION STEPS

Life in America has become a kaleidoscope of choices. Even in the arena of faith people tend to pick and choose, slice and dice. The resulting contours of people's beliefs and practices are unique and ever-changing. For a faith that has absolutes that cannot be compromised, acute awareness of the implications of this approach to spirituality is imperative.

Beware of the New Age. Because the New Age is not really a definable religion and has no real church or leadership, it is difficult to

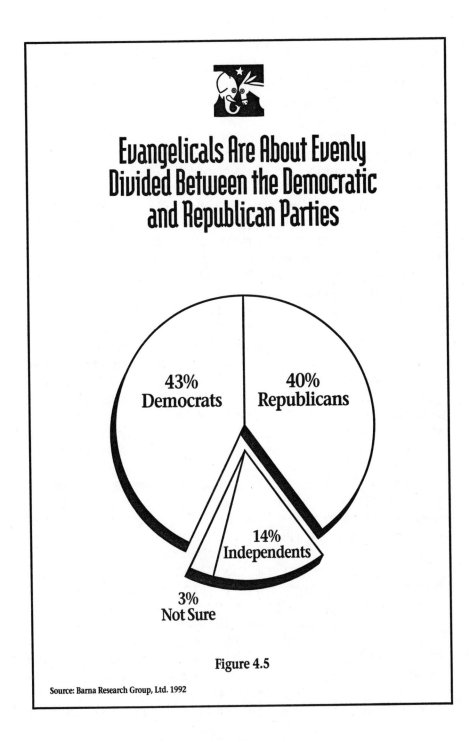

Evangelicals Are About Evenly Divided Between the Democratic and Republican Parties

43%
Democrats

40%
Republicans

14%
Independents

3%
Not Sure

Figure 4.5

Source: Barna Research Group, Ltd. 1992

identify. But make no mistake about it: the appeal of New Age ideas and practices is continuing to grow. Millions of Christians espouse New Age beliefs without realizing what they are doing. Many leaders in the Church are poorly informed and unaware of this subtle threat to Christian orthodoxy.

One of the critical ways we can combat the spread of aberrant theology is by covering all of the basics thoroughly when we teach and evangelize. For instance, when we discuss Christianity with a nonbeliever we cannot afford to assume that when the person indicates a belief in God he is referring to the same God in whom we believe. Knowing that 40% of all nonbelievers accept a different God than He who created and rules the world should motivate us to start from scratch to be certain we are not building on weak foundations of faith.

Discipling new believers. How encouraging it is to recognize growth in the ranks of the Christian Body. The increase in the proportion of adults who are born again brings with it the challenge to be sure these new believers are nurtured consistently and significantly in their faith. As other data in this year's survey revealed, many of the new Christians have accepted Christ but not the local church. Consequently, every believer must be sensitive to opportunities to disciple believers who may be apart from a spiritual body that provides the constant teaching and exhortation that is so desperately needed, especially in the early months of one's spiritual rebirth. Are the people in your church cognizant of and prepared to handle the responsibility they have to build up others in their faith?

Planning for growth. And what about the believers themselves? If we are called to replicate the early church in behavior and belief, perhaps we ought to establish a specific goal to increase the number of evangelicals. Again, we will confront the language barrier. Many Christians resist being labeled an evangelical, in the same way that many believers refuse to be known as "born again." Considerable negative baggage comes with labels, and the "evangelical" tag is no exception.

However, we need to focus on the meaning of evangelical—i.e. belief in the Bible, a relationship with Christ, reliance on grace alone for salvation, active participation in evangelism and prayer. We then might transcend the political and cultural barriers and focus on the desire of God's heart: to create and nurture people who are committed to becoming fully devoted followers of Christ.

If you agree that increasing the ranks of the evangelical Christian community is a worthy goal, create a plan for your church to lead people from their current spiritual state to a more advanced level of faith. It will not happen unless you commit to it, and you probably will not commit to it unless you have a tangible, articulated plan to reap such an outcome. Set your goals high and allocate your ministry resources toward that end.

THE LIFE OF THE BODY

CHAPTER HIGHLIGHTS

- Half of all adults who described themselves as Christian most frequently attend Catholic or Baptist churches.
- Just one out of five self-described Christians usually attend a mainline Protestant church.
- Various types of churches attract different types of adults. Mainline Protestant churches have greater success at reaching the white, upscale segment. Catholics are most successful among Hispanics. Baptist churches fare well among blacks, older adults, Southerners, and born-again Christians. Evangelical churches are strong in the Western states and among born-again Christians.
- Church attendance is relatively stable, but boomers appear to be less committed to attend than previously.
- Four out of ten church-going people do not limit their attendance to a single church. One out of every ten attenders regularly rotates between two or more churches.
- One out of every eight adults claimed to be involved in some type of church leadership position.

WHAT WE DISCOVERED

Among people who called themselves Christian, the vast majority maintain traditional views about the local church. For instance, most adults acknowledged the importance of being somehow connected to a church and the importance of at least occasionally attending services or events at the church.

The depth of commitment to a given church, though, does not appear to be strengthening, even in the wake of the reported increase in the spiritual commitment and interest of Americans.

The New Alignment

Formerly, people who defined themselves as Christian were either Catholic or mainline Protestant. A few smaller denominations drew people to their churches, but together those groups represented a minor slice of the church-going public.

Since World War II, however, a religious realignment has been taking place. Mainline churches—Church of Christ, Episcopal, Lutheran, Methodist and Presbyterian—have been consistently losing members and their attendance figures reflect this decline. Some church analysts now call them the "sideline" churches rather than "mainline." The rising stars have been the independent Bible, nondenominational and evangelical churches. Baptist churches have also continued to grow, particularly the Southern Baptist denomination.

In 1992, the most popular affiliations among self-described Christians were Catholic (25%) and Baptist (24%). No other denominational identity reached double figures. The next most prolific were Methodist (7%), Lutheran (6%) and Church of Christ (3%). Charismatic and Pentecostal churches, including the Assemblies of God and Church of God groups, represented 8%. Nondenominational churches were listed at 4%. Small denominations, which are typically considered evangelical (e.g. Evangelical Free, Presbyterian Church in America) accounted for about 10% of the total. (See data table 93.)

The demographic profiles of the people who associate with these church classifications is quite different.

- Mainline churches attracted an above-average proportion of college graduates (32%), upper-income people (30%) and people from the Midwest (35%). They were less successful than

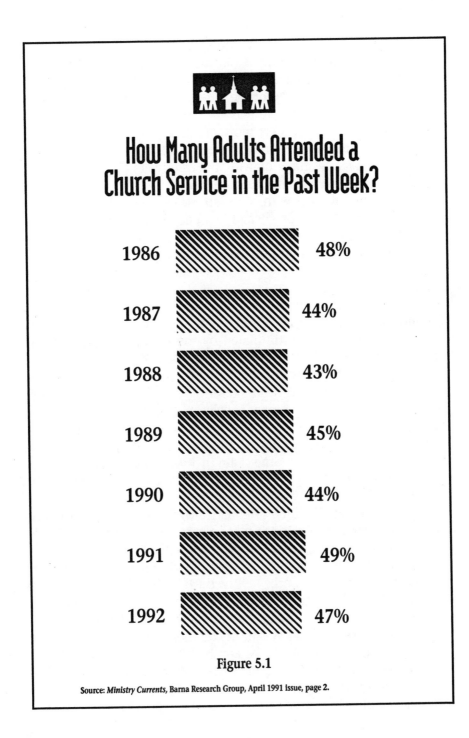

How Many Adults Attended a Church Service in the Past Week?

1986 48%

1987 44%

1988 43%

1989 45%

1990 44%

1991 49%

1992 47%

Figure 5.1

Source: *Ministry Currents*, Barna Research Group, April 1991 issue, page 2.

the norm at drawing nonwhites (9%). (See data table 93.)

- Baptist churches tended to attract older adults (32% of all those 65 or older), blacks (53%), born-again Christians (32%) and Southerners (43% of the self-described Christians in that region).
- Catholic churches drew more prolifically from the Hispanic community (62%) and the Northeast (48%). They were relatively unsuccessful at drawing the elderly (14%), Southerners (13%) and born-again Christians (12%).
- Churches aligned with non-Baptist, evangelical denominations appealed more heavily to people living in the West (22%) and to born-again Christians (25% of all born-again adults attended such churches).

Attending Services

On a given Sunday, slightly less than half of all adults claim they attend worship services at a church. This measure hit a high mark of 49% last year (perhaps stimulated by the pending Gulf War) and dropped slightly to 47% in 1992. (See data table 47.)

What is most interesting about the decline in attendance is that baby boomers, who had been exploring churches for the past five years, experienced a *ten percentage point drop* in attendance compared to one year earlier. Fifty percent of the boomers claimed to have attended church services during the week preceding the survey in 1991; just 40% made the same claim in 1992. This decline cannot be explained away by sampling error, given the number of boomers who were interviewed. (See data table 94.)

Overall, reported church attendance over the course of a typical month has not changed in the past year. Among self-described Christians, one out of every five (21%) said they generally do not attend services. One-third of the group said they attend from one to three times a month (13% once a month, 12% twice, 10% three times). The largest group, 41%, said they attend services four or more times each month. Three percent could not judge their attendance. (See data table 94.)

Attendance every week was most common among those who were 46 or older (53%), people in the South (47%), married adults (46%), born-again Christians (57%, double the proportion among nonbelievers), Bible readers (59%), and charismatics and Pentecostals (60%). (See data table 94.)

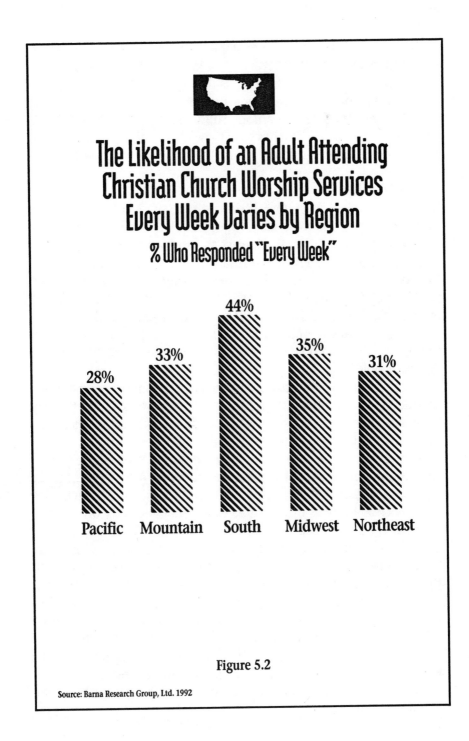

The Likelihood of an Adult Attending Christian Church Worship Services Every Week Varies by Region

% Who Responded "Every Week"

Pacific — 28%
Mountain — 33%
South — 44%
Midwest — 35%
Northeast — 31%

Figure 5.2

Source: Barna Research Group, Ltd. 1992

The aggregate trend is one of stability, but some shifting is occurring within the Body of believers. Most importantly, boomers are still attending church but not as often as in the past. This may be a temporary decline or it may be the precursor of a coming exodus from the Church. Since boomers are among those leading the cadre of adults who charge that local churches tend to be irrelevant, this possibility of a generational retreat from the Church must be taken seriously.

Brand Loyalty

In a mobile society that shows little loyalty to product brands or even to other people, it is reasonable to assume that people might visit a variety of churches rather than select and support a single church.

Among the self-described Christians who attend church services at least once in a typical month, six out of every ten (61%) said they always attend the same church every time they go to a service. Three out of ten adults said they usually attend the same church but occasionally go to others. About one out of every ten (9%) indicated that they divide their attendance between two or more churches they like. (See data table 95.)

Unexpectedly, Catholics were more likely than most people to say they do not always attend the same church every week. Given the way Catholics are assigned to a parish based upon location of residence, this level of mobility was not anticipated.

The most mobile church attenders, however, were those people who attend charismatic or Pentecostal churches. A majority of those adults (54%) stated they attend a variety of churches. In fact, they were twice as likely as other adults to say they regularly divide their attendance between two or more churches. (See data table 95.)

Not very many people who regularly attend a specific church are planning to leave that church within the coming year. Just 4% said they are very likely to change from their current church to a different church. An additional 11% said a transition was somewhat likely. Thirteen percent said a switch was not too likely, but the vast majority (71%) stated that such was not at all likely. (See data table 96.)

Who was most likely to consider a switch? Divorced adults led the way (35% very or somewhat likely), followed by residents of the Northeast (24%) and people from households earning less than $20,000 (22%).

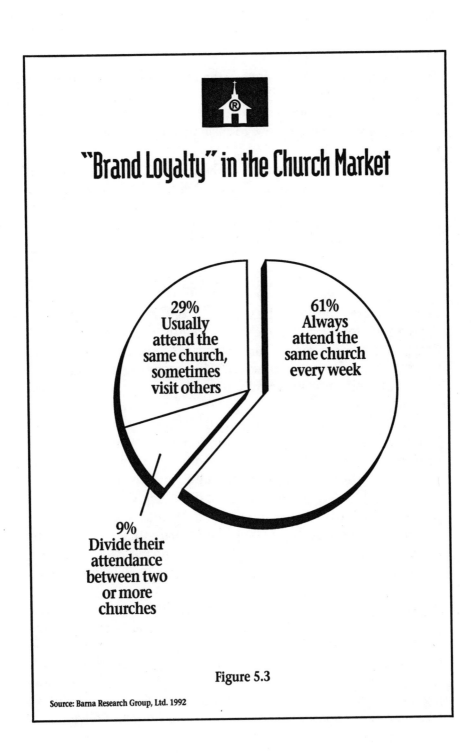

"Brand Loyalty" in the Church Market

29%
Usually
attend the
same church,
sometimes
visit others

61%
Always
attend the
same church
every week

9%
Divide their
attendance
between two
or more
churches

Figure 5.3

Source: Barna Research Group, Ltd. 1992

Leadership Obligations

The church, as any organization, rises and falls on the strength of the leadership it receives from those who fill key positions. Unlike most organizations, the church relies heavily upon unpaid volunteers (whom we call "the laity") to spearhead much of the ministry undertaken by the church.

One out of every twelve adults (8%) claimed they are involved in regularly leading or teaching a Sunday School class. An even larger proportion (13%) said they serve on a board or committee within the church. (See data tables 97,99.)

ACTION STEPS

In the aggregate, the life of the Church is constantly changing. Sometimes we are too close to the changes to realize they are happening. Often, church leaders are not sure how to best address the changes and therefore choose to ignore these shifts in behavior and attitude. This strategy of benign neglect typically gives rise to serious problems down the line.

Tending to the boomers. It is hard to love a generation as self-absorbed and selfish as the baby boom cohort. But boomers need the Church as much, if not more, than any other generation America has experienced. The possibility that they are about to exit from the community of believers in record numbers is disturbing. Can the exodus be prevented without compromising what the Church stands for?

Certainly! But such an effort will require sharp strategic thinking by church leaders, diligent efforts by the people who make the ministry of the Body happen, consistent prayer on the part of all believers and a willingness to explore new avenues for outreach.

Why are boomers disenchanted with the Church? Largely because it fails to consistently meet their needs with quality outreach and teaching. If you are serious about stabilizing your church's congregation and about effectively applying the Christian faith to the real challenges of people's lives, examine how you are developing and deploying your ministry. Pose the tough questions boomers would ask regarding the purposes and practices of the Church. Be willing to change what is negotiable, and to stand firm for what is not. Whatever you do, do not take this challenge sitting down.

Earn their loyalty. You cannot assume people perceive involvement with a church as a reasonable or valuable experience. The typical young adult who attends a church these days has three equally viable options: continue to participate in the life of that church, change to another church or give up on churches altogether. How you respond to their needs—i.e. the consistency and perceived quality of the teaching and events, the quality of the friendships developed through the church, the apparent viability of Christianity in the face of a challenging world—will greatly influence their commitment to your church.

Understand mobility. The natural tendency among church leaders is to view people's mobility between churches as an evil. You may view such church hopping as evidence of disloyalty and spiritual schizophrenia. However, that pattern of mobility might be one of the best circumstances toward building God's Kingdom.

Why do people make the rounds from church to church? Generally it is because no one church has the ability to meet all the complex needs of a person. People do not visit a variety of churches simply to observe the differences across congregations. Their time is too valuable to engage in sociological study. Their purpose is to deal with the needs, hurts and doubts with which they struggle. Praise God that they believe His Church has some answers to provide.

If we allow for the possibility that people may best grow spiritually by attending multiple churches, what opportunities does that open up to you? How should that reshape your thinking about the meaning of ministry and community? What does this mean in terms of viewing ministry as a multichurch effort rather than the sum of your own church's best attempt?

CHAPTER 6 | A RELIGIOUSLY ACTIVE PEOPLE

CHAPTER HIGHLIGHTS

- Nearly two-thirds of the public (64%) said they had either watched religious television or listened to Christian radio programming within the past month. Overall, 49% watched religious television, 45% had listened to a radio station airing Christian music, and 39% had listened to Christian teaching or preaching on the radio. One-third of the adult population (32%) had been exposed to both religious television and Christian radio programming during that period.

- Four out of ten adults said they had shared their faith in the past month with someone who believed differently than themselves.

- More than one-third of all adults (37%) claimed to have read a Christian magazine during the preceding month. One-third said they had read a Christian book, other than the Bible, during that same time frame.

- One out of every four adults said they were currently involved in a small group for Bible study, prayer or fellowship.

- Just over half of all adults said they had read from the Bible in the prior month, other than when they were at church. Although the frequency with which people had read the Bible did not change in the past year, the data revealed that one out of every eight adults reads the Bible daily.

WHAT WE DISCOVERED

Americans tend to be among the most religious people on the face of the earth. This interest in religion is not always apparent to the observer because much of the religious activity takes place in private. Whether that practice is prayer, Bible reading or absorbing religious media, the majority of Americans do engage in some form of religious activity every month.

Religious Radio and TV

Nearly two-thirds of the public (64%) said they had either watched religious television or listened to Christian radio programming within the past month. Overall, 49% watched religious television; 45% had listened to a radio station airing Christian music; and 39% had listened to Christian teaching or preaching on the radio. One-quarter (28%) had listened to both Christian music and to Christian teaching on the radio during the past 30 days. One-third of the adult population (32%) had been exposed to both religious television and Christian radio programming during that period. (See data tables 100,101,105.)

The audience for these media tended to be older adults. Born-again Christians had a more pronounced tendency to interact with such broadcasts. Religious television was more commonly viewed by women than men. Notice, too, that the audience of non-Christians for religious television is about one-third larger than it is for Christian radio teaching and preaching programs.

The debate whether the Christian media truly reach the non-Christian public seems like a rather silly discussion. The statistics clearly show—and have for some time—that literally millions of non-Christian adults have some degree of exposure to Christian media programming.

If we project the percentages to the aggregate population, we discover that almost half of the aggregate viewing audience for religious television shows is non-Christian. A smaller proportion of nonbelievers watch these shows than do believers. However, because there are so many millions more nonbelievers than believers, their larger numbers compensate for their lower incidence of viewing the programs. Overall, the two groups are virtually the same size numerically.

As for Christian radio, slightly more than two out of five listeners

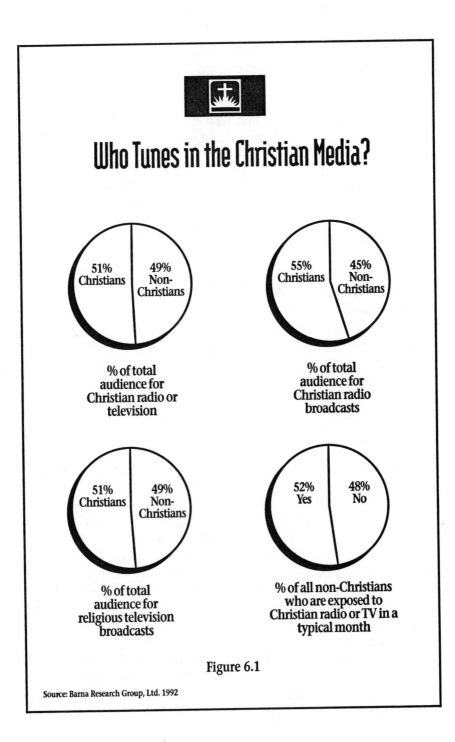

Who Tunes in the Christian Media?

51% Christians | 49% Non-Christians

% of total audience for Christian radio or television

55% Christians | 45% Non-Christians

% of total audience for Christian radio broadcasts

51% Christians | 49% Non-Christians

% of total audience for religious television broadcasts

52% Yes | 48% No

% of all non-Christians who are exposed to Christian radio or TV in a typical month

Figure 6.1

Source: Barna Research Group, Ltd. 1992

either to stations playing Christian teaching (43%) or to those airing Christian music (45%) are nonbelievers.

Who Tunes in to Christian Broadcasting in a Typical Month?
(Base: 1,013 adults)

		Born Again?	
Type of Broadcast	All Adults	Yes	No
radio: Christian music	45%	62%	33%
radio: Christian teaching	39	55	28
radio: Christian teaching and Christian music	28	44	18
television: religious	49	62	40
Christian radio and religious television	32	48	22
Christian radio or religious television	64	81	52
Christian radio, but *not* religious television	15	14	15
religious television, but *not* Christian radio	15	20	12

Why are these numbers so much larger than the figures produced by the ratings services, such as Nielsen or Arbitron? Indeed, these figures even surpass those achieved by top-rated television shows such as "Roseanne" and "60 Minutes."

One key reason may have to do with definitions. A radio station airing songs by Amy Grant, Michael W. Smith and Stryper may be deemed a Christian music station by some people. Programs such as "The Paul Harvey Report" are construed to be Christian programming by some adults. Watching programming on The Family Channel, which is operated by the Christian Broadcasting Network, may be thought of as Christian programming—even when the viewer is watching nonreligious shows on that channel, such as "The Waltons," "Father Dowling Mysteries," and "Bordertown." Since the ratings services provide figures for specific shows or stations, and they use different methodologies, they measure audience size in a different, noncomparable way.

The key to evaluating the Christian media, however, probably lies not so much in settling arguments over whether or not specific target groups are exposed to Christian programming, but whether such exposure has made any difference in the lives of those people. Since most

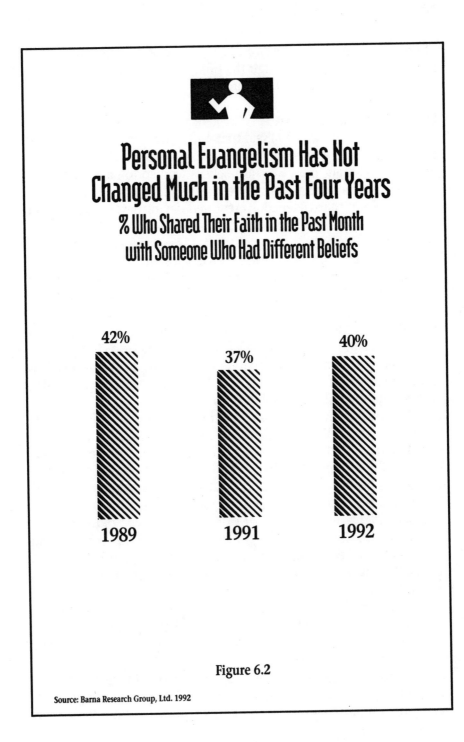

Personal Evangelism Has Not Changed Much in the Past Four Years

% Who Shared Their Faith in the Past Month with Someone Who Had Different Beliefs

42%

37%

40%

1989

1991

1992

Figure 6.2

Source: Barna Research Group, Ltd. 1992

of these programs raise their funds on the basis of claims that many people are being saved through the broadcast, evaluating the number of conversions might also be in order.

Other Spiritual Activities

Four out of ten adults (40%) said that during the past month they had shared their faith with someone who believed differently than themselves. Surprisingly, men were as likely as women to have engaged in such evangelistic efforts. Even more unexpectedly, a higher proportion of young adults than older adults reported having described their faith to others in the past month. (See data table 104.)

Just more than one-third of all adults (37%) claimed to have read a Christian magazine during the preceding month. This activity was most common among women, adults 46 or older and Christians. Recognizing that this translates to a total audience of about 70 million adults, we must assume that people have defined "Christian magazine" in the broadest sense. To stretch the numbers this much, exposure to magazines such as Reader's Digest may well be included in this count. Our research indicates that more Christians read Reader's Digest than read all of the independent, advertising-supported Christian magazines combined. (See data table 106.)

One-third of the population said they had read a Christian book, other than the Bible, during the last month. Although this pales in comparison to the proportion of all adults who had read a book during that time frame (less than half as many), it constitutes a huge amount of people: about 65 million adults. (See data tables 50,102.)

Once again, the magnitude of these numbers must cause us to wonder. Comparing the number of Christian books sold during the past year with this figure raises the question: What do people consider a "Christian" book? The figures may be somewhat inflated by people's generous perceptions of the definition of Christian literature. (See the following table.)

One-quarter of the population said they had donated money to a Christian ministry other than a church. This was most common among adults 46 or older (38%) and among born-again Christians (40%). (See data table 103.)

Participation in a small group was also common to one out of every four adults (25%). The small-group movement burst to this level several years ago and has plateaued there for at least the last three years.

The people most likely to engage in a small group, whether it be for Bible study, prayer or fellowship, were women (30%), people 46 to 64 years of age (37%), blacks (39%), born-again Christians (44%), and charismatics and Pentecostals (58%). (See data table 98.)

Religious Activities Engaged in During the Past Month
(Base: 1,013 adults)

Activity	All	Men	Women	18-26	27-45	46-64	65+	Born Again Yes	No
Helped needy people in the area	60%	54%	66%	43%	61%	66%	68%	65%	57%
Watched religious TV	49	41	56	32	45	55	69	62	40
Listened to Christian music radio station	45	42	47	34	42	50	58	62	33
Shared beliefs with a non-Christian	40	42	39	47	43	36	35	50	34
Listened to Christian preaching or teaching on radio	39	39	38	29	36	41	52	55	28
Read a Christian magazine	37	34	41	16	31	50	59	51	28
Read a Christian book (excluding Bible)	34	33	35	23	32	37	47	51	22
Donated money to a Christian ministry (excluding a church)	28	26	30	11	25	36	41	40	20
Participated in a small group	25	20	30	15	22	37	27	44	13
Helped needy people in other countries	24	23	25	14	19	34	31	33	18

In total, if the data are projected to the entire adult population we find that almost 50 million adults claim they are involved in a small group for spiritual purposes. One-third of those people are baby boomers, one-third are the pre-boomers. This means that two-thirds of the market is in the 27 to 64 age category. The other one-third are comprised of the busters and senior citizens. Numerically, twice as many elderly adults as young adults are involved in small groups.

At either end of the continuum of activities studied was assistance provided to other people, either through volunteering time or giving money. Six out of ten adults claimed they had offered such help within the past month to needy people in their own area; 24% claimed to have extended such help to needy people in other countries. Attitudinal research informs us that Americans are likely to help local needy

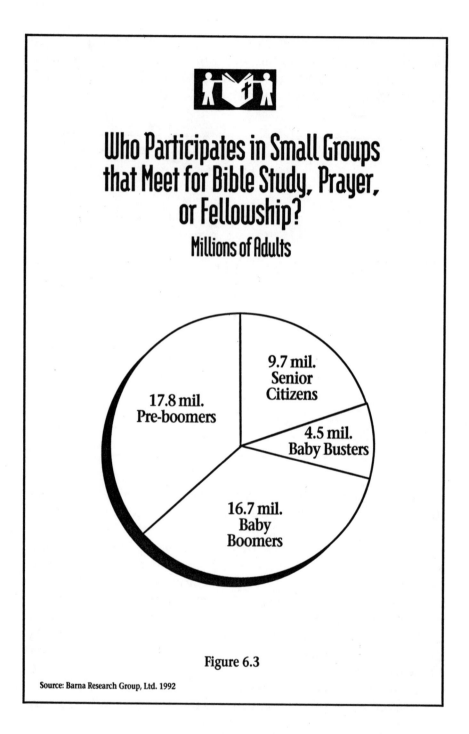

Who Participates in Small Groups that Meet for Bible Study, Prayer, or Fellowship?
Millions of Adults

9.7 mil.
Senior
Citizens

17.8 mil.
Pre-boomers

4.5 mil.
Baby Busters

16.7 mil.
Baby
Boomers

Figure 6.3

Source: Barna Research Group, Ltd. 1992

people because of convenience. But they also help out of a desire to commit resources to solve local problems rather than crises in other sections of the world. (See data tables 107,108.)

Participation in religious activity also varied significantly by region. As the figures in the accompanying table point out, involvement in any given activity was likely to be below average among residents of the Northeast, Mountain and Pacific states. Adults living in the South were generally substantially above the norm; Midwesterners vacillated above and below the average depending upon the activity in question.

Religious Activities Engaged in During the Past Month, by Region

Activity	All	North-east	Mid-west	South	Moun-tain	Pacific
Helped needy people in the area	60%	61%	61%	63%	52%	54%
Watched religious TV	49	38	53	64	28	33
Listened to Christian music radio station	45	36	43	59	29	35
Shared beliefs with a non-Christian	40	37	38	45	33	40
Listened to Christian preaching or teaching on radio	39	31	44	48	25	26
Read a Christian magazine	37	28	37	47	34	33
Read a Christian book (excluding Bible)	34	26	31	42	33	30
Donated money to a Christian ministry (excluding a church)	28	32	25	28	26	25
Participated in a small group	25	13	24	34	26	24
Helped needy people in other countries	24	28	20	25	21	22

Southerners were well above the average (at least 20% higher) when it came to involvement in activities that promoted their personal spiritual development. These included watching religious television, listening to Christian radio stations, reading Christian books and magazines, and attending small groups. However, they were merely average when it came to matters of sacrifice: giving money to nonchurch Christian ministries, helping needy people in their area and helping needy people in other countries.

Residents of the Mountain and Pacific states were substantially below the average (20% or more) regarding exposure to Christian television and radio. Adults in the Northeast were well below the mean when it came to reading Christian literature or being involved in a small group.

Bible Reading

A crucial factor in the spiritual growth of people is Bible reading. The importance people ascribed to the Bible may have risen significantly in the past year, but their tendency to actually read the Bible did not change at all.

In total, about half of all adults (53%) said they read the Bible in a typical week. One-quarter of all adults (25%) say they read the Bible once or twice a week, other than at church. Fifteen percent read the Scriptures between three and six days in a typical week; one out of every eight adults (13%) said they read the Bible every day, not including when they are in church. (See data table 109.)

The people most committed to reading the Bible during the week were women, older adults, those with limited education and lower levels of household income, blacks, rural residents, people in the South. Not surprisingly, born-again Christians were more than twice as likely as others to claim weekly Bible reading (79% versus 35%). Baptists (67%), charismatics and Pentecostals (83%) were much more likely to read the Bible during the week than were Catholics (38%), Lutherans (54%) or Methodists (56%). (See data table 109.)

ACTION STEPS

Even if the data are assumed to be inflated, the story remains the same: Americans are very active in spiritual activity and are still open to yet further means of exploring the spiritual realm. How can you exploit this window of opportunity for the glory of God?

Focus. Millions of Americans are wandering through the spiritual wilderness without adequate preparation and guidance. They are being exposed to many concepts and teachings that are erroneous or may be valid but are out of context. Undaunted, Americans continue to absorb religious information and attempt to piece the puzzle together in light of what they know and experience.

People need the Church to help them gain a proper perspective on spiritual matters. They need help focusing on that which is significant,

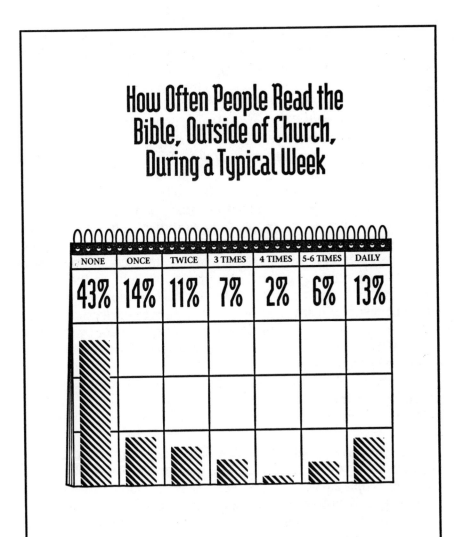

How Often People Read the Bible, Outside of Church, During a Typical Week

NONE	ONCE	TWICE	3 TIMES	4 TIMES	5-6 TIMES	DAILY
43%	14%	11%	7%	2%	6%	13%

Figure 6.4

Source: Barna Research Group, Ltd. 1992

and knowing how to use their energy to achieve a productive outcome. By getting to know the true spiritual condition of the people to whom you have the privilege of ministering, and responding on the basis of that knowledge, you can help them capture the insights they are seeking toward becoming a wiser person.

Build on the media. Tens of millions of dollars are poured into religious broadcasting every year. Thousands of hours of Christian teaching, exhortation, encouragement and guidance are available to the public. Yet, most church leaders are apt to steer their congregations away from such sources of information and teaching.

Can you identify certain broadcasts that are theologically acceptable and encourage your people to grow through exposure to those ministries? If your ultimate goal is to build up God's people so they can worship and minister more significantly, that task is too massive for you *not* to use every resource at your disposal. Build on the work of other qualified, godly teachers of the Word. Remember, your people will not devote as many hours or blocks of time to the local church as they used to. Maximize your time with your people not by retracing steps that others could cover for you but by going beyond where others have led your congregation.

Promote Bible use. It is exciting to learn that a growing number of people claim the Bible is very important in their lives. However, if there is no greater use of the Bible, of what value are those favorable impressions?

Many adults are frightened of the Bible. They cannot read it. They cannot understand it. They struggle to figure out how to apply its wisdom. As people are striving to make sense of the world, to leave a lasting mark on the planet and to identify resources that will assist them in their journey, seize the moment by aiding people in their attempts at integrating the Scriptures into their lives. Tutor them. Encourage them. Pray with and for them. Give them study tools. Gather people into study groups and provide effective leadership. Do whatever you can to capitalize upon the chance we presently have to prove the worth and relevance of the Bible.

THE TEN COMMANDMENTS

- When asked to describe how well their lives honor the spirit of the Ten Commandments, people were most likely to indicate they are completely satisfying the exhortations to abstain from murder, stealing and adultery.
- The commandments people admitted they were more likely to break were not working on the day of worship, swearing and lying.
- One-quarter of the respondents admitted they worship gods other than the God described in the Bible.
- Only 6% of the adult population said they were living in complete harmony with all Ten Commandments. This was true for 8% of the born-again adults and 4% of the nonbelievers.

WHAT WE DISCOVERED

Every year, in thousands of sermons, preachers pick on the Pharisees. Those ancient Jewish teachers are used as negative role models, examples of how Christians ought not to live their faith.

The Pharisees suffered from an acute case of spiritual legalism. It seems that no matter how hard they tried, they never truly grasped the spirit of the Law. Instead, they were devoted to, and extraordinarily skilled at, interpreting the letter of the Law and navigating around it. Jesus criticized them severely for their inability to catch the spirit of the commands of God.

Americans in the '90s can learn a lesson from the Pharisees. Although the Pharisees strove to fulfill the Law without understanding why, at least they were schooled in the Law. Modern Americans, to their discredit, cannot even be good legalists. A study conducted by George Gallup several years ago determined that most Americans could not even name half of the Ten Commandments. In other words, things have gotten so out of hand that when we sin now, we do not even realize it because we have no grounding in the original rules of the game.

Is there hope on the horizon? It depends how you define hope. One must wonder about the limits of God's patience when you hear people like Ted Turner campaigning to replace the Ten Commandments with his modernized version, known as the Ten Suggestions. Where is Moses when you need him?

WHERE THE RUBBER MEETS THE ROAD

In this year's survey, we read each of the Ten Commandments to people and asked them to describe how well their life-style coincides with each commandment.

What emerged was a profile of a nation whose people are steeped in sin. Given man's nature, of course, this is not surprising. The Bible leaves no ambiguities about the nature of the human heart. The human heart is sinful, wicked, deceitful, jealous, corrupt and selfish, to name but a few of the characteristics ascribed to it. What is discouraging about the current state of affairs in America is that so few people seem to care about this sin condition. Each passing day brings little desire or effort to change; it is life as usual for most Americans.

#1: Worship

Three-quarters of the adult public (76%) said they are completely true to the first commandment: "Thou shall not worship other gods." The other one-quarter of the population claimed to satisfy this commandment to varying, but lesser degrees. (See data table 81.)

Undeviating worship of the God of Israel was most commonly acknowledged by women (81%), residents of the South (86%) and born-again Christians (86%). The people least likely to claim they worship only the true God were men (69%), baby busters (64%), single adults (62%) and non-Christians (68%). Interestingly, only 70% of the residents of each region of the nation, other than the South, said they completely follow this commandment.

The Percentage of Adults Who Say They Completely Satisfy Each Commandment (Base: 1,013 adults)

Commandment	Completely Satisfy
Do not worship gods other than the God described in the Bible.	76%
You should not have any idols.	71
Do not swear or misuse God's name.	44
Do not work on the day of worship.	25
Honor your parents.	77
Do not commit murder.	93
Do not commit adultery.	82
Do not steal.	86
Do not lie.	48
Do not be jealous of the things other people have.	53

#2: No Idols

Following this law was a bit tougher for Americans. Just 71% claimed their lives are completely free of idol worship. (See data table 82.)

Young adults struggle with this the most. Barely half of the baby busters (53%) said their lives are in complete harmony with this commandment. The group that experienced the least struggle with this was widowed adults: 86% said they are completely following this mandate.

One of the cultural idols of our time is money. The dangers of pursuing money as an idol may be clear to the people who face the greatest temptation. Note that 74% of the people earning average or below average household incomes said this command was not a problem for them; 65% of those making an above-average salary made the same claim.

Naturally, the question assumes that people are able to identify idols in their lives. You probably know a few people who are so blinded to the idols they cherish that they are incapable of even seeing those false gods for what they are in their own lives. Consider the 71% figure a very conservative estimate.

#3: Swearing
Most Americans seem to realize that their language offends God. Less than half of our adult population (44%) said they completely live by the exhortation to not swear or otherwise abuse God's name. (See data table 83.)

Swearing was a more widespread problem among men, busters and boomers, college graduates, singles, upper-income adults and Lutherans than among other people groups. Who would have expected the better-educated adults, whose training theoretically instills a refined life-style, to acknowledge a problem with offensive language more than less well-educated and highly paid folk?

#4: Keep the Sabbath
Do you remember when it was illegal for a business to be open on Sunday? That, of course, is history now, as Sunday has become a major day of commerce in America. (See data table 84.)

The commandment to keep the Sabbath day holy was not limited simply to the idea of avoiding the workplace. The connotations are much broader. Yet, given that most Americans would interpret the commandment to mean not going to work on the day of worship, recognize that only one out of four adults (25%) say their lives are completely in tune with this command. In fact, less than half of the nation claims to be even "mostly" responsive to this commandment.

The elderly were more likely than most other people to say they completely keep this commandment (31%). Others who were more likely than average to do so were Baptists (36%), charismatics and Pentecostals (40%). People who attended church in the past week were nearly twice as likely as those absent from church to follow this portion of the Law.

#5: Honor Your Parents

The value of family is undergoing a resurgence in our culture and the survey discovered three out of four adults claim they are completely faithful to this demand. (See data table 85.)

Baby boomers and baby busters were less likely to make this claim (73%) than were their elders (82%). Born-again Christians (82%) were also somewhat more likely than non-Christians (73%) to state they are completely following this guideline.

#6: No Murders

Crime statistics from the Department of Justice tell us quite convincingly that murders are increasing in frequency. Gangs walk the streets in most of our major urban areas. In some cities, these youth-based groups are responsible for an average of one killing a day. Our television programs and movies are filled with incidents of violence, often resulting in the death of the fictional characters. Some sociologists have given warnings that we are so surrounded by acts and portrayals of violence and killing that young people, as an emotional defense mechanism, have become hardened to this reality. (See data table 86.)

Even so, it is quite a shock to speak with adults and realize many of them have committed murders. In our interviews, 7% were unable to claim that their lives were completely true to the commandment against murder.

#7: No Adultery

Psychologists tell us marital affairs are common these days. Many of the millions of adults who have been divorced (nearly one-quarter of the adult population) dissolved their marriages on the grounds of their spouse's unfaithfulness. (See data table 87.)

About 8 out of 10 adults (82%) claim they are completely trustworthy in this area of their lives. Among married people, the reported fidelity rate is even higher (91%).

The demographic comparisons of this sin are striking. Among baby busters, nearly one-quarter describe themselves as either a little or not at all living in ways that satisfy this commandment. One out of five single adults also answered the query in the same manner. Sexual

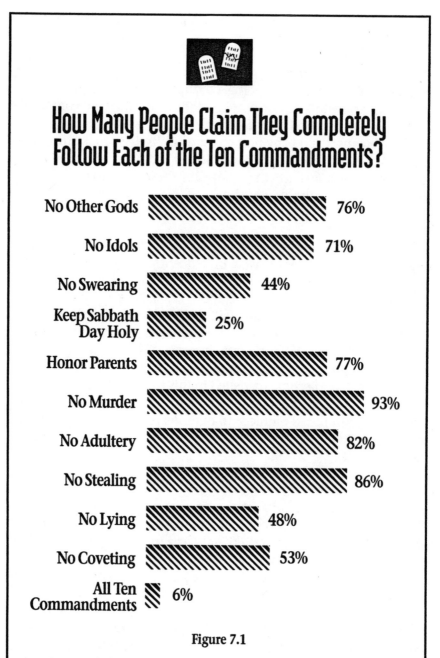

How Many People Claim They Completely Follow Each of the Ten Commandments?

No Other Gods	76%
No Idols	71%
No Swearing	44%
Keep Sabbath Day Holy	25%
Honor Parents	77%
No Murder	93%
No Adultery	82%
No Stealing	86%
No Lying	48%
No Coveting	53%
All Ten Commandments	6%

Figure 7.1

Source: Barna Research Group, Ltd. 1992

promiscuity is practiced most frequently by young adults, although they do not have exclusive rights to such misbehavior. Also notice that about one-third of the ethnic minorities (31%) indicated they are not completely reliable in this matter.

Inappropriate sexual behavior was more likely to be admitted by men (28%) than by women (9%). Most born-again Christians (90%) stated they were completely honorable in this regard. This means that among non-Christians, one-quarter of the public engage in sexual sin.

#8: No Stealing
Despite reports that petty larceny and other forms of theft have reached record proportions in our country, 86% of all adults claim they are completely satisfying God's command regarding abstinence from stealing. (See data table 88.)

Admission of theft was much more common among men (23%) than women (6%). It was also more likely among baby busters (28%), Hispanics (28%), single adults (24%) and people in the Midwest (20%). Nine percent of the born-again adults indicated they are less than completely following this code.

#9: Do Not Lie
The survey revealed that about one-third of the public say lying is sometimes necessary, but more than half (52%) sometimes lie.

The older a person was, the more likely they were to state they are completely satisfying the commandment to always tell the truth. (Ah, but how do we know they are not lying about this?) Deceitful language was more common among men than women; among college-educated adults than those with less formal education; among people without young kids than among parents; among people in metropolitan areas than among rural residents; among people who do not attend church and those who do not read the Bible. Just over half of the born-again adults (53%) said they were completely fulfilling this commandment; 44% of the non-Christians claimed compliance. (See data table 89.)

#10: No Jealousy over Possessions
How tough it is to fulfill this commandment in a society that prides itself on progress, and in which progress and success are measured materialistically. In fact, barely half of the adults in America (53%) say

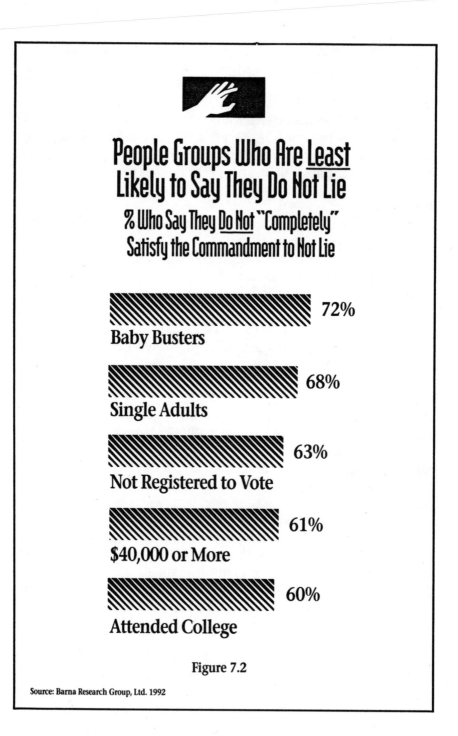

People Groups Who Are <u>Least</u> Likely to Say They Do Not Lie

% Who Say They <u>Do Not</u> "Completely" Satisfy the Commandment to Not Lie

72%
Baby Busters

68%
Single Adults

63%
Not Registered to Vote

61%
$40,000 or More

60%
Attended College

Figure 7.2

Source: Barna Research Group, Ltd. 1992

they are completely honoring this part of the Law. (See data table 90.)

Again, the older a person was, the more likely they were to believe they satisfy this Law. It may be easier to do so as one ages because it is the older people in America who own all the "right stuff." The people groups least likely to say they are completely in line with this commandment were college graduates (36%), single adults (37%), baby busters (38%) and people with above-average incomes (42%). Nearly half of the born-again segment (43%) experience lapses in this area.

THE BIG PICTURE

Remember the passage in Genesis 18 when Abraham beseeched God to spare Sodom if just 50 righteous people could be found? God agreed, so Abraham pressed Him further. Would He be willing to spare the city if just 45 righteous ones could be found? If just 40 righteous beings could be found? If just 30 righteous people were identified? If only 20 righteous ones were located? If a mere 10 righteous people were found? Graciously, God agreed to not destroy the city if even that handful of obedient people were found. Perhaps Abraham should be credited with originating the idea of the lowest common denominator.

Were Abraham alive today, he might find reason for holding a similar conversation with God regarding the decay of American society. In America, 1992, we have great reason to thank God for His grace through Jesus. The survey data reveal that just 6% of the adult population indicated they are living in complete fulfillment of all ten of the Commandments. This was true for 8% of the born-again adults and 4% of the nonbelievers.

The statistics also indicate that faith in Christ, and the related commitment to God and His Word, do seem to make a difference in people's life-styles. For every one of the commandments, born-again Christians demonstrated a slightly higher likelihood of saying they completely satisfy the admonition in question. The difference in response levels between believers and nonbelievers was not always as significant as might have been desired. However, the encouraging finding is that if people's responses concerning their behavior in light of the commandments are reliable, Christians *do* lead a different type of life than do non-Christians.

ACTION STEPS

Denial of sin is rampant in America. The probability is great that many people who claimed to be completely satisfying any given commandment were fooling themselves. The prevailing mind-set in our nation is that yes, people are sinful creatures but that they, themselves, have no deep-rooted, frequently manifested sin problem.

Granted, righteousness is not the product of works but of faith in Christ. Nevertheless, we are called to demonstrate our faith by our behavior and the condition of our hearts. And we are able to strengthen our relationship with God through obedience to His Word—which includes the commandments.

How can we build a greater commitment among people to a life-style that reflects His will?

Know the rules. People cannot consciously follow what they do not know. We must studiously avoid the temptation or the trap of becoming legalistic in our faith and life-style. God's rules were provided to help us negotiate the snares of life. Rather than permitting people to view the Ten Commandments as an outdated series of rules that are irrelevant to a high-tech world, help people comprehend the value of knowing and following the basic rules God intended for us to follow—for our own best interests.

Celebrate righteous behavior. One of the tragedies of the Church today is that it rarely celebrates the good works of its people. We fear that praising men for their efforts will lead to pride and ultimately to a fall. Unfortunately, in the process of ignoring what people do well, we send a message that such laudable efforts do not matter. Can you discover ways of encouraging people to continue their righteous efforts without giving them cause for boasting or pride?

Offer practical help. For the most part, Americans do not need detailed lectures identifying what is wrong about their life-styles. In most cases, they are cognizant of their moral and behavioral failures. Guilt trips simply do not motivate change. In more cases than not, shaming people for their weaknesses creates the opposite response of that intended.

People admit they are most likely to sin in the areas of swearing, lying and coveting what others have. One of the primary complaints regarding Christianity is that it is irrelevant to people's lives. Knowing this, perhaps we can fashion a positive response to people's needs.

Can we understand and respond to these known areas of difficulty, and assist adults in satisfying the dictates of Scripture? It is this type of partnership people are looking for in addressing their acknowledged deficiencies.

By promoting behavior that is acceptable to God, and more personally pleasing, we may be able to change people's perception of the Bible from one of an ancient Holy Book of wisdom to a modern guidebook for successful living. That process might help to reposition the Church as a Body of imperfect but loving and compassionate people supporting each other in a cooperative drive to live a better, more fulfilling, more righteous life.

CHAPTER 8
THE NINETIES LIFE-STYLE

CHAPTER HIGHLIGHTS

- Despite the growing problem of functional illiteracy, two-thirds of all adults had read part of a book other than the Bible in the past week.
- Young adults were about twice as likely to have read part of a book as to have watched MTV during the past week.
- Christian baby busters were actually more likely than their non-Christian counterparts to have watched MTV in the past week.
- The vast majority of the adult population participates in some form of organized religious activity during the course of an average month.
- Participation in even some of the most common religious activities appears to be seasonal in nature.
- Born-again Christians were more likely to participate in religious activities than were non-Christians. Few areas of life-style, apart from religious involvement, made Christians discernible from non-Christians.
- Adults identified the church as a place to meet new friends more often than they named any other place.
- The most common way people donate money to charitable organizations is through the church collection plate.

WHAT WE DISCOVERED

You can learn a lot about people based on how they spend their time. How do Americans allocate their jealously guarded free time?

Despite the fears that America will become a nation that does not read, two-thirds of all adults interviewed in January 1992 said they had read part of a book, other than the Bible, during the prior week. Reading as a leisure pursuit was most common among baby boomers, college graduates, people of average or above-average incomes, adults employed in white-collar positions, and city residents.

Concerned that literacy skills will continue to be eroded by slavish attention to television, some social critics have warned that young adults are abandoning books in favor of tele-trash, the televised programs offering questionable morality and aberrant views about life. The data from this research, however, suggest that young adults have neither given up on reading nor exhibited total devotion to tele-trash.

If we examine viewing habits related to MTV, cited by many church leaders as a chief supplier of tele-trash, the data show that young adults are more likely to pick up a book than to view music videos and rockumentaries. Reading was much more common among baby busters and baby boomers than was watching MTV. Among busters, 64% said they had read part of a book in the last week; 36% claimed to have viewed portions of MTV. Among the boomers, 72% indicated having read from a book, which is four times as many as claimed to have tuned into the music channel (19%). One must wonder if the same pattern holds true among teenagers and adolescents. (See data tables 50, 53.)

But get this: *Christian baby busters were more likely to watch MTV during the past week than were non-Christian busters!* Among boomers, there was no difference in the likelihood of tuning into MTV between believers and nonbelievers. The study did not evaluate how many times people turned to MTV, or how much time they spent watching the channel, but this information has some frightening implications for the Church.

In the week prior to the interview, almost half of the adults had attended a church worship service (47%) or had read the Bible (47%). About one out of four adults is likely to volunteer some time to a church (24%); one out of four will volunteer time to a nonprofit orga-

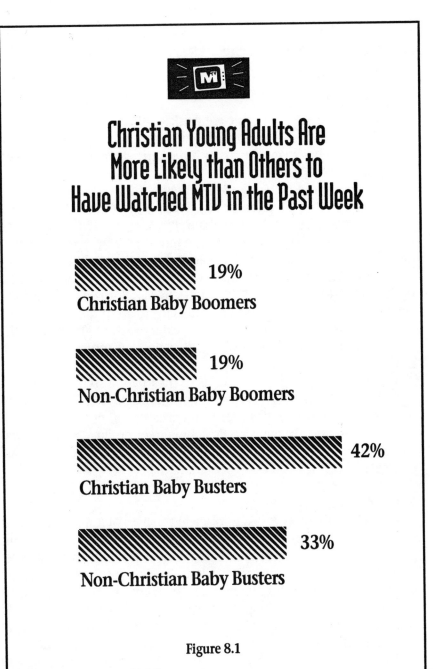

Christian Young Adults Are More Likely than Others to Have Watched MTV in the Past Week

19% **Christian Baby Boomers**

19% **Non-Christian Baby Boomers**

42% **Christian Baby Busters**

33% **Non-Christian Baby Busters**

Figure 8.1

Source: Barna Research Group, Ltd. 1992

nization other than a church (24%); and nearly one out of four will attend a church Sunday School class (22%). (See data tables 47-49,51,52.)

On a Monthly Basis

In the July 1991 survey people were asked which of several different activities they had engaged in during the prior month. Their behavior showed that religion remained an important element in their lives, along with entertainment.

More than 9 out of 10 people say they watch television and listen to the radio during a typical month. What may be more surprising is that about half of all adults (47%) said they had attended a movie at a theater in the last 30 days. Trips to the movie theater were most common among men (56%), people earning more than $40,000 (60%), Hispanics (72%), baby busters (80%), single adults (69%), Catholics (57%) and residents of the Pacific states (60%). Born-again Christians were notably less likely than non-Christians to go to the movies (39% versus 53%, respectively). The most theater-resistant group were the elderly, among whom only 12% had gone to a movie in the past month. (See data table 7.)

Other monthly, nonreligious activities people had engaged in included attending a class at a school or training center (21%), volunteering time to assist a nonprofit organization other than a church (35%), and refusing to buy a particular brand or product because it was being boycotted by a group or cause supported by the person (14%). (See data tables 4-6.)

Religious Activity

Much religious activity is taking place in the lives of millions of Americans on a regular basis. In a typical month, three-quarters of the adult public (76%) say they would attend a church worship service at least once. There are some seasonal variations, though. Just 54% actually did attend in June of 1991. Church attendance appears to drop substantially from June through August. Six out of ten people claim they would read the Bible, excluding while they were in a church, during a typical month. Again, the hypothetical exceeds the actual; just 42% said they had actually read part of the Bible in the month preceding the July 1991 interviews. On the average, 30% had attended a Sunday School class during the month before the July study. (See data tables 1,2,9.)

Religious Activities We Engage in During a Typical Month

Attend Church — 76%

Read the Bible — 59%

Attend Sunday School — 30%

Figure 8.2

Source: Barna Research Group, Ltd. 1992

In general, the people most likely to participate in any of the religious activities evaluated were women, blacks, adults 27 or older, married people, Protestants, born-again Christians and residents of the South.

Notice the discrepancy regarding weekly and monthly Bible reading. In January 1992, 47% said they had read the Bible in the past *week,* but just 42% of those interviewed in July 1991 said they had read the Bible in the past *month.* This highlights the inconsistent nature of people's spiritual involvement. Much of our behavior (religious and otherwise) is seasonal. Bible reading and church attendance tend to peak during the Christmas and Easter seasons, and to slack off during other times of the year. Participation in small groups is highest during the fall and winter months, but drops off substantially during the spring and summer. (See data tables 9,49.)

Standing out from the Crowd
Over the years, surprisingly little research shows evidence that the life-styles of born-again Christians differ from those of nonbelievers, apart from involvement in religious activities. Of the activities measured this year regarding common activities, believers were much more involved in every aspect of religious involvement.

In nonreligious activities, the profile was nearly identical among believers and nonbelievers concerning reading books, boycotting products and services, volunteering free time, attending classes and watching MTV.

Christians were somewhat less likely to attend movies (39%) than were non-Christians (53%). This gap is largely attributable to the fact that women, married people and the elderly—three dominant segments of the Christian population, numerically—were less likely than other adults to visit movie theaters. Whether this is due to their faith commitment or due to other life-style considerations cannot be determined from the available information. (See data table 7.)

Mating, Dating and Relating
Americans are still striving to develop a wider and deeper circle of friends. Almost half of all adults (45%) said they would like to have more close friends than they currently have. For many people, the pace of life seems to make friendships more difficult to develop. One-quarter (23%) claimed that "with society changing so fast, it's nearly impossible

Most Christian Women Avoid Movie Theaters

39% Yes	61% No

53% Yes	47% No

% of Christian women who go to the movies each month

% of non-Christian women who go to the movies each month

Figure 8.3

Source: Barna Research Group, Ltd. 1992

to have long-lasting friendships these days." This perspective was most common among ethnic minorities, lower-income people and those who are not presently married. Interestingly, baby boomers were the least likely generation to concur with this sentiment (18%, compared to 26% among other people). (See data tables 22,23.)

When people think about how they might meet new friends, two places dominate their thinking: work and church. Almost half of the adults interviewed said that if they wanted to make new friends, they would expect those new friends to be found from among their colleagues at work (45%) or among people who comprise their church (49%). Other potential places to find friends might be social or exercise clubs (listed by 20%), through community organizations or activities (18%), at school (18%), in the neighborhood (12%) or through involvement in sports activities (8%). (See data table 24.)

Although churches were the most commonly listed source of new friends, religious centers were not universally viewed as a viable meeting place. Women (61%) were much more likely than men (36%) to list churches. The older a person was, the more likely they were to name churches. Less than half of all busters and boomers cited churches as a high-potential source, while more than two-thirds of the older adults did so. Other segments listing churches more readily were blacks (65%), rural residents (55%), Southerners (61%), born-again Christians (75%) and Protestants (62%). Among the groups least likely to cite the church as a likely meeting place were single adults (27%).

Making the World a Better Place[1]
In January 1992, 46% of Americans said they had donated money to charitable organizations during the past 30 days. This timing, of course, encompasses end-of-year giving motivated by the holiday season and by the end of the tax year. (See data table 112.)

Baby boomers, it seems, have a bad reputation among many people as being unwilling to part with their money for good causes. The reality is that boomers are every bit as likely as prior generations were at this stage in their life cycle to donate money to charity. They are nearly as likely as older adults to give money to nonprofit organizations, although they give their money based on very different criteria than do their predecessors.

The survey also showed that the better educated and wealthier people were more likely to have donated money than were people of less-

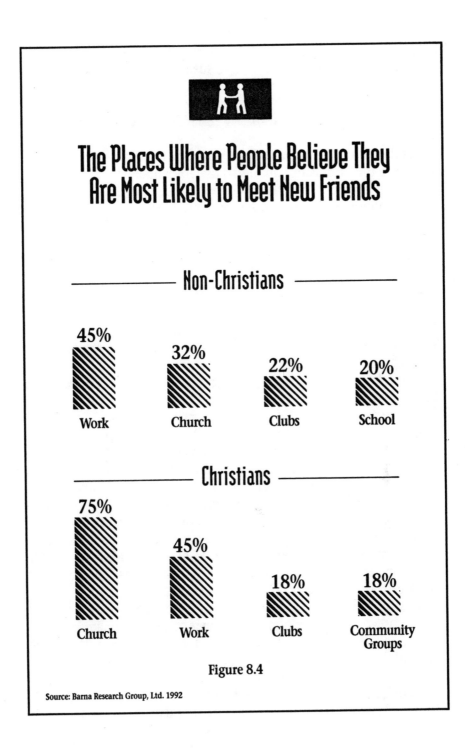

The Places Where People Believe They Are Most Likely to Meet New Friends

Non-Christians

- 45% Work
- 32% Church
- 22% Clubs
- 20% School

Christians

- 75% Church
- 45% Work
- 18% Clubs
- 18% Community Groups

Figure 8.4

Source: Barna Research Group, Ltd. 1992

er means and schooling. Whites were much more likely than ethnic minorities to donate funds (51% versus 30%). Those who were least likely to have donated any money were Southerners (39% had done so), adults not registered to vote (31%), Baptists (38%), those who had not attended church in the past week (39%), and charismatics and Pentecostals (39%).

Of the various ways available for donating money to worthy causes, here were the most common means used by donors:

Giving through a church collection/temple donation	69%
Responding to a person-to-person appeal	39%
Responding to a direct mail appeal	31%
Through an automatic deduction from a paycheck	24%
Responding to a television, radio or print advertisement	13%
Responding to a telephone appeal	12%

Ask and You May Receive

Who responds best to these different types of appeals? Here is the profile of who was most likely to have donated money in response to a specific type of funds request.

Church collections. Giving as part of a church offering was most likely among pre-boomers and senior citizens, ethnic minorities, married adults, suburbanites, Southerners, born-again Christians, Catholics, people who had attended church in the past week and those who had read the Bible in the last week. Notice that one out of five born-again Christians who had donated money to some charity did *not* give money to a church in the past month. (See data table 115.)

Interpersonal appeals. A face-to-face request for a gift was most likely to result in donations from white adults and from those who had not attended a church service in the prior week. (See data table 116.)

Mail solicitation. Appeals sent by mail were most likely to result in donations from women, older adults, retired adults, people in the Northeast, and born-again Christians. (See data table 113.)

Payroll deductions. Automatic deductions from one's paycheck were most common among baby boomers, college graduates, parents, people in the Midwest and South, and adults who had not read the Bible in the past week. (See data table 118.)

Media appeals. Requests for contributions made by television, radio or the print media had the highest chance of garnering results among blacks and lower-income adults. (See data table 117.)

Telemarketing. Many people have complained that fund-raising by telephone is a practice that exploits the people who can least afford to be ripped off. However, research suggests that the people most likely to provide a donation in response to an unsolicited telephone call were whites and people who had attended college—two segments usually not listed among the groups who need to be protected from unscrupulous telemarketers. (See data table 114.)

ACTION STEPS

Sometimes we minister on the basis of bad assumptions. Gaining valid insights into how Americans really behave can help shape your ministry so that it takes advantage of the existing opportunities and avoids the probable pitfalls.

Reading happens. For instance, although it is true that our nation is beset with rampant functional illiteracy, it would be wrong to assume this means people are no longer reading books and other materials. People will read if it is interesting material or clearly to their benefit to do so.

New-time religion. We used to assume that if a person indicated an interest in a church, they could be counted on for several blocks of time during the course of a typical week. Today, though, time being at a premium, we can probably expect to get two blocks of time from a young adult during the course of a week. If one of those blocks is committed to a worship service, how can you optimize the remaining time block you will receive from these people?[2]

Evangelism. Does it disturb you that fewer than 4 out of 10 Christians share their faith with nonbelievers during the course of a typical month? And did you notice that the competition is getting more aggressive? More than one-quarter of all nonbelievers are sharing their brand of faith with others, too.

Now is the time to determine how well-equipped the people in your church are to effectively build relationships with nonbelievers. How well-prepared and comfortable they are in sharing their faith in Christ, and to ascertain how a church can support people in their efforts to reach the community and the world for Christ. Simply holding witnessing seminars and other traditional programs may no longer meet the need for preparing the saints. Discuss the need for evangelism with your fellow partners in outreach and learn what types of resources and assistance might promote more effective evangelism.

Money for ministry. The offering plate is an accepted part of raising funds for the church's ministry. But the research also shows that to enhance the capital reserves available for ministry, it is important to use the personal touch in raising funds.

Other research we have conducted has shown that younger adults, in particular, respond favorably to tangible demonstrations of how donated money has been used. Video presentations of ministry projects and partners, or other forms of documentation showing money for ministry that has been well-spent, are critical when attempting to seek contributions from world-class skeptics. The money to sustain effective ministry is usually available, but it is generally given to those organizations that can best prove they not only need funds but will use them well. Assuming a church "deserves" people's giving is no longer part of Americans' vocabulary.

Notes
1. The research concerning charitable giving was conducted in cooperation with *The Non-Profit Times,* Skillman, NJ.
2. For a more detailed discussion of this trend, see "Time Is the Enemy" in *Ministry Currents,* January-March 1992, pp. 11-13.

POLITICS AND THE ISSUES THAT MOTIVATE US

CHAPTER HIGHLIGHTS

- A larger proportion of born-again Christians (77%) than non-Christians (67%) were registered to vote.
- Protestants and Catholics were equally likely to be registered to vote. However, two of the most politically conservative groups—those attending charismatic or Pentecostal churches and those associated with evangelical denominations—were less likely to be registered (66%) than were those affiliated with the less conservative, mainline Protestant churches (75%).
- Protestant adults were twice as likely as Catholic adults to be registered as Republicans. However, even among Protestants, more were Democrats than Republicans.
- About half of the mainline and evangelical Protestants were registered Republicans. Only one-fifth of the Baptists were Republicans.
- During the presidency of George Bush the Republican party has remained stable in the proportion of adherents while the Democratic party has gained ground.
- The key issues on which voters will be judging the 1992 presidential candidates will be their positions related to public education, crime, drug law enforcement, the economy and health care.
- Among the issues least important to voters were abortion and the separation of church and state.
- Most Americans disagree with the notion that boycotts of products or companies do not accomplish anything.

WHAT WE DISCOVERED

Over the past two decades, we have witnessed a decline in the proportion of adults who turn out to vote during key elections. Large-scale campaigns have been mounted to persuade adults of the value of being a registered voter. Millions of Americans are ineligible to vote because they failed to legally register to cast a ballot.

The elections that draw the largest numbers of voters are those in which the president is selected. Yet, even in presidential election years, barely half of the registered voters turn out to indicate their preference. The percentage of registered voters who participate in primary elections (the candidates whose names will appear on the November ballot are chosen) is even smaller—sometimes as few as just 10% of the electorate turn out for this critical winnowing process.

The implication is that an ever smaller body of people is making increasingly important choices on behalf of the growing population of Americans. Each person who votes these days represents a growing number of Americans who have consciously chosen to sit on the sidelines and watch the proceedings.

Voter Registration and Election Turnout Statistics, 1974-1988

Year	Voting Age Population Registered to Vote	Voting Age Population That Cast a Vote
1974	62.2%	35.9%
1976	66.7%	53.5%
1978	62.6%	34.9%
1980	66.9%	52.6%
1982	64.1%	38.0%
1984	68.3%	53.1%
1986	64.3%	33.4%
1988	66.6%	50.1%

Source: U.S. Bureau of the Census, *Statistical Abstract of the United States, 1991;* pages 268, 270.

Who Participates in the Process?

Voter registration data released by the government confirm the findings of surveys. The people who are most likely registered to vote are older adults, those who are better educated, married adults, whites and those who have higher household income levels. Notice that the people who most need the political process to fend for them—ethnic minorities, and those with less education, income and (in most cases) access to the reigns of political power—are least likely to be engaged in the electoral process.

Our surveys indicate that born-again Christians are somewhat more likely than non-Christians to be registered to vote. In January 1992 we found that 71% of the population was registered. Among born-again Christians, 77% were registered, and only 67% of the non-Christians were registered. Because the born-again population represents a minority of the nation's adults, however, they remain outnumbered in terms of total voters. Projecting these percentages to the adult population at large (190 million adults) shows that there are about 76 million non-Christians registered to vote, compared to about 58 million born-again Christians. (See data table 119.)

People associated with Protestant churches were no more likely to be registered to vote than were adults aligned with the Catholic church (74% compared to 73%). However, within the Protestant ranks there was substantial variation in the probability of being registered. Among the Methodist respondents, for instance, 86% were signed up to vote, but just 65% of the adults associated with charismatic and Pentecostal churches were registered.

Unexpectedly, the data showed that among people attending churches associated with noncharismatic, evangelical denominations, only 69% were registered. Thus, two of the most politically conservative groups—those attending charismatic or Pentecostal churches and those associated with evangelical denominations—were less likely to be registered (66%) than were those affiliated with mainline Protestant churches (75%).

Party Time

Party affiliation also varied across people groups. Democrats retained a substantial edge over those who claimed to be registered as Republicans or unaffiliated (i.e. independents). Overall, 44% said they were

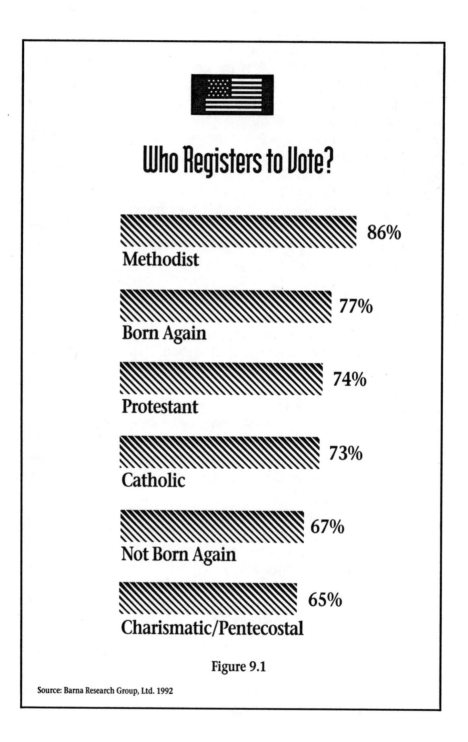

Who Registers to Vote?

86%
Methodist

77%
Born Again

74%
Protestant

73%
Catholic

67%
Not Born Again

65%
Charismatic/Pentecostal

Figure 9.1

Source: Barna Research Group, Ltd. 1992

registered as Democrats, 29% as Republicans, and 20% as independents. The remaining 6% could not recall their affiliation. (See data table 120.)

Each of the three affiliations had a different type of appeal to different people groups. For instance, women were least likely to be independents (17%), and men were more comfortable with being independents (24%) and somewhat less likely to be Democrats (41%, compared to 46% of the women). Age made an even bigger difference in people's inclinations. Among baby busters (adults 18-26 years old) 36% were independent; among baby boomers (adults 27-45) 24% were independent; among pre-boomers (adults 46 or older) just 17% were independents.

Voter Registration and Party Affiliation by Church Affiliation
(Base: 722 registered voters)

Type of church	Registered	Republican	Democrat	Independent
Protestant	74%	37%	47%	16%
Catholic	73%	16%	51%	27%
Mainline Protestant	75%	49%	34%	17%
Evangelical/Charismatic/Pentecostal	66%	50%	39%	11%
Baptist	81%	19%	58%	18%

People were more likely than average to register as Democrats if they were noncaucasian (74% of the blacks and 56% of the Hispanics were Democrats), from lower-income households, had low levels of formal education, were widowed, lived in urban or rural areas and were located in the South (57%). Perhaps surprisingly, Baptists were well above average in the probability of being Democrats (58%), along with Catholics (51%).

Looking at party affiliation by a different categorization, note that among all Protestants 37% were Republicans, nearly half were Democrats (47%), and the remainder independents. This was quite different from the registration of people attending churches of evangelical denominations. Among those adults, half were Republicans, 39% Democrats, and just 11% independents.

Adults more likely than average to be Republicans were college graduates, whites, parents of children under 18, those from upper-income households, suburbanites and adults living in the Midwest and Western states. Lutherans, Methodists and those attending charismatic or Pentecostal churches were well above the norm in their likelihood of being registered Republicans.

Democratic Believers

A plurality of born-again Christians were Democrats (43%). However, among believers, Republicans outnumbered independents by a two to one margin (33% versus 16%). Among non-Christians, a plurality were Democrats (45%), but the division between Republicans and independents was even (26% and 24%, respectively). (See data table 120.)

Voter Registration and Party Affiliation Among Christians and Non-Christians

Registration	Christians	Non-Christians	All Adults
Democratic	43% (25 million)	45% (34 million)	44% (59 million)
Republican	33% (20 million)	26% (20 million)	30% (40 million)
Independent	16% (9 million)	24% (18 million)	20% (27 million)
Not sure	8% (5 million)	6% (4 million)	6% (9 million)

Numerically, this means there are approximately 25 million Democrats, 20 million Republicans, and 9 million independents among the Christian population. Another five million Christians have no recollection of their party affiliation and would be scattered among the three designations. Among the non-Christians, the Democrats hold a much larger edge: 34 million voters, compared to 20 million Republicans and 18 million independents. There were about 4 million undesignated non-Christian voters.

Notice the different profile of each of these three voting groups. People registered as Republicans were equally divided between Christians and non-Christians. Among Democrats, non-Christians outnumbered Christians by 9 million people. Among independents, twice as many were non-Christians as Christians.

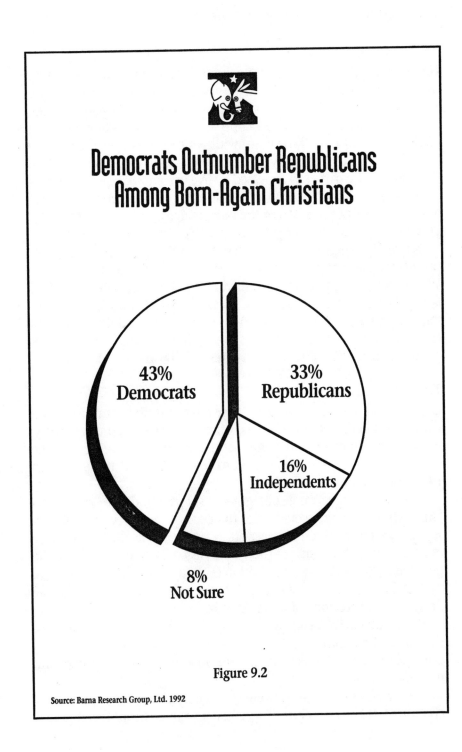

Democrats Outnumber Republicans Among Born-Again Christians

43%
Democrats

33%
Republicans

16%
Independents

8%
Not Sure

Figure 9.2

Source: Barna Research Group, Ltd. 1992

The Bush Influence

Has party registration changed much during the Bush era? Comparing the preceding figures to a similar survey we conducted four years earlier, we detect a minor but significant shift in party allegiance during the 1988-1991 period. When comparing the registration of those adults who could recall the party with which they were affiliated, we see that the Republican party (Bush's party) has remained stable (32%). The Democratic party has increased by five percentage points, jumping from 42% in 1988 to 47% at the beginning of 1992. This growth came at the expense of the ranks of the independents, who decreased from 26% of the electorate four years ago to 21% at the start of 1992.

Normally, when people are pleased with the performance of their president, the number of people registered in his party increases. When the voting public is dissatisfied with the president's efforts, there is a backlash effect in which there is growth in the ranks of the opposing party or among independents. The increasing number of Democrats coincides with recent polls showing a substantial proportion of people who are disenchanted with President Bush's record in office.

The Key Issues

Our political system is complex these days, and the list of issues on which presidents and other elected officials make decisions is lengthy. In election campaigns, the candidates attempt to carve out unique positions on issues of major interest to voters. What are those issues in 1992? (See data tables 121-135.)

Upon asking our sample of registered voters to indicate how important each of 15 issues would be in the decision of which candidate to support in the presidential election, 5 issues emerged as particularly important to people. Each of these 5 was listed by three-quarters of the population as being very important in their candidate selection process.

The five issues were public education, crime, enforcement of the drug laws, the economy and health care.

Four issues were deemed very important by about two-thirds of the voter population. Those issues were taxes, human rights protection, reducing the budget deficit, and policies related to welfare and unemployment.

A third echelon of issues were characterized as very important by about half of the electorate. Those issues were environmental policy, abortion, military and defense spending, separation of church and state, and women's rights.

Bringing up the rear, only one out of four voters cited the mass transportation policy issue as very important in their candidate selection.

Evaluating the broad message that this ranking sends, it appears that Americans are examining the presidential candidates (and, probably, other candidates for federal office) in light of what decisions they would make that will affect them most directly and personally. The five leading issues are all matters on which a president's leadership and decisions could significantly affect a person's life. The issues toward the bottom end of the continuum—e.g. mass transportation, separation of church and state, abortion and defense spending—were items that people perceive to have a less direct influence upon their lives.

How Many Voters Consider Each Issue Very Important in Their Candidate Selection (Base: 722 registered voters)

Rank	Issue	Very Important
1	public education	78%
1	crime	78%
1	enforcement of drug laws	78%
4	the economy	76%
5	health care	75%
6	taxes	66%
6	human rights protection	66%
8	budget deficit	64%
9	welfare, unemployment policy	63%
10	environmental policy	57%
11	abortion	56%
12	military, defense spending	51%
13	separation of church & state	50%
14	women's rights	49%
15	mass transportation policy	26%

Different Strokes for Different Folks

Not all voters are equally interested in a given issue. Briefly, consider which population segments are most and least interested in the candidates' stands on these issues.

Public education. Surveys continue to show that the majority of Americans believe our public school system is falling apart. International studies have demonstrated that American students perform at lower levels than do students in other nations. Interestingly, it is the very groups who are least likely to have been the recipients of a strong education who were most interested in how the candidates plan to address our educational dilemma. The groups particularly tuned in to this issue are those who have the lowest levels of education and income: blacks, Democrats and voters in the South. This issue is least important among Republicans, college graduates and people from households making $60,000 or more a year. (See data table 125.)

Crime. As crime rates continue to soar in the United States, it is little wonder that almost four out of five adults named this as a dominant theme in their own vote deliberations. Crime was especially important among women, the elderly, people with little education and low household incomes, and residents of the South. (See data table 126.)

Drug law enforcement. This issue was of paramount importance to people 46 or older, those with limited education and income levels, and adults living in urban or rural settings. The least concerned about the issue were college graduates and those voters with the highest levels of income. (See data table 132.)

The economy. During the past year it has been virtually impossible to escape the media's attention to the recession and the effect of our economy on people's lives. The handling of our economy is the issue that has the greatest across-the-board interest among voters. The only segment that emerged as especially interested in this issue was single adults. The sole group that seemed significantly less interested in this issue was the Hispanic population. (See data table 134.)

Health care. As millions of Americans live without any type of health care or medical insurance, and as tens of thousands of employers across the nation decrease the health care benefits paid on behalf of employees, this issue has rapidly risen to the top of people's list of concerns. Interestingly, the segments least focused on this issue are Republicans, Hispanics and the wealthy. (See data table 129.)

Christians and Non-Christians Do Not Agree on the Importance of Some Key Issues

Issue	Born-again Christians Very Important	Issue Rank	Non-Christians Very Important	Issue Rank
drug law enforcement	81%	1	76%	2
crime	80%	2	76%	2
public education	78%	3	78%	1
the economy	78%	3	75%	5
health care	74%	5	76%	2
taxes	66%	6	66%	7
welfare/unemployment	66%	6	61%	10
budget deficit	64%	8	65%	8
human rights protection	63%	9	69%	6
abortion	60%	10	53%	13
separation of church and state	56%	11	45%	14
environmental policy	50%	12	62%	9
military and defense spending	47%	13	55%	11
women's rights	44%	14	54%	12
mass transit	20%	15	30%	15
(respondent base)	315		407	

Taxes. What politician has not bemoaned having to take a stand on taxation? As a central "pocketbook issue," two out of three voters say a candidate's position on taxes is critical. Adults who are particularly focused on this issue include blacks and people with limited education and income. (See data table 123.)

Human rights protection. An emphasis upon this aspect of public policy is most important to people 46 and older, downscale adults, blacks, urban residents, Democrats and Southerners. Perhaps surprisingly, non-Christians were significantly more interested in this issue than were Christians (69% versus 63%). (See data table 133.)

Budget deficit. The national budget deficit is a more critical matter to people the older they get. It is also of greater importance to people of limited means and among whites. (See data table 128.)

Welfare and unemployment policies. Although most Americans know someone whose job has been eliminated or drastically cut back as a result of the economic slump, a relatively small proportion of Americans is unemployed or collecting welfare benefits. Even so, two-thirds said this policy was of major interest to them. The segments who were most keenly interested in candidates' views in this area were people 27 or older, adults who had low levels of education and household income, and rural residents. (See data table 130.)

Environmental policy. As might be expected, the baby busters demonstrated the highest interest in such policy positions. Other voter groups who reflected a similar interest in this issue were blacks, low-income adults, singles, urban residents and those in the northeast. Republicans were remarkably less interested in environmental policy (only 45% said this was a very important issue); and people living in the Mountain and Western states, often portrayed by the media as the home of the environmental extremists, were also substantially less moved by this issue (48%). (See data table 124.)

Born-again Christians were much less energized by the issue of environmental policy than were non-Christians (50% versus 62%). Similarly, people who had attended a church service in the past week were much less likely to cite such policy matters as very important to them than were adults who had not attended a church service (51% compared to 63%). Far from being leaders of the environmental movement, it appears that many (if not most) Christians are rather removed from the challenges of environmental protection and restoration.

Abortion. Although abortion has been a high-profile issue for the better part of the last 15 years, it appears that most Americans do not retain a burning interest in this matter. Half said the issue is one of great importance to them, but additional research on people's views regarding abortion indicates that their views are neither solid nor intensely felt. This issue was considered very important by an above-average proportion of Hispanics, people of low income and Southern-ers. (See data table 122.)

The adults who had attended a church service in the past week were more likely than others to describe abortion as a key issue to them (64% versus 47%, respectively). Incredibly, born-again Christians were barely more interested in this issue than were non-Christians (60% versus 53%).

Military and defense spending. This issue was most compelling to the elderly, Democrats, people living in the South and in the Western

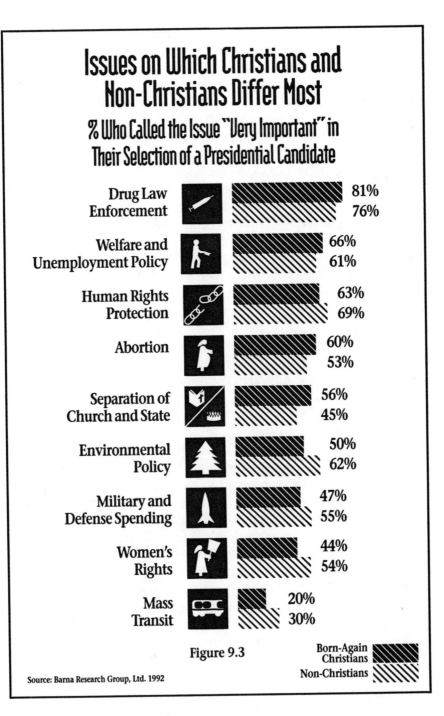

Issues on Which Christians and Non-Christians Differ Most

% Who Called the Issue "Very Important" in Their Selection of a Presidential Candidate

Issue	Born-Again Christians	Non-Christians
Drug Law Enforcement	81%	76%
Welfare and Unemployment Policy	66%	61%
Human Rights Protection	63%	69%
Abortion	60%	53%
Separation of Church and State	56%	45%
Environmental Policy	50%	62%
Military and Defense Spending	47%	55%
Women's Rights	44%	54%
Mass Transit	20%	30%

Figure 9.3

Born-Again Christians
Non-Christians

Source: Barna Research Group, Ltd. 1992

states, adults who had not attended church in the past week, non-Christians, and lower-income people. (See data table 127.)

Separation of church and state. The candidates' stands on this issue were of relatively higher importance to men (the only issue on which they exhibited greater interest than women) people 46 or older, blacks, people living in the South and West, born-again Christians, church attenders, and Protestants. (See data table 131.)

Women's rights. The segments demonstrating the greatest interest in this matter were blacks, single adults, low-income householders, people living in cities, non-Christians, and those who do not attend church services. The segment least likely to describe this as a very important issue were Republicans and adults living in upper-income households. (See data table 121.)

Mass transportation policy. People most likely to be affected by mass transit policies were those who exhibited the greatest interest in stands on this matter. Those groups included the elderly, low-income adults, and people from ethnic minority groups. (See data table 135.)

Faith and Perspective

Do the spiritual beliefs and religious practices of Americans influence their political views? Although the information collected in this year's survey is, in itself, inconclusive, when combined with data from other studies conducted in the recent past the answer is that the influence is relatively minor.

The problem is not so much a disinterest in participation in the political process as a lack of insight into the problems and situations in which Christians might have an influence. When it comes to being informed about the issues (i.e. depth of understanding) or having a coherent worldview (i.e. a philosophy of life based upon biblical prin-ciples), Christians emerge no different from nonbelievers.

On the other hand, the belief in the value of participation in per-suasive action remains firm. When survey respondents were asked for their reaction to the statement "participating in a boycott of products or companies does not really accomplish anything," two-thirds dis-agreed with the statement (32% strongly disagreed, 35% moderately disagreed). Although this is a different approach from direct involve-ment in political election campaigns, the underlying concept— attempting to exert influence upon the entities that shape our daily environment—is the same. (See data table 46.)

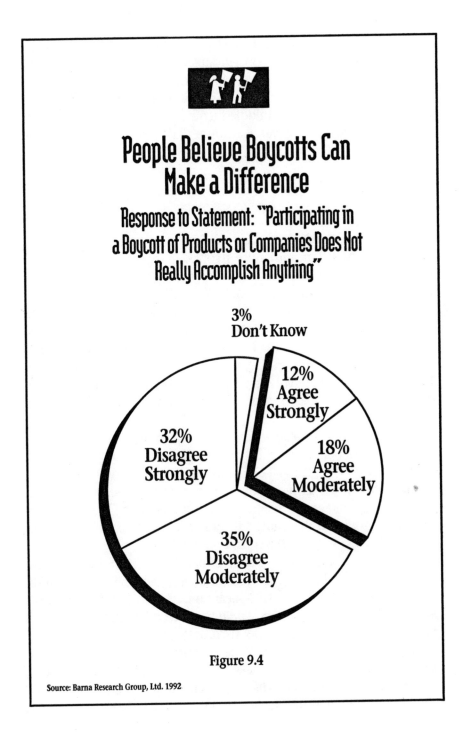

People Believe Boycotts Can Make a Difference

Response to Statement: "Participating in a Boycott of Products or Companies Does Not Really Accomplish Anything"

3%
Don't Know

12%
Agree
Strongly

18%
Agree
Moderately

32%
Disagree
Strongly

35%
Disagree
Moderately

Figure 9.4

Source: Barna Research Group, Ltd. 1992

Christians and non-Christians were indistinguishable in the reaction to this statement. The people groups who were most supportive of the idea of boycotting offensive products or companies were adults 45 or younger (70%, compared to 60% of the older adults), college graduates (70%), people from middle-income households (70%), adults living in the suburbs (70%), Catholics (71%), and residents of the Pacific states (77%).

ACTION STEPS

What can the Church do to help Christians be better informed and more integrally and meaningfully involved in American public policy? Here are a few ideas to consider that do not require local churches or pastors to endorse specific candidates for public office.

Register to vote. Churches can encourage people to be registered voters. People often do not know how to go about becoming registered, or need an extra push to make the effort. If your church can facilitate the registration process, more people might become involved. Many churches initiate voter registration drives within their churches or their community as a means of expanding participation in the political process.

Teach about social responsibility. Many church leaders have had positive experiences by teaching people the connection between biblical principles and our responsibility to society. Some pastors have preached about the connection of these matters. Others have taught elective classes or Sunday School groups on this topic. Others have led the small groups in the church to uniformly address political issues and social responsibility in a short-term series.

Provide information for consideration. Your church can become a convenient and effective center to distribute resources about the candidates and propositions that will appear on the ballot. Providing printed, audio and video resources for people to explore can enhance people's participation. Even simple tasks such as highlighting books in your church's library or identifying good books available at nearby bookstores can encourage people to take this responsibility more seriously.

Pray for the process and the people. Encourage your people to pray about the candidates, the election and the political process we live by.

This may be the most significant manner of influence we can exert on the system and upon the world Christ has called us to influence.

Motivate involvement in key situations. Despite all the media attention focused upon elections, it is astounding how many adults forget the date of elections. Others claim they were undecided about the value of casting a ballot and simply lacked the final push to make a trip to the polling booth. Reminding people to get out and vote can make a big difference. Someone, or some organization, must champion the process and assume responsibility for exhorting people to exercise their right to vote. What a great opportunity for the Church to demonstrate its desire to influence lives and to be a part of the world, without necessarily accepting worldly values.

CLOSING THOUGHTS

Perhaps you have heard the story. The well-known actor has just entered his dressing room after a taxing evening of performing on stage. True to his customary form, he launches into a post-performance tirade about his own miscues during the play.

"Did you hear me blow the opening line in the third scene? And what was going through my mind during the confrontation with Nicole? No emotion, no nuance, total lack of expression, it was as if I was a corpse doing a brain-dead imitation of my own work."

On and on he rants and raves for several minutes. Finally, one of the stage hands helping him with his costume asks the key question. "So, overall, how did you think the show went tonight?"

Following a moment of reflection, the respected thespian knits his brow and replies, "On the whole, I think it was a very solid performance, a very solid performance, indeed. The people certainly got their money's worth tonight."

What a surprising turnabout from a man who seconds earlier had been verbally lacerating himself and his colleagues for the failure to achieve total excellence. His ultimate conclusion, though, reflected his ability to grasp not just the minutest details of the performance, but also the big picture.

Reviewing the data revealed in this year's study requires the same type of big picture detachment to arrive at a reasonable conclusion as to what it all means.

In the end, we might conclude that although some dark clouds are on the horizon, and some aspects of our culture are in clear need of major transformation, these weaknesses are at least partially offset by some of the positive developments that have been revealed.

To paraphrase the sixteenth-century French commentator François Rabelais, we are a work in process and must be judged accordingly at any given moment in time.

BE ENCOURAGED...

The Church can take heart that Americans are taking the importance of family seriously. How this becomes translated into practical responses is an area of opportunity for the Church. People admit they have more questions than answers when it comes to gaining fulfillment through family activity. But the focus on family realities represents a turn for the better in a culture that might not have been expected to place a premium on family life and the commitments it requires.

The renewed interest in religion is also encouraging for the Church. Although there is certainly a significant gap between religious interest and Christian commitment, the process moves forward one step at a time. May this be a sign that people intend to pursue a deeper understanding of the Christian faith and to make a decision to follow Jesus Christ.

Recognizing that most Americans have an accurate base of impressions about Christianity is also cause for celebration. The task of moving people from their current spiritual state to a place of deeper insight and commitment is made easier by the reality that most adults already hold some reasonable beliefs about the Bible, sin, the Ten Commandments, prayer and astrology. The task before us is to effectively and efficiently build upon the foundation that has already been laid.

IMPOSING CHALLENGES

The excitement we might feel about the window of opportunity ought not to overshadow the truth about the magnitude of the challenge we are facing. Empowered by God, we can certainly prove to be equal to the task. But moving forward in the battle against the forces of darkness will not come without sacrifices and crises along the way.

For instance, clarifying the moral madness that permeates the minds and hearts of millions of adults and providing them with a compelling alternative to their current thinking and behavior is a long-term task of no small dimension. Successfully moving adults to embrace a worldview that is comprehensive and biblically sound is a monumental undertaking. Yet, it is one of the fundamental building blocks to enable Americans to understand why so many of the moral and ethical stands and behaviors they support are in error.

As in every circumstance where change is the solution, it is inappropriate for us to simply tell people they are wrong and to outline what they must say or do to reverse the error. That is the superficial approach that has caused so many people to perceive Christianity to be a series of do's and don'ts (mostly don'ts), without an underlying rationale or baseline principles. It is this very strategy that has earned Christians the image of being judgmental and uncaring.

Recall the wisdom of the missionaries who learned that if they gave a man a fish, he would return the next day, hungry and helpless still. But by teaching that man how to catch a fish, he became self-sufficient and was able to help others. We, too, in addressing the moral and ethical confusions of the age, must help others to make decisions based on a deeper understanding of the nature of truth. In a culture where most people reject the idea of absolute truth and believe that personal experience is the only validation of truth, Christians have to develop methods of demonstrating and communicating the absolute truths that exist and that prescribe righteous activity.

Churches must address other practical and immediate needs, too. For instance, the image of churches needs enhancement. The swiftest means of upgrading the image is by sincerely caring for people. When a majority of people deny that Christian churches are in touch with, and responsive to, the needs of any given people group, there is real trouble. Perhaps the problem is one of image and awareness. Perhaps the problem is deeper and more critical.

Determine how your church is seen by different types of people; ways you can ensure that your people are ministry-driven and consistently sensitive to people's needs. The pattern evident within Jesus' ministry was to understand people's needs; address those physical or emotional needs; and then to proclaim a permanent, spiritual solution to the deepest of needs. His model certainly remains viable today.

Sensitivity to people groups includes possessing and applying special knowledge about those segments. The mass media belatedly and erroneously proclaim that baby boomers are flooding our churches; the data suggest otherwise. Are you ready to respond to millions of boomers who may be ready to exit our churches? What strategies have you developed for discipling the recent surge of people who apparently have chosen to commit their lives to Christ, but are seeking to develop spiritually outside the parameters of an organized church? It is the answers to such probing and complex matters on which the future of the American church is hinged.

In the course of reaching out to others, we cannot always rely upon them to tell us the nature of their needs or even of their spiritual commitment. The survey data underscore the danger of taking people's statements about faith at face value.

- More than four out of every five adults describe themselves as Christian. Two-thirds of the population claim they have made a personal commitment to Jesus Christ. Yet, less than half of the adults in our nation trust Jesus Christ as their means to salvation. (See data table 92,110.)
- More than 9 out of 10 people state that they believe in God, but 4 out of every 10 non-Christians are placing their faith in a different god than the God of the Bible. (See data table 91.)
- Large majorities of people now claim that the Bible and religion are very important in their lives, but there is little evidence that this change in attitude has influenced the way they live.

Are you and your ministry colleagues discerning enough to know the right questions to ask to determine the nature of the people you encounter? Perhaps one reason we do not experience increased evangelistic efforts is because believers ask questions that get the wrong answers. Ask the average adult and he or she will claim to be a Christian. Can you and your church prepare the true saints to be wise as serpents; to identify the people who need to encounter Jesus Christ; to know how to most effectively introduce nonbelievers to the living God?

It is also critical to constantly ask the tough questions that may result in answers we do not necessarily want to hear. One such question concerns people's perceptions about salvation. Most Americans know that Jesus lived and died, most believe He was resurrected. Yet, half of all non-Christians also believe that all good people will go to heaven after they die, regardless of their commitment to Christ. (See data table 111.)

Diligently question your assumptions about people and about ministry. Too frequently we base our outreach efforts on what we think is reality as opposed to reality. The problem is not that the truth about our circumstances is hidden from us, but that we do not take the time to check every element of our perceptions to verify their accuracy. Do not be trapped by bad assumptions or by seeking shortcuts to ministry.

APPENDICES

I   Information About the Information:
    Research Methodology and Related Insights   161

II Data Tables Directory   173
    July 1991 Survey Tables   179
    January 1992 Survey Tables   227

III About Barna Research Group   321

IV Index   323

Information About the Information: Research Methodology and Related Insights

The statistics in this book are drawn from a pair of annual nationwide telephone surveys conducted by the Barna Research Group, Ltd. These surveys cover a broad range of topics (some of which were excluded from this book) encompassing people's values, attitudes, beliefs and experiences.

The overall thrust of the book is to give you an overview of America in 1992 by exploring some important and telling components of the thinking and behavior that characterize Americans at this moment in time. As described at length in previous books (*The Frog in the Kettle* and *What Americans Believe* [1991]), I believe the '90s are a turning point for the Christian church in America.

The information in the preceding chapters is designed to enable you to better understand the dimensions of our changing world. To help you understand the call to the Christian community in the midst of such change. And to spark some ideas on how to have a more effective ministry in a culture that changes so rapidly and significantly that we are sometimes caught off-guard and unprepared. May resources like this one help us all to see another piece of the ever-changing puzzle toward serving God more meaningfully.

One of the conditions that hinders the Church today is its penchant for making or accepting bad assumptions as the basis of ministry decisions and efforts. The data and interpretations in this book should help you see through some of the deceptions and myths that prevent otherwise capable ministries from radically influencing a culture that is searching for meaning and substance.

MAKING SENSE OF THE STATISTICS

Throughout this book, I have tried to place the information within a meaningful context but with a minimum of subjective interpretation. It is my hope that this approach will enable you to arrive at your own conclusions, using the information as a springboard for intelligent and carefully conceived ministry decisions.

This book is the second in a series of such volumes. Regal Books publishes each year's updated edition of the series based on the results of our semiannual tracking studies (conducted in July 1991 and January 1992). Having the most recent data at your disposal will aid you in making more sophisticated, data-based decisions about ministry. By understanding and sometimes foreseeing cultural trends, you will be better positioned to determine what you, personally, can do to maximize your influence for the cause of Christ.

Can You Trust the Data?

The surveys described in this book are based upon the opinions of a national, representative sample of adults. The geodemographic profile of the people interviewed very closely reflects that of the population at large. Further, based on statistical tests, we can be 95% sure that the figures derived from this survey are accurate to within four percentage points of what would be found among the total adult population had we conducted a census rather than the survey.

People sometimes ask me how respondents are chosen for such research. Most reputable marketing research firms that conduct telephone interviews, including Barna Research, use a "random digit dial" sample (RDD). This means that a computer generates telephone numbers randomly, based upon the working blocks of numbers assigned by the telephone company within any given community.

Every adult living in a household that has a telephone (which is about 96% of all households) is therefore a potential respondent, even if they have an unlisted or unpublished phone number, or if they just had their telephone service installed that afternoon! We do not work from telephone books or other types of lists because of the inherent biases and limitations in those lists.

Since the sample itself consists of little more than a list of telephone numbers, we do not know the identity or specific location of the people we interview. This is not a problem since we neither ask to speak to people by name nor ask people to tell us their names. Knowing such information is of no value to us since we are only interested in their opinions and attitudes. To enable people to feel comfortable answering questions that are sometimes quite personal, we extend the promise of anonymity to each respondent and hold their answers in total confidence.

Of course, not everyone we contact agrees to participate in the survey. On the average, telephone surveys gain about a 60% cooperation rate. This means that of every 10 people we contact, 6 will answer our questions.

Why Interview Just 1,000 People?

A common concern about survey results and the projections made on the basis of those results is how the opinions of 1,000 people can possibly represent the opinions of the 190 million adults currently living in the United States.

Based on exhaustive statistical research conducted over many years, social scientists and mathematicians have learned that if random sampling techniques are properly used, it is possible to derive a representative understanding of a population by measuring the attitudes or behaviors of a small but carefully chosen portion of that larger population. A certain number of times the sample will be off the mark by more than the estimated rate of error due to chance. In the vast majority of instances, however, the statistics collected by the random sample survey will be an accurate reflection of the population from which the sample was drawn.

Reading the Data Tables

Many people look at a page filled with data—percentages, raw scores, indexes, frequencies or whatever—and break out in a cold sweat. Let me emphasize that you can get a multitude of insights out of this book without having to look at the data tables in the appendix. The statistics on which the survey commentary is based are provided for those hearty souls who can make sense out of the data, and who may wish to do some of their own data interpretation.

If you want to examine the data tables, here are a few clues to help you through the process. The sample data table on page 165 is coded to help you understand what each of the elements on the page represents.

A This is similar wording of the question asked in the survey.

B Each of these columns represents one of the answers that respondents might have given. Also remember that each of the figures in any of the columns is a percentage, not the total number of respondents who gave that particular answer.

C This is the total number (not a percentage) of survey respondents who are described by the label in the far left column of the row, and who answered this question. For the question on the sample page, 1,060 adults were asked the question. The second row, which is the results among males, shows the responses of the 510 people in that age group who were interviewed for the survey.

D The "total responding" row presents the aggregate survey data. Among all of the people involved in the survey who answered the question, their answers are always shown in the top row.

E The rest of the population segments listed on the page represent the other people groups who were interviewed, and how they responded. In this table, for instance, six independent variables were measured: gender, age, education, ethnicity, marital status, and having kids under 18. The statistics across from the male respondents tell us that 14% agreed strongly with the statement "one person cannot make a difference in the world," 8% agreed somewhat, 25% disagreed somewhat, 52% disagreed strongly, and 1% volunteered that they did not know (which is what DK stands for). The data in the row labeled "total responding" and beneath the column label "male" tells us that 510 men answered this question. The next row of data shows the responses of the female respondents. Among them, 9% agreed strongly with the statement, 13% agreed somewhat, 26% disagreed somewhat, 51% disagreed strongly, and 1% did not know. The subgroup size was 549 women. Notice that for any row of data shown in the table, the answers will add up to 100%. If the numbers are off by one or two percentage points, it is due to the rounding off of the figures.

A

Do you you agree strongly, agree somewhat, disagree somewhat, or disagree strongly with the statement: "One person cannot make a difference in the world"?

B

D   **C**

		N	Agree Strongly	Agree Somewhat	Disagree Somewhat	Disagree Strongly	Don't Know
Total Responding		1060	11%	11%	25%	51%	1%
Gender:	Male	510	14	8	25	52	1
	Female	549	9	13	26	51	1
Age:	18 to 26	226	13	9	33	45	1
	27-45	476	10	11	26	53	1
	46-64	234	10	10	23	56	0
	65 Plus	115	18	12	16	50	4
Education:	High School or Less	480	16	13	25	44	2
	Some College	289	7	8	28	57	0
	College Graduate	286	8	9	25	58	0
Ethnicity:	White	778	9	9	26	55	1
	Black	131	25	15	14	46	0
	Hispanic	90	18	9	34	36	3
Marital:	Married	575	10	10	26	54	0
	Single	311	13	10	27	50	0
	Divorced/Separated	100	8	14	26	48	4
	Widowed	70	19	15	19	43	3
Kids Under 18:	Yes	453	10	11	28	52	0
	No	607	13	11	24	51	2

E

Know Whom You Are Studying

For most of the questions addressed in this book, all of the survey respondents spoken to were asked to respond to that particular survey question. However, some questions have a smaller group of respondents. For instance, one series of questions was asked only of the 722 people who were currently registered to vote.

Keep these things in mind as you evaluate the data, remembering that the smaller the sample size, the greater the potential for sampling error in the resulting data. Later in this appendix a table provides the degree of error associated with different sample sizes at the 95% confidence level.

When you describe the data, be careful how you describe differences in the data. For instance, look at the proportions who said "disagree strongly" in the accompanying table among those who had a high school or lesser education and those who were college graduates. Among the less educated group, 44% strongly disagreed; among the college graduates 58% strongly disagreed. You should describe the gap between the two segments as a 14 percentage point difference. It is *not* a "14 percent difference." Those two descriptions offer a radically different perspective on the responses given by people.

DEFINITIONS

The following represent the definitions for each of the population subgroups referred to in the data tables throughout the book.

Total Population: The 1,013 adults (January 1992 survey) or 1,060 adults (July 1991 survey) who were interviewed as part of the study.

Age: These categories reflect the age of the adult who was interviewed. Only people 18 or older were included in the survey. Note that people in the 18 to 26 age group are sometimes referred to as baby busters (part of the generation born between 1965-1983). Those in the 27 to 45 age bracket are sometimes called baby boomers (born between 1946-1964).

Education: People with formal education through a high school diploma are included in the "high school or less" group. Those who attended college but did not graduate are in the "some college" category. Those termed "college graduate" have received a college degree;

this includes Bachelors, Masters, doctorates and other professional degrees.

Ethnicity: People classified themselves according to their racial or ethnic background. The categories provided for their choices were "white," "black," "Hispanic," "Asian" and "some other ethnic origin."

Household Income: These categories refer to the total combined annual household income earned by all household members before taxes are removed.

Married: This refers to the person's current marital status; currently married, single and have never been married, divorced or widowed. People who have been divorced but remarried are included in the "married" category.

Community: The categories listed here were read to respondents, who then made a choice of one of the three options to describe the area they live in.

Region: The following states were included in these five regional groupings:

Northeast: ME, VT, NH, MA, RI, CT, NY, NJ, PA, DE, MD
South: VA, WV, KY, TN, NC, SC, GA, FL, AL, LA, MS, AR, OK, TX
Midwest: OH, MI, IN, IL, IA, WI, ND, SD, MO, KS, NE, MN
Mountain: AZ, NM, UT, CO, ID, WY, MT, NV
Pacific: CA, OR, WA

Born Again: To qualify for the "yes" category, people had to say that they had made a personal commitment to Jesus Christ that is still important in their lives today; *and* believe that when they die they will go to heaven because they have confessed their sins and have accepted Jesus Christ as their Savior. Anyone who did not concur with both of those conditions was in the "no" category. Classification in this category does *not* depend upon whether or not the individual calls himself or herself "born again."

Kids Under 18: People in the "yes" row constitute those who currently had children under the age of 18 living in their household. Those in the "no" row were those who did not have children under 18 in the household.

Job Type: People were asked to classify their jobs into 1 of 10 categories. People in the "white collar" group indicated they were employed as a professional, manager, administrator or business owner. Those in the "blue collar" group were employed as a laborer, craftsman, service worker, secretary or clerical worker. "Not employed" encompassed homemakers, students, retired adults and unemployed people.

Voter Registration: People not registered to vote are listed in the "no" row. Among registered voters, they were distributed into their voter designation: Democrat, Republican, or no party affiliation—"independent."

Denominational Affiliation: Enough people were interviewed for each of the denominations shown to present their data separately. These show the adults who identified the given denomination as the church they attend most often. In the July 1991 survey, the data were categorized differently. Those respondents were placed in the "Protestant" or "Catholic" category, according to the type of church they attended most often.

Read Bible This Week: People were asked if they had read a part of the Bible during the last seven days. Those who had done so were in the "yes" row; those who had not were in the "no" group.

Attended Church This Week: Those in the "yes" category were adults who said that in the past seven days they had attended a church service. Those in the "no" category said they had not done so.

HOW THE SURVEYS WERE CONDUCTED

The data referred to in this book were collected through nationwide telephone surveys conducted by the Barna Research Group, Ltd., during July 1991 and January 1992. In total, 1,060 adults were interviewed in July, and 1,013 in January. Those adults were chosen through the use of a random digit dial sample provided by Maritz, Inc. The response rate for these surveys was 61% for the July 1991 survey, 62% for the January 1992 survey.

The average interview length was 17 minutes in the July survey and 22 minutes in the January survey. All of the interviews were conducted from the centralized telephone facility of the Barna Research Group in Glendale, California. Calls were placed between 5:00 P.M. and 9:00 P.M. in a given time zone on week nights, from 10:00 A.M. to 4:00 P.M. on Saturdays, and from noon to 8:00 P.M. on Sundays.

Quotas were established on the interviews to ensure that the number of completed interviews in a given geographic area corresponded with the population in that area.

To balance the sample according to true population proportions, statistical weighting was employed, based upon gender. The population and survey sample distributions by demographic categories are shown below.

Adult Population Demographics

		Population	Sample
Gender:	Male	48%	47%
	Female	52	53
Age:	18-26	16	17
	27-45	44	42
	46-64	25	26
	65+	15	15
Ethnicity:	White	76	72
	Black	12	14
	Asian	3	2
	Hispanic	8	9
Region:	Northeast	23	22
	South	36	36
	Midwest	21	22
	Mountain	5	5
	Pacific	15	15

Source: *Statistical Abstract of the United States, 1991;* U.S. Department of Commerce, Washington, D.C.

SOME RULES FOR ANALYZING SURVEY DATA

Every survey of people's attitudes and experiences based upon a sample of the population is a representation of the attitudes and experiences of the people who comprise the aggregate population.

Sampling Error

If the sample is selected properly—that is, survey respondents are chosen in accordance with the principles of probability sampling—then it is possible to estimate the potential amount of error attributable to sampling inaccuracies in the survey data. The only way to fully eliminate that potential error is to conduct a census rather than a sample.

In other words, we would have to interview every member of the population rather than a selected few. You can imagine the time and expense involved in such an operation.

Statisticians have developed means of identifying how much error could be in survey measurements due to sampling inaccuracies, assuming that random sampling procedures are conscientiously applied. The table on the next page outlines estimates of how much error might be found in surveys, based upon the sample size and the response levels to survey questions. All the figures shown assume we are working at the 95% confidence interval, meaning that we would expect these statistics to be accurate in 95 out of 100 cases. This is the standard confidence level used in most survey research work.

In general, the following conditions are true:

- The larger the sample size, the more reliable the survey data. However, there is not a simple one-to-one relationship between sample size and sampling error reduction.
- The larger the difference in opinion evident through the response distribution related to the question, the less likely that the survey statistics are erroneous due to sampling.

Response Levels and Accuracy

The data in the table on the next page indicate how accurate the data are at specific response levels, and at different sample sizes.

For instance, in a survey of 1,000 people, if the answers were about evenly divided—50% said "yes," 50% said "no"—those responses are probably accurate to within plus or minus three percentage points of what the survey actually found. Thus, you could say that the most likely response to the question was 50% saying "yes," with a 3-point margin of error at the 95% confidence interval. This means that in this situation, the true population response would be somewhere between 47% and 53% in 95 out of 100 cases.

Here is another example. Let's say you ask the question regarding whether or not people say they have attended a church worship service in the past year. You find that 71% say they have, and 29% say they have not. Assume the question was asked of 380 adults.

To determine the approximate level of sampling error associated with this finding you would look under the 30%/70% column (since the 71%-29% outcome is closest to the 30%-70% distribution); you would use the figures on the row representing the sample size of 400 people. The intersection point of that row with the 30%/70% column indicates a maximum sampling error of four percentage points.

You might say that 71% of all adults have attended a church worship service in the past year; this information is accurate to within plus or minus four percentage points at the 95% confidence level.

In some cases, the sample size or response distributions you use might vary markedly from the parameters shown in this data table. You can either extrapolate from the figures shown to arrive at a closer interpretation of the error statistic or consult a good statistics book that contains a more detailed table.

Sampling Accuracy Table

.05 Confidence Interval

Sample Size	Response Distribution				
	50/50	40/60	30/70	20/80	10/90
2,000	2	2	2	2	2
1,500	3	3	2	2	2
1,200	3	3	3	2	2
1,000	3	3	3	2	2
800	3	3	3	3	2
600	4	4	4	3	2
400	5	5	4	4	3
200	7	7	6	5	4
100	10	10	9	8	6
50	14	14	13	12	8

DATA TABLES DIRECTORY

JULY 1991 SURVEY TABLES

I. Our Activities in an Average Month

1. Attend church worship service
2. Attend church Sunday School class
3. Attend small group Bible study
4. Avoid buying products being boycotted
5. Volunteer time to a nonprofit organization
6. Attend a class at a school or training center
7. Go to a theater to see a movie
8. Explain religious beliefs to someone
9. Read part of the Bible when not in church

II. Our Impressions of Established Organizations

10. Presbyterian Church
11. Baptist Church
12. Lutheran Church
13. Methodist Church
14. Roman Catholic Church
15. Republican Party
16. Democratic Party
17. Ford Motor Company
18. Chrysler Corporation
19. Salvation Army

20. American Cancer Society
21. Mormon Church

III. Our Relationships
22. Need for more close friends
23. Are long-lasting friendships possible?
24. Likely places to find new friends

IV. Are Protestant Churches Meeting Needs of the Following People Groups?
25. Women under 35
26. Women 35 or older
27. Men under 35
28. Men 35 or older
29. The elderly
30. Blacks
31. Hispanics
32. Asians
33. Single adults
34. Single parents
35. Teenagers
36. Non-Christians
37. The poor
38. Families
39. Children under age 13
40. Opportunities for women to serve in the church

V. How We View Various Aspects of Life
41. Men are better leaders than women
42. Everything in life is negotiable
43. Most poor people are poor because they are lazy
44. The world is out of control these days
45. You need to look out for your own best interests
46. Boycotting products doesn't accomplish anything

January 1992 Survey Tables

VI. Our Activities in an Average Week
47. Attend a church worship service
48. Attend a Sunday School class
49. Read part of the Bible
50. Read a book
51. Volunteered time at church
52. Volunteered time to a nonprofit organization other than a church
53. Watched MTV

VII. Our Values and Beliefs About Various Aspects of Life
54. Religion
55. Bible
56. Money
57. Time
58. Living comfortably
59. Friends
60. Family
61. Free time
62. Career
63. Health
64. Community
65. Government and politics

VIII. Our Views About Life in General
66. Popular music has a negative influence
67. Music videos reflect the ways most people live and think
68. Abortion is morally wrong
69. Lying is sometimes necessary
70. The only certainty is what you experience in your own life
71. One person can make a real difference
72. Money is still the main symbol of success in life

IX. Our Values and Beliefs About Religious Aspects
73. The Bible is the written Word of God

74. The Christian faith has all the answers for a successful life
75. People's prayers do not have the power to change circumstances
76. Horoscopes and astrology provide an accurate prediction of the future
77. The Ten Commandments are not relevant today
78. The whole idea of sin is outdated
79. The Bible does not command people to attend church
80. All good people will live in heaven after they die

X. How We View the Ten Commandments
81. Do not worship other gods
82. Do not have idols
83. Do not swear or misuse God's name
84. Do not work on the day of worship
85. Honor your parents
86. Do not commit murder
87. Do not commit adultery
88. Do not steal
89. Do not lie
90. Do not be jealous

XI. Our Beliefs, Our Church Affiliation
91. Beliefs about God
92. Religious faith
93. Denomination (self-described Christians)
94. Monthly church attendance (Christians)
95. Church attendance habits (Christians)
96. Consider a change in church affiliation (Christians)

XII. Our Involvement in Church
97. Teach a Sunday School class
98. Participate in a small group
99. Serve as a leader in the church

XIII. Religious Activities and Views: TV, Magazines, Books, Radio, Volunteerism, Beliefs
100. Watched religious TV

101. Listened to Christian teaching on radio
102. Read a Christian book other than the Bible
103. Donated money to a Christian ministry, other than a church
104. Shared religious beliefs with someone with different beliefs
105. Listened to Christian music on radio
106. Read a Christian magazine
107. Volunteered time or money to needy people in own area
108. Volunteered time or money to needy people in other countries
109. Read Bible, other than at church
110. A personal commitment to Jesus Christ still important today
111. Views on life after death
112. Contributions to nonprofit organizations

XIV. Methods of contributions
113. Direct mail appeal
114. Telephone appeal
115. Church collection or temple donation
116. Person-to-person appeal
117. TV, radio or print ad
118. Automatic deduction from paycheck

XV. 1992 Presidential Election Year—Voter Status
119. Registered to vote
120. Registered voters' party affiliation

XVI. 1992 Presidential Election Year—Issues
121. Women's rights
122. Abortion
123. Taxes
124. Environmental policy
125. Public education
126. Crime
127. Military and defense spending
128. Budget deficit
129. Health care

130. Welfare and unemployment policies
131. Separation of Church and State
132. Drug enforcement
133. Human rights protection
134. Economy
135. Mass transportation

July 1991
Survey Tables

TABLE 1   181

During the past month did you "attend a church worship service"?

		N	Yes	No
Total Responding		1060	54%	46%
Gender:	Male	510	47	53
	Female	549	62	38
Age:	18 to 26	226	41	59
	27-45	476	56	44
	46-64	234	57	43
	65 Plus	115	66	34
Education:	High School or Less	480	50	50
	Some College	289	58	42
	College Graduate	286	58	42
Ethnicity:	White	778	55	45
	Black	131	64	36
	Hispanic	90	47	53
Marital:	Married	575	60	40
	Single	311	43	57
	Divorced/Separated	100	57	43
	Widowed	70	61	39
Kids Under 18:	Yes	453	57	43
	No	607	52	48
Household Income:	Under $20,000	211	54	46
	$20,000 to $39,999	397	52	48
	$40,000 to $59,999	195	59	41
	$60,000 or more	137	52	48
Community:	Urban	306	53	47
	Suburban	395	52	48
	Rural	303	60	40
Region:	Northeast	230	54	46
	Midwest	246	53	47
	South	354	61	39
	Mountain	55	46	54
	Pacific	174	45	55
Born Again:	Yes	412	80	20
	No	648	38	62
Denominational Affiliation:	Protestant	589	62	38
	Catholic	286	59	41
Attended Church This Week:	Yes	576	100	0
	No	483	0	100
Read Bible This Week:	Yes	449	81	19
	No	611	35	65

TABLE 2

During the past month did you "attend a church Sunday School class"?

		N	Yes	No
Total Responding		1060	29%	71%
Gender:	Male	510	26	74
	Female	549	33	67
Age:	18 to 26	226	23	77
	27-45	476	29	71
	46-64	234	34	66
	65 Plus	115	33	67
Education:	High School or Less	480	29	71
	Some College	289	30	70
	College Graduate	286	30	70
Ethnicity:	White	778	29	71
	Black	131	42	58
	Hispanic	90	18	82
Marital:	Married	575	34	66
	Single	311	22	78
	Divorced/Separated	100	26	74
	Widowed	70	31	69
Kids Under 18:	Yes	453	32	68
	No	607	27	73
Household Income:	Under $20,000	211	25	75
	$20,000 to $39,999	397	30	70
	$40,000 to $59,999	195	32	68
	$60,000 or more	137	33	67
Community:	Urban	306	29	71
	Suburban	395	27	73
	Rural	303	35	65
Region:	Northeast	230	22	78
	Midwest	246	29	71
	South	354	42	58
	Mountain	55	28	72
	Pacific	174	16	84
Born Again:	Yes	412	52	48
	No	648	15	85
Denominational Affiliation:	Protestant	589	41	59
	Catholic	286	18	82
Attended Church This Week:	Yes	576	53	47
	No	483	2	98
Read Bible This Week:	Yes	449	52	48
	No	611	13	87

TABLE 3   183

During the past month did you "attend a small group that met to pray or study the Bible, other than in a Sunday School class or church service"?

		N	Yes	No
Total Responding		1060	18%	82%
Gender:	Male	510	15	85
	Female	549	20	80
Age:	18 to 26	226	16	84
	27-45	476	18	82
	46-64	234	17	83
	65 Plus	115	21	79
Education:	High School or Less	480	17	83
	Some College	289	19	81
	College Graduate	286	18	82
Ethnicity:	White	778	17	83
	Black	131	28	72
	Hispanic	90	13	87
Marital:	Married	575	19	81
	Single	311	13	87
	Divorced/Separated	100	21	79
	Widowed	70	21	79
Kids Under 18:	Yes	453	19	81
	No	607	16	84
Household Income:	Under $20,000	211	18	82
	$20,000 to $39,999	397	18	82
	$40,000 to $59,999	195	14	86
	$60,000 or more	137	19	81
Community:	Urban	306	20	80
	Suburban	395	15	85
	Rural	303	19	81
Region:	Northeast	230	15	85
	Midwest	246	16	84
	South	354	20	80
	Mountain	55	18	82
	Pacific	174	17	83
Born Again:	Yes	412	29	71
	No	648	11	89
Denominational Affiliation:	Protestant	589	23	77
	Catholic	286	10	90
Attended Church This Week:	Yes	576	29	71
	No	483	4	96
Read Bible This Week:	Yes	449	36	64
	No	611	4	96

TABLE 4

During the past month did you "avoid buying a specific product or brand because it is being boycotted by a group or cause you support"?

		N	Yes	No	Don't Know
Total Responding		1060	14%	85%	1%
Gender:	Male	510	14	86	0
	Female	549	15	84	1
Age:	18 to 26	226	19	81	0
	27-45	476	13	86	1
	46-64	234	16	83	1
	65 Plus	115	9	90	1
Education:	High School or Less	480	10	89	1
	Some College	289	17	82	0
	College Graduate	286	18	81	1
Ethnicity:	White	778	16	83	1
	Black	131	9	91	0
	Hispanic	90	14	86	0
Marital:	Married	575	13	86	1
	Single	311	17	83	0
	Divorced/Separated	100	16	83	1
	Widowed	70	11	88	1
Kids Under 18:	Yes	453	14	85	1
	No	607	15	85	0
Household Income:	Under $20,000	211	15	84	1
	$20,000 to $39,999	397	14	85	1
	$40,000 to $59,999	195	11	88	0
	$60,000 or more	137	19	80	1
Community:	Urban	306	15	85	0
	Suburban	395	17	82	0
	Rural	303	11	87	1
Region:	Northeast	230	19	81	0
	Midwest	246	14	85	0
	South	354	12	87	1
	Mountain	55	5	94	1
	Pacific	174	15	83	1
Born Again:	Yes	412	15	85	1
	No	648	14	85	1
Denominational Affiliation:	Protestant	589	12	88	1
	Catholic	286	16	83	0
Attended Church This Week:	Yes	576	15	84	1
	No	483	14	86	0
Read Bible This Week:	Yes	449	16	83	1
	No	611	13	86	0

TABLE 5   185

During the past month did you "volunteer your time to help a nonprofit organization, other than a church"?

		N	Yes	No
Total Responding		1060	35%	65%
Gender:	Male	510	33	67
	Female	549	36	64
Age:	18 to 26	226	23	77
	27-45	476	36	64
	46-64	234	40	60
	65 Plus	115	44	56
Education:	High School or Less	480	30	70
	Some College	289	35	65
	College Graduate	286	43	57
Ethnicity:	White	778	37	63
	Black	131	33	67
	Hispanic	90	19	81
Marital:	Married	575	37	63
	Single	311	27	73
	Divorced/Separated	100	37	63
	Widowed	70	47	53
Kids Under 18:	Yes	453	35	65
	No	607	35	65
Household Income:	Under $20,000	211	29	71
	$20,000 to $39,999	397	34	66
	$40,000 to $59,999	195	42	58
	$60,000 or more	137	42	58
Community:	Urban	306	37	63
	Suburban	395	33	67
	Rural	303	36	64
Region:	Northeast	230	40	60
	Midwest	246	34	66
	South	354	34	66
	Mountain	55	39	61
	Pacific	174	29	71
Born Again:	Yes	412	39	61
	No	648	32	68
Denominational Affiliation:	Protestant	589	37	63
	Catholic	286	32	68
Attended Church This Week:	Yes	576	41	59
	No	483	27	73
Read Bible This Week:	Yes	449	41	59
	No	611	30	70

TABLE 6

During the past month did you "attend a class at a school or training center"?

		N	Yes	No
Total Responding		1060	21%	79%
Gender:	Male	510	24	76
	Female	549	17	83
Age:	18 to 26	226	34	66
	27-45	476	20	79
	46-64	234	17	83
	65 Plus	115	1	99
Education:	High School or Less	480	13	87
	Some College	289	20	80
	College Graduate	286	33	67
Ethnicity:	White	778	18	82
	Black	131	21	79
	Hispanic	90	25	75
Marital:	Married	575	17	83
	Single	311	32	68
	Divorced/Separated	100	18	82
	Widowed	70	7	93
Kids Under 18:	Yes	453	23	77
	No	607	18	81
Household Income:	Under $20,000	211	12	87
	$20,000 to $39,999	397	19	81
	$40,000 to $59,999	195	24	76
	$60,000 or more	137	35	65
Community:	Urban	306	23	77
	Suburban	395	25	75
	Rural	303	13	87
Region:	Northeast	230	20	80
	Midwest	246	19	81
	South	354	21	79
	Mountain	55	15	85
	Pacific	174	24	76
Born Again:	Yes	412	19	81
	No	648	21	79
Denominational Affiliation:	Protestant	589	18	82
	Catholic	286	26	74
Attended Church This Week:	Yes	576	21	79
	No	483	20	79
Read Bible This Week:	Yes	449	19	81
	No	611	21	78

TABLE 7   187

During the past month did you "go to a theater to see a movie"?

		N	Yes	No	Don't Know
Total Responding		1060	47%	53%	0%
Gender:	Male	510	56	44	0
	Female	549	39	60	0
Age:	18 to 26	226	80	20	0
	27-45	476	50	50	0
	46-64	234	27	73	0
	65 Plus	115	12	88	0
Education:	High School or Less	480	36	64	0
	Some College	289	56	44	0
	College Graduate	286	56	43	0
Ethnicity:	White	778	43	57	0
	Black	131	45	55	0
	Hispanic	90	72	28	0
Marital:	Married	575	39	61	0
	Single	311	69	31	0
	Divorced/Separated	100	52	48	0
	Widowed	70	13	87	0
Kids Under 18:	Yes	453	53	47	0
	No	607	43	57	0
Household Income:	Under $20,000	211	37	63	0
	$20,000 to $39,999	397	45	55	0
	$40,000 to $59,999	195	58	42	0
	$60,000 or more	137	63	37	1
Community:	Urban	306	49	51	0
	Suburban	395	51	49	0
	Rural	303	41	59	0
Region:	Northeast	230	49	51	0
	Midwest	246	41	59	0
	South	354	45	55	0
	Mountain	55	45	55	0
	Pacific	174	60	40	0
Born Again:	Yes	412	39	61	0
	No	648	53	47	0
Denominational Affiliation:	Protestant	589	38	62	0
	Catholic	286	57	43	0
Attended Church This Week:	Yes	576	44	56	0
	No	483	51	49	0
Read Bible This Week:	Yes	449	40	60	0
	No	611	53	47	0

During the past month did you "explain your religious beliefs to someone who you felt did not have the same beliefs as you"?

		N	Yes	No	Don't Know
Total Responding		1060	31%	68%	1%
Gender:	Male	510	30	68	1
	Female	549	32	67	1
Age:	18 to 26	226	36	63	1
	27-45	476	30	69	1
	46-64	234	32	68	1
	65 Plus	115	26	74	1
Education:	High School or Less	480	30	70	1
	Some College	289	35	64	1
	College Graduate	286	30	69	1
Ethnicity:	White	778	31	69	1
	Black	131	41	56	4
	Hispanic	90	30	70	0
Marital:	Married	575	31	69	0
	Single	311	33	65	2
	Divorced/Separated	100	33	67	0
	Widowed	70	24	75	1
Kids Under 18:	Yes	453	32	67	1
	No	607	31	68	1
Household Income:	Under $20,000	211	34	66	0
	$20,000 to $39,999	397	34	65	1
	$40,000 to $59,999	195	29	71	0
	$60,000 or more	137	29	68	3
Community:	Urban	306	38	61	1
	Suburban	395	29	70	1
	Rural	303	25	75	0
Region:	Northeast	230	28	70	2
	Midwest	246	31	69	1
	South	354	37	63	0
	Mountain	55	27	73	0
	Pacific	174	27	72	1
Born Again:	Yes	412	37	62	1
	No	648	27	72	1
Denominational Affiliation:	Protestant	589	33	67	1
	Catholic	286	24	74	2
Attended Church This Week:	Yes	576	36	62	1
	No	483	25	74	1
Read Bible This Week:	Yes	449	45	54	1
	No	611	22	78	1

TABLE 9   189

During the past month did you "read part of the Bible, other than while you were at a church"?

		N	Yes	No
Total Responding		1060	42%	58%
Gender:	Male	510	32	68
	Female	549	52	48
Age:	18 to 26	226	35	65
	27-45	476	39	61
	46-64	234	44	56
	65 Plus	115	65	35
Education:	High School or Less	480	46	54
	Some College	289	42	58
	College Graduate	286	37	63
Ethnicity:	White	778	42	58
	Black	131	58	42
	Hispanic	90	34	66
Marital:	Married	575	44	56
	Single	311	33	67
	Divorced/Separated	100	47	53
	Widowed	70	63	37
Kids Under 18:	Yes	453	44	56
	No	607	41	59
Household Income:	Under $20,000	211	54	46
	$20,000 to $39,999	397	42	58
	$40,000 to $59,999	195	36	64
	$60,000 or more	137	34	66
Community:	Urban	306	41	59
	Suburban	395	37	63
	Rural	303	51	49
Region:	Northeast	230	34	66
	Midwest	246	44	56
	South	354	53	47
	Mountain	55	36	64
	Pacific	174	31	69
Born Again:	Yes	412	68	32
	No	648	26	74
Denominational Affiliation:	Protestant	589	53	47
	Catholic	286	31	69
Attended Church This Week:	Yes	576	63	37
	No	483	18	82
Read Bible This Week:	Yes	449	100	0
	No	611	0	100

TABLE 10

What is your impression of the "Presbyterian church"? Is it very favorable, somewhat favorable, somewhat unfavorable, or very unfavorable?

		N	Very Favorable	Somewhat Favorable	Somewhat Unfavorable	Very Unfavorable	Don't Know
Total Responding		1060	12%	38%	8%	4%	38%
Gender:	Male	510	9	39	9	3	39
	Female	549	14	37	8	4	37
Age:	18 to 26	226	3	29	9	8	51
	27-45	476	11	40	9	3	38
	46-64	234	14	42	9	3	32
	65 Plus	115	29	35	5	2	28
Education:	High School or Less	480	12	33	10	4	40
	Some College	289	9	38	9	5	39
	College Graduate	286	13	46	6	2	33
Ethnicity:	White	778	13	41	9	3	35
	Black	131	12	31	10	7	40
	Hispanic	90	6	28	8	11	47
Marital:	Married	575	13	44	8	3	32
	Single	311	7	31	8	5	50
	Divorced/Separated	100	8	37	13	5	38
	Widowed	70	28	24	8	3	36
Kids Under 18:	Yes	453	8	38	10	3	41
	No	607	15	38	8	4	36
Household Income:	Under $20,000	211	13	29	8	7	44
	$20,000 to $39,999	397	10	39	13	2	36
	$40,000 to $59,999	195	10	45	7	3	36
	$60,000 or more	137	13	44	5	7	32
Community:	Urban	306	12	39	10	5	35
	Suburban	395	11	40	6	2	41
	Rural	303	14	37	11	3	35
Region:	Northeast	230	11	38	9	6	37
	Midwest	246	11	39	8	2	40
	South	354	14	38	8	3	37
	Mountain	55	16	23	8	12	40
	Pacific	174	9	41	10	2	37
Born Again:	Yes	412	16	41	10	2	32
	No	648	9	36	8	5	42
Denominational Affiliation:	Protestant	589	15	43	8	2	33
	Catholic	286	8	33	8	6	46
Attended Church This Week:	Yes	576	13	43	7	4	32
	No	483	10	32	10	3	45
Read Bible This Week:	Yes	449	15	40	9	4	32
	No	611	10	36	8	4	43

TABLE 11   191

What is your impression of the "Baptist church"? Is it very favorable, somewhat favorable, somewhat unfavorable, or very unfavorable?

		N	Very Favorable	Somewhat Favorable	Somewhat Unfavorable	Very Unfavorable	Don't Know
Total Responding		1060	29%	36%	10%	5%	20%
Gender:	Male	510	24	38	11	5	21
	Female	549	33	35	9	5	18
Age:	18 to 26	226	19	32	13	9	27
	27-45	476	29	38	11	4	18
	46-64	234	33	40	7	4	16
	65 Plus	115	40	30	7	1	22
Education:	High School or Less	480	34	35	9	4	18
	Some College	289	28	34	10	6	21
	College Graduate	286	21	42	13	5	20
Ethnicity:	White	778	25	39	11	4	20
	Black	131	68	21	4	3	4
	Hispanic	90	12	39	15	14	20
Marital:	Married	575	30	39	10	5	16
	Single	311	21	34	12	6	27
	Divorced/Separated	100	34	36	7	6	17
	Widowed	70	46	25	8	0	21
Kids Under 18:	Yes	453	30	38	11	5	16
	No	607	28	35	10	5	22
Household Income:	Under $20,000	211	40	30	7	5	18
	$20,000 to $39,999	397	28	39	10	4	18
	$40,000 to $59,999	195	22	40	11	5	22
	$60,000 or more	137	26	36	14	8	16
Community:	Urban	306	32	33	11	5	19
	Suburban	395	22	39	12	5	22
	Rural	303	32	40	10	3	15
Region:	Northeast	230	20	39	11	4	27
	Midwest	246	26	35	12	4	23
	South	354	45	34	8	5	9
	Mountain	55	6	37	17	12	28
	Pacific	174	19	40	10	5	25
Born Again:	Yes	412	46	36	7	2	9
	No	648	18	37	13	7	26
Denominational Affiliation:	Protestant	589	41	39	7	3	11
	Catholic	286	13	36	14	7	31
Attended Church This Week:	Yes	576	36	38	9	4	14
	No	483	21	34	12	6	26
Read Bible This Week:	Yes	449	43	36	8	3	10
	No	611	18	37	12	6	27

TABLE 12

What is your impression of the "Lutheran church"? Is it very favorable, somewhat favorable, somewhat unfavorable, or very unfavorable?

		N	Very Favorable	Somewhat Favorable	Somewhat Unfavorable	Very Unfavorable	Don't Know
Total Responding		1060	12%	35%	8%	5%	40%
Gender:	Male	510	11	35	9	4	41
	Female	549	13	35	7	6	40
Age:	18 to 26	226	6	27	7	9	51
	27-45	476	11	37	9	3	40
	46-64	234	16	39	7	6	32
	65 Plus	115	18	32	5	1	44
Education:	High School or Less	480	12	30	8	7	43
	Some College	289	10	37	8	4	42
	College Graduate	286	14	42	7	2	35
Ethnicity:	White	778	14	39	8	3	36
	Black	131	7	23	7	14	50
	Hispanic	90	7	28	13	4	48
Marital:	Married	575	14	38	9	5	35
	Single	311	9	30	6	6	49
	Divorced/Separated	100	11	31	14	3	11
	Widowed	70	13	35	3	2	47
Kids Under 18:	Yes	453	9	35	9	6	41
	No	607	14	35	7	4	40
Household Income:	Under $20,000	211	9	30	6	7	48
	$20,000 to $39,999	397	13	35	10	4	38
	$40,000 to $59,999	195	11	40	6	2	41
	$60,000 or more	137	15	40	10	7	28
Community:	Urban	306	11	36	9	5	40
	Suburban	395	12	37	7	4	41
	Rural	303	15	36	8	3	38
Region:	Northeast	230	10	37	7	6	39
	Midwest	246	21	39	4	5	31
	South	354	8	30	9	6	48
	Mountain	55	11	34	10	3	43
	Pacific	174	12	37	11	2	39
Born Again:	Yes	412	16	33	8	4	39
	No	648	9	36	8	5	42
Denominational Affiliation:	Protestant	589	15	35	7	5	38
	Catholic	286	9	37	6	3	44
Attended Church This Week:	Yes	576	13	36	8	5	39
	No	483	10	34	8	5	43
Read Bible This Week:	Yes	449	14	33	8	6	39
	No	611	10	37	8	4	41

TABLE 13   193

What is your impression of the "Methodist church"? Is it very favorable, somewhat favorable, somewhat unfavorable, or very unfavorable?

		N	Very Favorable	Somewhat Favorable	Somewhat Unfavorable	Very Unfavorable	Don't Know
Total Responding		1060	18%	42%	8%	4%	29%
Gender:	Male	510	12	44	9	3	31
	Female	549	23	40	7	4	26
Age:	18 to 26	226	10	32	10	8	40
	27-45	476	14	46	9	2	29
	46-64	234	24	46	6	3	21
	65 Plus	115	38	35	1	2	23
Education:	High School or Less	480	18	41	9	4	29
	Some College	289	19	36	10	5	31
	College Graduate	286	18	50	5	1	26
Ethnicity:	White	778	18	45	8	3	26
	Black	131	23	44	8	6	18
	Hispanic	90	13	29	11	7	40
Marital:	Married	575	19	47	8	2	25
	Single	311	12	36	9	6	38
	Divorced/Separated	100	19	43	12	3	24
	Widowed	70	41	31	1	3	24
Kids Under 18:	Yes	453	14	42	9	4	30
	No	607	21	42	7	3	27
Household Income:	Under $20,000	211	21	39	9	4	27
	$20,000 to $39,999	397	16	44	8	3	28
	$40,000 to $59,999	195	15	45	5	3	32
	$60,000 or more	137	20	41	9	3	27
Community:	Urban	306	17	40	7	5	32
	Suburban	395	17	45	5	3	30
	Rural	303	22	44	11	2	21
Region:	Northeast	230	17	44	9	3	28
	Midwest	246	19	43	6	4	28
	South	354	22	45	7	3	24
	Mountain	55	17	29	11	10	34
	Pacific	174	12	37	10	2	39
Born Again:	Yes	412	25	47	8	2	18
	No	648	14	39	8	4	35
Denominational Affiliation:	Protestant	589	25	47	7	3	19
	Catholic	286	11	36	7	4	41
Attended Church This Week:	Yes	576	22	46	7	4	22
	No	483	13	38	9	3	37
Read Bible This Week:	Yes	449	24	46	7	4	18
	No	611	13	39	8	3	36

TABLE 14

What is your impression of the "Catholic church"? Is it very favorable, somewhat favorable, somewhat unfavorable, or very unfavorable?

		N	Very Favorable	Somewhat Favorable	Somewhat Unfavorable	Very Unfavorable	Don't Know
Total Responding		1060	23%	36%	16%	7%	18%
Gender:	Male	510	23	39	18	6	15
	Female	549	24	33	15	8	20
Age:	18 to 26	226	24	33	18	8	16
	27-45	476	21	37	17	6	18
	46-64	234	23	35	14	11	17
	65 Plus	115	29	36	11	4	20
Education:	High School or Less	480	23	32	16	9	20
	Some College	289	25	39	11	8	17
	College Graduate	286	22	39	21	4	14
Ethnicity:	White	778	22	37	17	8	17
	Black	131	14	36	15	12	24
	Hispanic	90	55	32	4	0	8
Marital:	Married	575	24	37	16	7	16
	Single	311	22	32	19	8	18
	Divorced/Separated	100	18	45	12	8	18
	Widowed	70	31	33	9	5	22
Kids Under 18:	Yes	453	24	36	16	7	17
	No	607	23	36	16	8	18
Household Income:	Under $20,000	211	24	28	16	8	24
	$20,000 to $39,999	397	21	36	16	8	19
	$40,000 to $59,999	195	26	43	12	5	15
	$60,000 or more	137	24	38	22	11	5
Community:	Urban	306	23	36	17	8	16
	Suburban	395	26	39	17	5	12
	Rural	303	20	34	15	8	23
Region:	Northeast	230	27	33	18	10	12
	Midwest	246	22	39	15	7	17
	South	354	18	36	13	9	24
	Mountain	55	32	35	18	3	12
	Pacific	174	26	35	22	3	14
Born Again:	Yes	412	20	35	18	8	19
	No	648	25	36	15	7	17
Denominational Affiliation:	Protestant	589	9	40	20	9	22
	Catholic	286	64	30	4	0	2
Attended Church This Week:	Yes	576	29	34	15	7	15
	No	483	16	38	17	8	21
Read Bible This Week:	Yes	449	22	34	17	10	17
	No	611	24	37	15	5	18

TABLE 15   195

What is your impression of the "Republican Party"? Is it very favorable, somewhat favorable, somewhat unfavorable, or very unfavorable?

		N	Very Favorable	Somewhat Favorable	Somewhat Unfavorable	Very Unfavorable	Don't Know
Total Responding		1060	20%	38%	18%	14%	10%
Gender:	Male	510	24	37	18	14	7
	Female	549	16	38	17	15	13
Age:	18 to 26	226	22	36	18	13	11
	27-45	476	17	41	19	15	8
	46-64	234	23	39	17	12	10
	65 Plus	115	22	29	15	19	15
Education:	High School or Less	480	23	32	13	15	16
	Some College	289	20	37	24	15	4
	College Graduate	286	15	49	19	12	6
Ethnicity:	White	778	24	40	17	10	9
	Black	131	4	25	17	41	14
	Hispanic	90	16	37	24	9	13
Marital:	Married	575	22	39	17	13	10
	Single	311	20	38	18	16	9
	Divorced/Separated	100	11	37	22	16	14
	Widowed	70	19	31	20	14	17
Kids Under 18:	Yes	453	20	37	18	14	12
	No	607	20	38	17	15	9
Household Income:	Under $20,000	211	14	36	16	20	14
	$20,000 to $39,999	397	20	37	21	13	8
	$40,000 to $59,999	195	24	43	14	11	9
	$60,000 or more	137	24	41	16	17	3
Community:	Urban	306	18	37	21	16	7
	Suburban	395	22	37	18	15	8
	Rural	303	21	42	14	12	12
Region:	Northeast	230	18	34	20	21	6
	Midwest	246	23	33	15	15	14
	South	354	20	44	16	10	10
	Mountain	55	25	34	23	12	6
	Pacific	174	16	38	20	15	11
Born Again:	Yes	412	22	41	14	12	11
	No	648	18	36	20	16	10
Denominational Affiliation:	Protestant	589	21	39	14	15	11
	Catholic	286	22	40	23	10	6
Attended Church This Week:	Yes	576	22	38	18	12	9
	No	483	17	37	17	17	12
Read Bible This Week:	Yes	449	21	39	17	12	11
	No	611	19	37	18	16	10

What is your impression of the "Democratic Party"? Is it very favorable, somewhat favorable, somewhat unfavorable, or very unfavorable?

		N	Very Favorable	Somewhat Favorable	Somewhat Unfavorable	Very Unfavorable	Don't Know
Total Responding		1060	23%	39%	19%	10%	9%
Gender:	Male	510	19	39	22	14	7
	Female	549	27	39	16	7	11
Age:	18 to 26	226	14	42	21	12	10
	27-45	476	24	39	19	10	8
	46-64	234	23	41	17	11	7
	65 Plus	115	34	32	20	4	10
Education:	High School or Less	480	27	34	15	10	13
	Some College	289	21	40	21	12	5
	College Graduate	286	17	46	23	7	7
Ethnicity:	White	778	18	41	21	11	9
	Black	131	54	22	6	8	9
	Hispanic	90	21	43	16	9	10
Marital:	Married	575	21	41	18	11	9
	Single	311	20	40	22	11	8
	Divorced/Separated	100	34	30	17	10	9
	Widowed	70	33	34	18	4	11
Kids Under 18:	Yes	453	20	41	18	10	10
	No	607	25	37	20	10	8
Household Income:	Under $20,000	211	31	35	17	10	8
	$20,000 to $39,999	397	25	38	18	9	9
	$40,000 to $59,999	195	15	45	23	9	8
	$60,000 or more	137	18	42	21	16	4
Community:	Urban	306	24	38	23	8	7
	Suburban	395	22	40	20	10	7
	Rural	303	21	39	18	13	9
Region:	Northeast	230	22	44	16	11	7
	Midwest	246	25	33	21	8	12
	South	354	24	39	19	10	8
	Mountain	55	15	41	21	15	9
	Pacific	174	20	39	22	9	9
Born Again:	Yes	412	24	36	19	10	10
	No	648	22	41	19	10	8
Denominational Affiliation:	Protestant	589	25	37	18	11	10
	Catholic	286	20	43	22	10	5
Attended Church This Week:	Yes	576	24	38	20	10	8
	No	483	22	40	19	10	10
Read Bible This Week:	Yes	449	24	37	19	11	9
	No	611	22	41	19	9	9

TABLE 17   197

What is your impression of the "Ford Motor Company"? Is it very favorable, somewhat favorable, somewhat unfavorable, or very unfavorable?

		N	Very Favorable	Somewhat Favorable	Somewhat Unfavorable	Very Unfavorable	Don't Know
Total Responding		1060	20%	46%	11%	6%	18%
Gender:	Male	510	21	51	12	6	10
	Female	549	19	40	11	6	25
Age:	18 to 26	226	17	49	9	9	16
	27-45	476	20	46	14	6	15
	46-64	234	21	48	9	5	17
	65 Plus	115	25	31	9	1	35
Education:	High School or Less	480	24	39	10	8	19
	Some College	289	17	48	11	5	18
	College Graduate	286	15	54	13	3	15
Ethnicity:	White	778	20	46	12	5	16
	Black	131	24	32	7	10	28
	Hispanic	90	19	51	15	4	10
Marital:	Married	575	21	47	11	5	16
	Single	311	16	49	11	8	17
	Divorced/Separated	100	23	46	12	4	15
	Widowed	70	25	20	12	3	41
Kids Under 18:	Yes	453	19	47	13	6	15
	No	607	20	44	10	6	19
Household Income:	Under $20,000	211	23	37	8	7	25
	$20,000 to $39,999	397	20	46	12	6	16
	$40,000 to $59,999	195	17	55	12	6	10
	$60,000 or more	137	20	48	13	8	10
Community:	Urban	306	17	48	10	7	18
	Suburban	395	18	50	12	5	15
	Rural	303	24	40	13	6	17
Region:	Northeast	230	15	44	12	8	20
	Midwest	246	19	45	14	7	15
	South	354	25	46	8	4	16
	Mountain	55	8	58	12	5	17
	Pacific	174	20	43	11	5	21
Born Again:	Yes	412	19	44	10	5	22
	No	648	20	46	12	7	15
Denominational Affiliation:	Protestant	589	22	44	9	6	20
	Catholic	286	19	51	12	5	13
Attended Church This Week:	Yes	576	19	47	9	5	20
	No	483	20	44	14	7	15
Read Bible This Week:	Yes	449	21	43	11	5	20
	No	611	19	47	12	7	16

What is your impression of the "Chrysler Corporation"? Is it very favorable, somewhat favorable, somewhat unfavorable, or very unfavorable?

		N	Very Favorable	Somewhat Favorable	Somewhat Unfavorable	Very Unfavorable	Don't Know
Total Responding		1060	16%	44%	9%	5%	25%
Gender:	Male	510	20	49	10	6	16
	Female	549	13	41	9	4	33
Age:	18 to 26	226	12	48	10	8	23
	27-45	476	15	49	9	4	23
	46-64	234	19	42	10	6	23
	65 Plus	115	21	26	10	1	42
Education:	High School or Less	480	21	40	8	5	26
	Some College	289	15	44	11	5	26
	College Graduate	286	10	52	11	5	22
Ethnicity:	White	778	16	47	9	4	24
	Black	131	25	29	4	9	33
	Hispanic	90	15	48	14	3	20
Marital:	Married	575	16	45	10	5	24
	Single	311	14	48	9	6	23
	Divorced/Separated	100	21	45	9	5	19
	Widowed	70	18	22	6	2	52
Kids Under 18:	Yes	453	15	47	9	5	24
	No	607	17	42	10	5	26
Household Income:	Under $20,000	211	18	40	5	4	33
	$20,000 to $39,999	397	17	45	10	5	22
	$40,000 to $59,999	195	16	52	5	7	20
	$60,000 or more	137	12	46	19	9	14
Community:	Urban	306	18	44	9	6	22
	Suburban	395	14	49	9	4	24
	Rural	303	17	43	11	5	24
Region:	Northeast	230	15	44	7	10	23
	Midwest	246	16	44	12	5	23
	South	354	17	48	9	4	23
	Mountain	55	13	56	5	2	23
	Pacific	174	15	35	12	2	36
Born Again:	Yes	412	15	41	10	3	30
	No	648	16	47	9	6	22
Denominational Affiliation:	Protestant	589	17	44	9	3	27
	Catholic	286	14	48	10	7	21
Attended Church This Week:	Yes	576	14	45	9	5	27
	No	483	19	44	10	5	22
Read Bible This Week:	Yes	449	15	47	9	4	26
	No	611	17	43	10	6	25

TABLE 19 199

What is your impression of the "Salvation Army"? Is it very favorable, somewhat favorable, somewhat unfavorable, or very unfavorable?

		N	Very Favorable	Somewhat Favorable	Somewhat Unfavorable	Very Unfavorable	Don't Know
Total Responding		1060	57%	35%	2%	1%	5%
Gender:	Male	510	53	40	2	1	4
	Female	549	61	31	2	1	5
Age:	18 to 26	226	58	32	1	1	7
	27-45	476	51	41	3	1	3
	46-64	234	61	33	1	1	4
	65 Plus	115	68	25	1	2	5
Education:	High School or Less	480	56	35	3	1	5
	Some College	289	62	32	1	1	3
	College Graduate	286	53	40	2	1	4
Ethnicity:	White	778	56	37	2	1	5
	Black	131	66	25	4	3	3
	Hispanic	90	49	42	5	0	3
Marital:	Married	575	56	37	3	1	4
	Single	311	56	36	1	1	6
	Divorced/Separated	100	57	32	2	4	5
	Widowed	70	70	25	1	0	4
Kids Under 18:	Yes	453	54	39	3	0	4
	No	607	59	33	1	2	5
Household Income:	Under $20,000	211	67	27	1	1	4
	$20,000 to $39,999	397	56	36	3	1	4
	$40,000 to $59,999	195	52	40	1	1	6
	$60,000 or more	137	53	42	2	3	1
Community:	Urban	306	58	35	3	2	3
	Suburban	395	55	37	2	0	4
	Rural	303	58	36	1	0	5
Region:	Northeast	230	53	39	3	2	3
	Midwest	246	61	31	2	0	5
	South	354	57	36	1	1	4
	Mountain	55	56	36	4	0	4
	Pacific	174	56	36	2	0	5
Born Again:	Yes	412	61	32	2	0	5
	No	648	54	37	2	1	5
Denominational Affiliation:	Protestant	589	60	32	2	1	4
	Catholic	286	53	41	3	0	2
Attended Church This Week:	Yes	576	59	34	2	1	3
	No	483	54	37	2	2	6
Read Bible This Week:	Yes	449	64	27	2	1	5
	No	611	52	41	2	1	4

TABLE 20

What is your impression of the "American Cancer Society"? Is it very favorable, somewhat favorable, somewhat unfavorable, or very unfavorable?

		N	Very Favorable	Somewhat Favorable	Somewhat Unfavorable	Very Unfavorable	Don't Know
Total Responding		1060	63%	27%	1%	2%	7%
Gender:	Male	510	60	29	1	1	8
	Female	549	66	25	2	2	6
Age:	18 to 26	226	64	23	0	1	12
	27-45	476	64	29	2	2	3
	46-64	234	61	25	3	2	9
	65 Plus	115	59	30	0	1	10
Education:	High School or Less	480	64	24	2	2	9
	Some College	289	66	26	2	3	4
	College Graduate	286	59	34	1	0	7
Ethnicity:	White	778	62	29	2	1	6
	Black	131	68	22	0	4	7
	Hispanic	90	69	14	2	2	14
Marital:	Married	575	61	29	2	2	6
	Single	311	63	25	0	1	11
	Divorced/Separated	100	70	24	1	0	5
	Widowed	70	62	29	1	1	7
Kids Under 18:	Yes	453	63	27	1	2	7
	No	607	63	27	2	1	7
Household Income:	Under $20,000	211	62	23	1	3	11
	$20,000 to $39,999	397	64	28	2	1	5
	$40,000 to $59,999	195	66	27	0	1	6
	$60,000 or more	137	60	30	2	2	6
Community:	Urban	306	59	32	1	1	7
	Suburban	395	66	24	1	2	7
	Rural	303	64	27	2	1	6
Region:	Northeast	230	63	32	2	1	2
	Midwest	246	62	24	1	3	10
	South	354	65	27	1	1	6
	Mountain	55	50	38	5	3	4
	Pacific	174	63	22	1	1	13
Born Again:	Yes	412	65	28	2	1	4
	No	648	61	27	1	2	9
Denominational Affiliation:	Protestant	589	63	28	2	2	6
	Catholic	286	69	22	1	1	7
Attended Church This Week:	Yes	576	66	27	2	1	4
	No	483	59	27	1	2	10
Read Bible This Week:	Yes	449	64	27	2	1	6
	No	611	62	27	1	2	8

TABLE 21　　　　　　　　　201

What is your impression of the "Mormon Church"? Is it very favorable, somewhat favorable, somewhat unfavorable, or very unfavorable?

		N	Very Favorable	Somewhat Favorable	Somewhat Unfavorable	Very Unfavorable	Don't Know
Total Responding		1060	6%	21%	18%	19%	35%
Gender:	Male	510	6	24	17	18	36
	Female	549	7	18	18	21	35
Age:	18 to 26	226	2	18	23	19	38
	27-45	476	7	21	16	19	36
	46-64	234	7	24	17	20	31
	65 Plus	115	8	20	14	18	39
Education:	High School or Less	480	5	21	14	22	39
	Some College	289	7	19	22	19	32
	College Graduate	286	7	23	21	16	33
Ethnicity:	White	778	6	24	19	19	32
	Black	131	9	12	11	21	47
	Hispanic	90	9	21	14	24	32
Marital:	Married	575	6	24	18	21	31
	Single	311	5	16	19	18	42
	Divorced/Separated	100	10	22	14	16	39
	Widowed	70	8	18	16	16	41
Kids Under 18:	Yes	453	6	20	17	21	36
	No	607	6	22	19	18	35
Household Income:	Under $20,000	211	8	17	18	14	43
	$20,000 to $39,999	397	5	25	15	20	35
	$40,000 to $59,999	195	6	19	22	19	34
	$60,000 or more	137	6	23	19	27	25
Community:	Urban	306	6	22	15	21	35
	Suburban	395	6	21	22	17	33
	Rural	303	6	21	17	20	36
Region:	Northeast	230	6	20	16	18	40
	Midwest	246	2	24	17	19	38
	South	354	7	20	15	21	36
	Mountain	55	12	21	28	16	24
	Pacific	174	9	21	23	20	27
Born Again:	Yes	412	5	18	18	28	31
	No	648	7	23	18	14	38
Denominational Affiliation:	Protestant	589	5	19	18	23	36
	Catholic	286	8	27	15	15	35
Attended Church This Week:	Yes	576	7	19	18	25	31
	No	483	5	23	17	13	41
Read Bible This Week:	Yes	449	8	17	20	27	28
	No	611	5	24	16	14	41

Table 22

Do you agree or disagree with the statement: "You wish you had more close friends"?

		N	Yes	No	Don't Know
Total Responding		1060	45%	54%	1%
Gender:	Male	510	49	49	2
	Female	549	41	59	1
Age:	18 to 26	226	42	56	2
	27-45	476	49	50	1
	46-64	234	36	63	1
	65 Plus	115	49	50	1
Education:	High School or Less	480	49	50	1
	Some College	289	33	65	1
	College Graduate	286	48	50	2
Ethnicity:	White	778	44	55	1
	Black	131	44	56	0
	Hispanic	90	55	42	3
Marital:	Married	575	43	56	1
	Single	311	46	52	2
	Divorced/Separated	100	44	56	0
	Widowed	70	48	50	2
Kids Under 18:	Yes	453	43	56	1
	No	607	46	53	1
Household Income:	Under $20,000	211	46	52	1
	$20,000 to $39,999	397	46	52	2
	$40,000 to $59,999	195	48	51	1
	$60,000 or more	137	36	64	0
Community:	Urban	306	44	54	2
	Suburban	395	43	56	1
	Rural	303	47	53	1
Region:	Northeast	230	40	60	0
	Midwest	246	43	55	1
	South	354	49	50	1
	Mountain	55	41	58	1
	Pacific	174	45	52	3
Born Again:	Yes	412	46	53	0
	No	648	43	55	2
Denominational Affiliation:	Protestant	589	44	55	1
	Catholic	286	47	51	2
Attended Church This Week:	Yes	576	45	54	1
	No	483	44	54	1
Read Bible This Week:	Yes	449	47	52	1
	No	611	43	56	2

TABLE 23 203

Do you agree or disagree with the statement: "With society changing so fast, it's nearly impossible to have long-lasting friendships these days"?

		N	Yes	No	Don't Know
Total Responding		1060	23%	76%	1%
Gender:	Male	510	21	78	1
	Female	549	25	74	2
Age:	18 to 26	226	30	70	1
	27-45	476	18	82	1
	46-64	234	24	74	1
	65 Plus	115	27	69	4
Education:	High School or Less	480	29	69	2
	Some College	289	17	82	1
	College Graduate	286	18	81	1
Ethnicity:	White	778	20	79	1
	Black	131	37	60	2
	Hispanic	90	29	71	0
Marital:	Married	575	20	80	1
	Single	311	26	73	1
	Divorced/Separated	100	26	71	2
	Widowed	70	29	66	6
Kids Under 18:	Yes	453	22	78	1
	No	607	24	74	2
Household Income:	Under $20,000	211	32	64	4
	$20,000 to $39,999	397	25	74	1
	$40,000 to $59,999	195	17	83	0
	$60,000 or more	137	17	83	0
Community:	Urban	306	21	77	2
	Suburban	395	22	76	1
	Rural	303	24	75	1
Region:	Northeast	230	23	76	1
	Midwest	246	20	78	2
	South	354	24	74	1
	Mountain	55	19	81	0
	Pacific	174	26	74	1
Born Again:	Yes	412	22	76	2
	No	648	23	76	1
Denominational Affiliation:	Protestant	589	24	75	1
	Catholic	286	22	76	2
Attended Church This Week:	Yes	576	22	76	2
	No	483	24	75	1
Read Bible This Week:	Yes	449	22	75	2
	No	611	23	76	1

If you wanted to make new friends, where would you be most likely to find the people who would become your new friends? (Probe: "Are there any other places?") ** Multiple Response **

		N	Work	Church	Neighbor-hood	Sports	School	Social/ Exercise Clubs	Community Activities/ Organizations	Other	Don't Know
Total Responding		1060	45%	49%	12%	8%	18%	20%	18%	19%	11%
Gender:	Male	510	48	36	9	12	17	22	14	20	13
	Female	549	43	61	14	5	19	18	22	18	9
Age:	18 to 26	226	41	28	9	8	42	23	9	32	10
	27-45	476	57	48	11	9	14	20	18	15	11
	46-64	234	42	61	14	9	8	20	23	16	10
	65 Plus	115	16	72	18	4	8	18	23	17	12
Education:	High School or Less	480	37	51	14	8	13	17	12	22	15
	Some College	289	47	50	11	9	25	20	21	18	7
	College Graduate	286	58	45	10	8	20	25	24	15	8
Ethnicity:	White	778	46	49	14	9	14	20	20	18	12
	Black	131	36	65	8	5	14	18	11	22	8
	Hispanic	90	55	38	4	8	31	28	13	25	10
Marital:	Married	575	51	58	14	9	13	19	21	15	8
	Single	311	42	27	8	8	32	22	12	26	15
	Divorced/Separated	100	47	51	9	8	10	22	13	19	15
	Widowed	70	13	71	16	2	3	19	25	17	13
Kids Under 18:	Yes	453	52	50	12	8	22	17	16	17	10
	No	607	41	48	12	9	15	22	20	21	12
Household Income:	Under $20,000	211	32	52	14	5	13	15	16	21	14
	$20,000 to $39,999	397	48	51	9	9	19	22	17	19	11
	$40,000 to $59,999	195	56	47	16	10	23	25	18	16	8
	$60,000 or more	137	53	36	11	11	15	16	17	22	8
Community:	Urban	306	43	48	11	11	17	20	15	18	14
	Suburban	395	51	46	14	8	20	22	18	18	11
	Rural	303	42	55	11	8	15	19	21	18	8
Region:	Northeast	230	48	40	13	11	21	25	20	19	14
	Midwest	246	45	47	11	8	16	18	20	20	11
	South	354	44	61	12	6	14	17	13	18	8
	Mountain	55	60	47	14	12	15	19	19	22	14
	Pacific	174	41	40	12	8	27	21	22	18	11
Born Again:	Yes	412	45	75	12	8	15	18	18	13	6
	No	648	45	32	12	9	20	22	18	23	14
Denominational Affiliation:	Protestant	589	42	62	12	8	13	16	19	16	9
	Catholic	286	51	39	12	10	25	28	17	20	10
Attended Church This Week:	Yes	576	45	70	13	7	17	20	20	15	7
	No	483	46	24	11	10	19	20	16	24	16
Read Bible This Week:	Yes	449	40	73	13	7	15	18	19	16	6
	No	611	49	31	11	9	20	21	17	21	14

TABLE 25

205

Are Protestant churches very sensitive, somewhat sensitive, not too sensitive, or not sensitive at all to the needs of "women under 35"?

		N	Very Sensitive	Somewhat Sensitive	Not Too Sensitive	Not at All Sensitive	Don't Know
Total Responding		1060	17%	39%	7%	3%	34%
Gender:	Male	510	16	40	7	3	34
	Female	549	17	38	8	3	34
Age:	18 to 26	226	15	40	6	2	37
	27-45	476	15	38	8	3	36
	46-64	234	14	43	8	4	31
	65 Plus	115	32	34	4	1	29
Education:	High School or Less	480	19	39	5	3	33
	Some College	289	14	37	7	3	39
	College Graduate	286	15	41	11	2	31
Ethnicity:	White	778	15	41	7	2	35
	Black	131	31	34	6	8	21
	Hispanic	90	20	36	5	2	38
Marital:	Married	575	17	41	8	4	31
	Single	311	15	37	8	3	37
	Divorced/Separated	100	15	39	3	1	42
	Widowed	70	23	35	4	3	35
Kids Under 18:	Yes	453	15	42	7	3	33
	No	607	18	37	7	3	35
Household Income:	Under $20,000	211	24	33	7	4	33
	$20,000 to $39,999	397	17	42	6	3	33
	$40,000 to $59,999	195	12	48	8	3	30
	$60,000 or more	137	11	33	11	4	41
Community:	Urban	306	18	34	9	4	35
	Suburban	395	14	40	6	2	37
	Rural	303	18	44	7	3	28
Region:	Northeast	230	8	40	6	4	41
	Midwest	246	18	39	8	2	33
	South	354	23	41	7	2	27
	Mountain	55	15	47	1	4	32
	Pacific	174	16	31	9	3	41
Born Again:	Yes	412	25	43	6	2	24
	No	648	11	36	8	4	40
Denominational Affiliation:	Protestant	589	21	45	7	3	24
	Catholic	286	11	35	5	2	47
Attended Church This Week:	Yes	576	22	41	6	3	27
	No	483	10	37	8	3	42
Read Bible This Week:	Yes	449	27	41	4	3	24
	No	611	9	37	9	3	42

TABLE 26

Are Protestant churches very sensitive, somewhat sensitive, not too sensitive, or not sensitive at all to the needs of "women 35 or older"?

		N	Very Sensitive	Somewhat Sensitive	Not Too Sensitive	Not at All Sensitive	Don't Know
Total Responding		1060	22%	38%	5%	2%	34%
Gender:	Male	510	22	37	4	2	35
	Female	549	22	38	7	1	32
Age:	18 to 26	226	21	35	6	2	37
	27-45	476	18	39	4	1	38
	46-64	234	26	40	6	3	25
	65 Plus	115	31	33	7	1	29
Education:	High School or Less	480	24	38	4	2	32
	Some College	289	21	35	4	1	39
	College Graduate	286	20	41	8	1	30
Ethnicity:	White	778	20	39	6	2	33
	Black	131	35	36	4	2	24
	Hispanic	90	30	31	3	3	34
Marital:	Married	575	23	41	6	2	29
	Single	311	20	34	6	1	39
	Divorced/Separated	100	20	36	1	2	41
	Widowed	70	22	35	4	2	37
Kids Under 18:	Yes	453	19	42	5	1	34
	No	607	24	35	6	2	33
Household Income:	Under $20,000	211	30	30	4	3	33
	$20,000 to $39,999	397	21	40	6	2	31
	$40,000 to $59,999	195	17	48	6	1	28
	$60,000 or more	137	17	32	5	1	45
Community:	Urban	306	20	36	5	2	37
	Suburban	395	20	39	6	1	34
	Rural	303	25	41	4	2	28
Region:	Northeast	230	17	37	6	2	39
	Midwest	246	22	37	6	2	34
	South	354	27	39	6	2	26
	Mountain	55	18	47	0	1	33
	Pacific	174	18	34	5	2	40
Born Again:	Yes	412	30	42	5	1	22
	No	648	16	35	6	2	41
Denominational Affiliation:	Protestant	589	28	44	5	1	22
	Catholic	286	16	34	4	1	44
Attended Church This Week:	Yes	576	26	41	5	1	27
	No	483	16	34	6	3	41
Read Bible This Week:	Yes	449	32	39	5	1	23
	No	611	14	37	5	2	41

Table 27   207

Are Protestant churches very sensitive, somewhat sensitive, not too sensitive, or not sensitive at all to the needs of "men under 35"?

		N	Very Sensitive	Somewhat Sensitive	Not Too Sensitive	Not at All Sensitive	Don't Know
Total Responding		1060	12%	38%	9%	4%	36%
Gender:	Male	510	11	42	7	5	36
	Female	549	14	36	11	2	37
Age:	18 to 26	226	10	38	9	6	37
	27-45	476	11	38	10	2	40
	46-64	234	15	42	10	4	30
	65 Plus	115	20	36	5	3	37
Education:	High School or Less	480	14	38	9	4	36
	Some College	289	12	36	7	3	41
	College Graduate	286	11	42	12	2	33
Ethnicity:	White	778	13	39	9	2	37
	Black	131	20	35	13	6	26
	Hispanic	90	6	42	8	9	34
Marital:	Married	575	13	39	11	4	34
	Single	311	11	38	8	5	38
	Divorced/Separated	100	13	39	4	1	44
	Widowed	70	16	34	7	2	41
Kids Under 18:	Yes	453	9	41	10	3	36
	No	607	15	36	9	4	36
Household Income:	Under $20,000	211	18	32	11	3	36
	$20,000 to $39,999	397	13	40	9	5	33
	$40,000 to $59,999	195	8	47	11	3	31
	$60,000 or more	137	8	36	8	4	45
Community:	Urban	306	13	37	10	3	38
	Suburban	395	12	38	8	4	39
	Rural	303	14	42	10	2	31
Region:	Northeast	230	8	38	11	3	40
	Midwest	246	12	38	9	4	36
	South	354	17	40	9	3	32
	Mountain	55	9	41	8	9	33
	Pacific	174	11	36	8	3	42
Born Again:	Yes	412	20	43	10	2	25
	No	648	8	35	9	5	44
Denominational Affiliation:	Protestant	589	17	43	10	3	27
	Catholic	286	6	36	8	4	46
Attended Church This Week:	Yes	576	17	41	10	3	30
	No	483	7	36	8	5	45
Read Bible This Week:	Yes	449	20	41	9	3	27
	No	611	7	36	9	4	43

TABLE 28

Are Protestant churches very sensitive, somewhat sensitive, not too sensitive, or not sensitive at all to the needs of "men 35 or older"?

		N	Very Sensitive	Somewhat Sensitive	Not Too Sensitive	Not at All Sensitive	Don't Know
Total Responding		1060	19%	36%	7%	2%	35%
Gender:	Male	510	20	36	6	3	35
	Female	549	18	37	8	1	36
Age:	18 to 26	226	19	33	11	1	36
	27-45	476	17	37	6	2	39
	46-64	234	22	39	6	4	29
	65 Plus	115	25	33	6	1	35
Education:	High School or Less	480	19	37	6	3	35
	Some College	289	16	35	6	2	40
	College Graduate	286	22	36	10	1	31
Ethnicity:	White	778	19	38	6	2	36
	Black	131	29	36	6	4	25
	Hispanic	90	15	31	12	5	36
Marital:	Married	575	20	39	6	3	32
	Single	311	17	32	10	2	38
	Divorced/Separated	100	20	34	1	1	43
	Widowed	70	20	36	5	2	37
Kids Under 18:	Yes	453	15	40	7	2	35
	No	607	22	34	7	2	35
Household Income:	Under $20,000	211	25	27	10	4	35
	$20,000 to $39,999	397	20	37	7	2	33
	$40,000 to $59,999	195	15	48	7	1	29
	$60,000 or more	137	17	32	6	2	43
Community:	Urban	306	19	34	8	2	37
	Suburban	395	18	35	7	2	38
	Rural	303	22	43	6	2	28
Region:	Northeast	230	17	38	4	1	41
	Midwest	246	22	34	6	2	36
	South	354	22	39	7	3	29
	Mountain	55	9	37	16	3	34
	Pacific	174	15	32	10	3	41
Born Again:	Yes	412	29	40	6	1	24
	No	648	13	34	8	3	42
Denominational Affiliation:	Protestant	589	24	41	8	2	25
	Catholic	286	12	32	5	2	48
Attended Church This Week:	Yes	576	23	39	7	2	29
	No	483	14	33	7	3	43
Read Bible This Week:	Yes	449	27	38	7	2	26
	No	611	13	35	7	2	42

TABLE 29   209

Are Protestant churches very sensitive, somewhat sensitive, not too sensitive, or not sensitive at all to the needs of "the elderly"?

		N	Very Sensitive	Somewhat Sensitive	Not Too Sensitive	Not at All Sensitive	Don't Know
Total Responding		1060	39%	26%	4%	2%	28%
Gender:	Male	510	38	26	3	3	30
	Female	549	40	27	5	2	27
Age:	18 to 26	226	39	24	2	3	33
	27-45	476	36	27	4	2	31
	46-64	234	42	30	4	3	22
	65 Plus	115	44	23	6	1	25
Education:	High School or Less	480	41	25	3	4	28
	Some College	289	37	26	5	1	32
	College Graduate	286	38	30	4	1	26
Ethnicity:	White	778	39	27	4	2	29
	Black	131	49	28	1	5	17
	Hispanic	90	36	21	8	5	30
Marital:	Married	575	41	28	4	2	25
	Single	311	35	27	3	3	33
	Divorced/Separated	100	42	17	5	1	36
	Widowed	70	35	28	6	3	28
Kids Under 18:	Yes	453	39	27	4	2	27
	No	607	39	26	4	2	29
Household Income:	Under $20,000	211	42	22	4	3	28
	$20,000 to $39,999	397	39	27	4	3	27
	$40,000 to $59,999	195	40	29	5	0	26
	$60,000 or more	137	32	29	3	3	33
Community:	Urban	306	38	23	5	3	31
	Suburban	395	38	28	3	2	29
	Rural	303	42	29	4	2	23
Region:	Northeast	230	36	27	2	2	33
	Midwest	246	41	25	4	2	28
	South	354	43	27	5	3	23
	Mountain	55	29	35	4	3	29
	Pacific	174	36	24	5	1	34
Born Again:	Yes	412	46	30	5	1	17
	No	648	34	24	4	3	36
Denominational Affiliation:	Protestant	589	48	29	4	2	17
	Catholic	286	30	24	3	2	41
Attended Church This Week:	Yes	576	46	27	4	2	21
	No	483	30	26	4	3	37
Read Bible This Week:	Yes	449	47	27	5	3	18
	No	611	33	26	3	2	36

Are Protestant churches very sensitive, somewhat sensitive, not too sensitive, or not sensitive at all to the needs of "blacks"?

		N	Very Sensitive	Somewhat Sensitive	Not Too Sensitive	Not at All Sensitive	Don't Know
Total Responding		1060	14%	35%	10%	3%	38%
Gender:	Male	510	13	36	10	3	38
	Female	549	16	34	10	3	38
Age:	18 to 26	226	11	37	10	1	41
	27-45	476	12	34	10	3	40
	46-64	234	19	34	10	4	33
	65 Plus	115	21	37	6	2	34
Education:	High School or Less	480	16	36	6	3	38
	Some College	289	12	32	10	3	44
	College Graduate	286	14	36	17	2	32
Ethnicity:	White	778	13	35	10	2	40
	Black	131	31	34	11	4	20
	Hispanic	90	14	31	11	5	38
Marital:	Married	575	15	35	10	4	36
	Single	311	12	36	11	1	40
	Divorced/Separated	100	19	32	5	2	43
	Widowed	70	15	37	10	5	33
Kids Under 18:	Yes	453	12	38	10	3	39
	No	607	16	33	10	3	37
Household Income:	Under $20,000	211	21	31	11	5	33
	$20,000 to $39,999	397	15	41	9	2	33
	$40,000 to $59,999	195	13	35	12	2	37
	$60,000 or more	137	9	30	13	3	45
Community:	Urban	306	15	34	10	3	37
	Suburban	395	13	36	11	2	39
	Rural	303	15	37	10	3	36
Region:	Northeast	230	11	34	9	2	43
	Midwest	246	12	35	9	3	41
	South	354	17	37	12	3	31
	Mountain	55	24	34	6	2	34
	Pacific	174	13	33	9	3	42
Born Again:	Yes	412	22	38	11	2	28
	No	648	10	33	9	3	44
Denominational Affiliation:	Protestant	589	19	39	11	2	29
	Catholic	286	11	30	9	2	48
Attended Church This Week:	Yes	576	20	35	11	2	32
	No	483	8	35	9	4	45
Read Bible This Week:	Yes	449	23	37	11	3	27
	No	611	8	34	9	3	46

TABLE 31   211

Are Protestant churches very sensitive, somewhat sensitive, not too sensitive, or not sensitive at all to the needs of "Hispanics"?

		N	Very Sensitive	Somewhat Sensitive	Not Too Sensitive	Not at All Sensitive	Don't Know
Total Responding		1060	12%	30%	11%	4%	43%
Gender:	Male	510	13	31	11	5	41
	Female	549	12	30	10	4	44
Age:	18 to 26	226	14	26	12	4	45
	27-45	476	9	32	11	3	45
	46-64	234	12	32	10	7	39
	65 Plus	115	21	30	9	1	39
Education:	High School or Less	480	15	30	7	5	43
	Some College	289	9	30	9	5	46
	College Graduate	286	10	30	17	3	39
Ethnicity:	White	778	11	32	11	4	43
	Black	131	16	26	14	8	36
	Hispanic	90	24	30	3	5	38
Marital:	Married	575	11	32	12	5	41
	Single	311	13	27	12	4	45
	Divorced/Separated	100	16	28	5	2	49
	Widowed	70	15	38	6	2	39
Kids Under 18:	Yes	453	8	33	10	5	44
	No	607	15	28	11	4	42
Household Income:	Under $20,000	211	19	27	9	2	42
	$20,000 to $39,999	397	10	34	11	5	40
	$40,000 to $59,999	195	9	34	11	5	42
	$60,000 or more	137	10	24	16	5	45
Community:	Urban	306	13	29	12	5	41
	Suburban	395	9	29	11	4	46
	Rural	303	13	36	9	3	39
Region:	Northeast	230	11	27	12	4	47
	Midwest	246	7	31	10	5	47
	South	354	15	32	12	3	37
	Mountain	55	19	24	9	9	39
	Pacific	174	13	32	7	3	45
Born Again:	Yes	412	19	33	10	3	35
	No	648	8	29	11	5	48
Denominational Affiliation:	Protestant	589	15	34	12	4	35
	Catholic	286	12	28	8	3	49
Attended Church This Week:	Yes	576	16	32	12	4	37
	No	483	7	28	9	5	50
Read Bible This Week:	Yes	449	19	31	12	4	34
	No	611	7	29	10	5	49

TABLE 32

Are Protestant churches very sensitive, somewhat sensitive, not too sensitive, or not sensitive at all to the needs of "Asians"?

		N	Very Sensitive	Somewhat Sensitive	Not Too Sensitive	Not at All Sensitive	Don't Know
Total Responding		1060	10%	29%	11%	4%	45%
Gender:	Male	510	9	31	12	6	43
	Female	549	11	28	10	3	48
Age:	18 to 26	226	6	36	11	4	44
	27-45	476	9	28	11	4	48
	46-64	234	15	27	13	5	40
	65 Plus	115	17	26	7	1	50
Education:	High School or Less	480	11	29	10	3	48
	Some College	289	8	31	8	5	47
	College Graduate	286	12	28	16	5	40
Ethnicity:	White	778	11	30	10	3	46
	Black	131	15	25	14	5	41
	Hispanic	90	8	26	16	7	42
Marital:	Married	575	11	27	14	4	44
	Single	311	7	35	9	4	45
	Divorced/Separated	100	14	25	4	5	52
	Widowed	70	14	32	7	2	45
Kids Under 18:	Yes	453	7	33	12	4	45
	No	607	13	27	11	4	45
Household Income:	Under $20,000	211	17	29	9	3	42
	$20,000 to $39,999	397	10	32	10	5	44
	$40,000 to $59,999	195	7	30	15	7	42
	$60,000 or more	137	7	24	18	2	49
Community:	Urban	306	12	29	12	5	43
	Suburban	395	10	28	11	4	47
	Rural	303	9	32	11	4	43
Region:	Northeast	230	9	28	11	4	49
	Midwest	246	10	30	11	3	46
	South	354	12	28	13	5	42
	Mountain	55	7	46	2	2	43
	Pacific	174	10	27	10	5	46
Born Again:	Yes	412	16	31	12	3	38
	No	648	7	28	10	5	50
Denominational Affiliation:	Protestant	589	14	33	12	3	38
	Catholic	286	6	28	11	4	52
Attended Church This Week:	Yes	576	14	30	11	4	41
	No	483	6	28	11	5	50
Read Bible This Week:	Yes	449	17	31	11	4	38
	No	611	6	28	11	4	51

TABLE 33   213

Are Protestant churches very sensitive, somewhat sensitive, not too sensitive, or not sensitive at all to the needs of "single adults"?

		N	Very Sensitive	Somewhat Sensitive	Not Too Sensitive	Not at All Sensitive	Don't Know
Total Responding		1060	16%	36%	12%	3%	32%
Gender:	Male	510	14	36	14	4	32
	Female	549	18	37	11	2	32
Age:	18 to 26	226	11	34	15	3	36
	27-45	476	14	36	11	3	36
	46-64	234	16	42	14	3	24
	65 Plus	115	33	28	9	1	28
Education:	High School or Less	480	19	33	12	4	33
	Some College	289	13	38	12	2	35
	College Graduate	286	14	40	14	2	29
Ethnicity:	White	778	16	37	12	2	32
	Black	131	23	39	10	7	21
	Hispanic	90	13	25	21	5	36
Marital:	Married	575	18	37	14	2	28
	Single	311	12	38	11	4	35
	Divorced/Separated	100	15	29	8	5	42
	Widowed	70	19	32	11	3	35
Kids Under 18:	Yes	453	14	37	13	3	33
	No	607	18	36	12	3	32
Household Income:	Under $20,000	211	19	31	13	5	32
	$20,000 to $39,999	397	17	39	13	3	29
	$40,000 to $59,999	195	11	44	15	2	28
	$60,000 or more	137	19	24	14	3	40
Community:	Urban	306	15	36	11	4	33
	Suburban	395	15	35	13	2	34
	Rural	303	19	39	13	2	26
Region:	Northeast	230	13	32	13	3	39
	Midwest	246	16	35	14	3	32
	South	354	21	39	11	3	25
	Mountain	55	14	32	19	0	35
	Pacific	174	12	39	10	3	36
Born Again:	Yes	412	24	41	13	1	20
	No	648	11	33	12	4	40
Denominational Affiliation:	Protestant	589	23	42	13	2	21
	Catholic	286	9	29	12	3	47
Attended Church This Week:	Yes	576	21	39	12	2	26
	No	483	10	34	13	4	39
Read Bible This Week:	Yes	449	25	37	12	3	23
	No	611	9	36	13	3	39

TABLE 34

Are Protestant churches very sensitive, somewhat sensitive, not too sensitive, or not sensitive at all to the needs of "single parents"?

		N	Very Sensitive	Somewhat Sensitive	Not Too Sensitive	Not at All Sensitive	Don't Know
Total Responding		1060	17%	37%	10%	3%	33%
Gender:	Male	510	15	38	9	4	34
	Female	549	19	35	11	2	31
Age:	18 to 26	226	17	35	9	3	36
	27-45	476	15	36	11	3	35
	46-64	234	21	41	10	2	26
	65 Plus	115	21	36	9	1	33
Education:	High School or Less	480	21	37	6	4	33
	Some College	289	14	39	8	2	36
	College Graduate	286	15	35	18	2	30
Ethnicity:	White	778	17	39	9	2	33
	Black	131	19	39	13	7	22
	Hispanic	90	23	32	4	7	34
Marital:	Married	575	19	38	11	3	29
	Single	311	14	36	10	3	37
	Divorced/Separated	100	19	34	8	3	37
	Widowed	70	19	38	7	0	36
Kids Under 18:	Yes	453	17	37	12	2	32
	No	607	18	37	9	4	33
Household Income:	Under $20,000	211	22	33	7	5	33
	$20,000 to $39,999	397	18	40	11	3	29
	$40,000 to $59,999	195	13	43	14	3	28
	$60,000 or more	137	14	31	11	4	39
Community:	Urban	306	19	33	10	4	34
	Suburban	395	16	38	11	1	33
	Rural	303	18	41	10	3	28
Region:	Northeast	230	11	37	10	4	37
	Midwest	246	18	35	11	3	32
	South	354	22	38	10	1	29
	Mountain	55	22	34	11	1	32
	Pacific	174	12	37	9	6	36
Born Again:	Yes	412	25	41	10	2	23
	No	648	13	34	10	4	39
Denominational Affiliation:	Protestant	589	21	43	11	2	23
	Catholic	286	16	30	7	3	45
Attended Church This Week:	Yes	576	22	39	10	2	26
	No	483	12	34	9	4	40
Read Bible This Week:	Yes	449	25	37	10	3	24
	No	611	11	37	10	3	39

TABLE 35   215

Are Protestant churches very sensitive, somewhat sensitive, not too sensitive, or not sensitive at all to the needs of "teenagers"?

		N	Very Sensitive	Somewhat Sensitive	Not Too Sensitive	Not at All Sensitive	Don't Know
Total Responding		1060	28%	31%	9%	4%	29%
Gender:	Male	510	24	31	8	6	30
	Female	549	31	30	9	2	28
Age:	18 to 26	226	18	35	10	4	32
	27-45	476	26	29	8	5	33
	46-64	234	35	34	8	4	19
	65 Plus	115	41	24	7	1	26
Education:	High School or Less	480	30	29	8	5	28
	Some College	289	28	30	6	4	32
	College Graduate	286	24	34	12	3	27
Ethnicity:	White	778	28	33	7	3	29
	Black	131	33	26	14	9	18
	Hispanic	90	25	25	8	8	33
Marital:	Married	575	31	30	9	3	27
	Single	311	19	34	11	6	31
	Divorced/Separated	100	28	29	4	6	33
	Widowed	70	40	24	5	2	30
Kids Under 18:	Yes	453	25	33	8	4	29
	No	607	29	29	9	5	28
Household Income:	Under $20,000	211	32	26	6	6	30
	$20,000 to $39,999	397	28	31	10	5	26
	$40,000 to $59,999	195	20	40	11	3	26
	$60,000 or more	137	27	25	11	4	33
Community:	Urban	306	28	25	11	6	31
	Suburban	395	27	33	8	3	30
	Rural	303	32	35	6	3	24
Region:	Northeast	230	21	30	6	8	35
	Midwest	246	26	37	7	2	27
	South	354	36	28	9	4	23
	Mountain	55	27	22	19	3	28
	Pacific	174	22	30	11	3	34
Born Again:	Yes	412	42	33	6	2	17
	No	648	19	29	10	5	36
Denominational Affiliation:	Protestant	589	38	33	9	4	17
	Catholic	286	18	29	6	4	43
Attended Church This Week:	Yes	576	37	30	8	2	23
	No	483	17	31	10	6	36
Read Bible This Week:	Yes	449	40	31	8	2	19
	No	611	19	31	9	6	36

Are Protestant churches very sensitive, somewhat sensitive, not too sensitive, or not sensitive at all to the needs of "non-Christians"?

		N	Very Sensitive	Somewhat Sensitive	Not Too Sensitive	Not at All Sensitive	Don't Know
Total Responding		1060	16%	31%	13%	7%	33%
Gender:	Male	510	14	29	14	8	35
	Female	549	17	33	12	6	31
Age:	18 to 26	226	14	34	13	6	34
	27-45	476	14	28	13	8	37
	46-64	234	18	32	15	8	28
	65 Plus	115	22	33	13	1	31
Education:	High School or Less	480	18	34	11	5	32
	Some College	289	13	26	13	10	38
	College Graduate	286	14	31	17	7	32
Ethnicity:	White	778	16	32	14	6	33
	Black	131	20	31	12	11	26
	Hispanic	90	14	27	12	9	37
Marital:	Married	575	17	33	13	7	31
	Single	311	12	30	15	7	36
	Divorced/Separated	100	15	28	10	9	38
	Widowed	70	18	26	14	5	37
Kids Under 18:	Yes	453	14	33	12	7	33
	No	607	16	29	14	7	34
Household Income:	Under $20,000	211	16	30	14	6	34
	$20,000 to $39,999	397	17	32	12	7	32
	$40,000 to $59,999	195	15	36	13	7	29
	$60,000 or more	137	13	26	19	8	34
Community:	Urban	306	17	27	11	8	36
	Suburban	395	14	29	16	7	35
	Rural	303	16	41	12	6	26
Region:	Northeast	230	10	30	17	8	37
	Midwest	246	13	38	10	4	34
	South	354	23	30	12	8	27
	Mountain	55	12	31	17	11	30
	Pacific	174	12	26	13	7	41
Born Again:	Yes	412	26	37	12	4	20
	No	648	9	27	14	9	42
Denominational Affiliation:	Protestant	589	23	36	15	5	21
	Catholic	286	6	28	11	6	49
Attended Church This Week:	Yes	576	21	34	12	6	27
	No	483	9	27	15	8	41
Read Bible This Week:	Yes	449	25	34	13	6	21
	No	611	8	29	13	7	42

TABLE 37   217

Are Protestant churches very sensitive, somewhat sensitive, not too sensitive, or not sensitive at all to the needs of "the poor"?

		N	Very Sensitive	Somewhat Sensitive	Not Too Sensitive	Not at All Sensitive	Don't Know
Total Responding		1060	28%	32%	9%	3%	29%
Gender:	Male	510	27	31	9	3	30
	Female	549	29	32	8	3	28
Age:	18 to 26	226	31	27	9	2	31
	27-45	476	24	33	9	3	31
	46-64	234	29	35	9	3	24
	65 Plus	115	37	32	3	2	26
Education:	High School or Less	480	31	29	7	4	29
	Some College	289	26	33	8	2	31
	College Graduate	286	25	36	11	2	27
Ethnicity:	White	778	27	32	8	3	30
	Black	131	32	32	13	4	18
	Hispanic	90	37	22	5	4	31
Marital:	Married	575	28	33	9	3	27
	Single	311	26	31	9	3	30
	Divorced/Separated	100	30	31	3	3	33
	Widowed	70	30	30	6	3	31
Kids Under 18:	Yes	453	27	33	8	3	29
	No	607	28	31	9	3	29
Household Income:	Under $20,000	211	33	25	6	5	31
	$20,000 to $39,999	397	28	36	8	4	24
	$40,000 to $59,999	195	27	34	10	1	28
	$60,000 or more	137	22	29	13	3	33
Community:	Urban	306	28	28	9	4	31
	Suburban	395	27	35	8	3	28
	Rural	303	30	34	8	3	25
Region:	Northeast	230	24	29	9	4	33
	Midwest	246	25	37	6	2	29
	South	354	31	31	11	3	23
	Mountain	55	46	19	2	2	31
	Pacific	174	24	33	7	3	33
Born Again:	Yes	412	38	35	7	2	18
	No	648	22	29	10	4	35
Denominational Affiliation:	Protestant	589	35	35	9	2	19
	Catholic	286	26	27	6	2	40
Attended Church This Week:	Yes	576	36	31	8	2	24
	No	483	18	32	10	5	35
Read Bible This Week:	Yes	449	38	32	9	2	18
	No	611	20	31	8	4	36

TABLE 38

Are Protestant churches very sensitive, somewhat sensitive, not too sensitive, or not sensitive at all to the needs of "families"?

		N	Very Sensitive	Somewhat Sensitive	Not Too Sensitive	Not at All Sensitive	Don't Know
Total Responding		1060	46%	23%	2%	1%	28%
Gender:	Male	510	43	26	2	2	28
	Female	549	48	21	3	1	28
Age:	18 to 26	226	43	20	3	1	33
	27-45	476	45	22	1	1	30
	46-64	234	47	28	3	1	21
	65 Plus	115	48	22	2	1	27
Education:	High School or Less	480	44	24	2	1	28
	Some College	289	45	22	2	1	30
	College Graduate	286	49	22	2	1	26
Ethnicity:	White	778	48	22	1	1	28
	Black	131	42	29	7	2	21
	Hispanic	90	41	33	3	0	23
Marital:	Married	575	47	24	2	1	25
	Single	311	44	21	2	1	31
	Divorced/Separated	100	43	23	0	1	34
	Widowed	70	40	24	3	2	32
Kids Under 18:	Yes	453	45	24	1	1	28
	No	607	46	22	3	1	28
Household Income:	Under $20,000	211	49	19	2	2	28
	$20,000 to $39,999	397	44	28	2	1	25
	$40,000 to $59,999	195	47	24	3	1	25
	$60,000 or more	137	43	19	3	1	33
Community:	Urban	306	47	19	3	2	30
	Suburban	395	42	27	2	1	28
	Rural	303	50	23	2	1	25
Region:	Northeast	230	45	21	0	1	33
	Midwest	246	45	22	4	1	27
	South	354	47	24	2	1	25
	Mountain	55	42	22	6	2	28
	Pacific	174	44	26	1	0	29
Born Again:	Yes	412	52	27	2	0	19
	No	648	41	21	2	2	34
Denominational Affiliation:	Protestant	589	54	25	3	1	18
	Catholic	286	38	20	1	1	40
Attended Church This Week:	Yes	576	54	21	3	1	21
	No	483	35	26	2	2	36
Read Bible This Week:	Yes	449	55	22	2	1	19
	No	611	38	24	2	1	34

TABLE 39   219

Are Protestant churches very sensitive, somewhat sensitive, not too sensitive, or not sensitive at all to the needs of "children under age 13"?

		N	Very Sensitive	Somewhat Sensitive	Not Too Sensitive	Not at All Sensitive	Don't Know
Total Responding		1060	37%	25%	5%	3%	30%
Gender:	Male	510	35	23	5	5	31
	Female	549	38	26	6	1	28
Age:	18 to 26	226	35	23	4	3	35
	27-45	476	32	26	5	3	33
	46-64	234	41	27	7	3	22
	65 Plus	115	50	19	7	1	24
Education:	High School or Less	480	39	24	5	3	28
	Some College	289	33	26	4	2	35
	College Graduate	286	37	25	7	4	27
Ethnicity:	White	778	39	25	5	2	30
	Black	131	30	32	11	9	18
	Hispanic	90	39	22	0	3	36
Marital:	Married	575	39	26	7	3	26
	Single	311	35	23	5	3	34
	Divorced/Separated	100	31	25	1	5	38
	Widowed	70	41	24	6	2	27
Kids Under 18:	Yes	453	36	28	5	3	28
	No	607	38	22	6	3	31
Household Income:	Under $20,000	211	37	27	4	3	29
	$20,000 to $39,999	397	39	24	6	3	28
	$40,000 to $59,999	195	34	29	7	4	25
	$60,000 or more	137	32	21	6	4	36
Community:	Urban	306	35	21	7	5	31
	Suburban	395	32	30	4	1	32
	Rural	303	47	22	6	2	23
Region:	Northeast	230	29	24	5	6	37
	Midwest	246	37	25	6	2	29
	South	354	44	24	5	3	24
	Mountain	55	42	25	4	2	27
	Pacific	174	32	27	6	2	33
Born Again:	Yes	412	51	24	5	2	18
	No	648	28	25	5	4	37
Denominational Affiliation:	Protestant	589	48	26	6	2	18
	Catholic	286	28	22	3	2	45
Attended Church This Week:	Yes	576	47	24	6	2	22
	No	483	25	26	5	5	39
Read Bible This Week:	Yes	449	49	25	6	2	18
	No	611	28	25	5	4	38

TABLE 40

Do you think that most Christian churches provide meaningful opportunities for women to serve in areas of ministry in which they have special talents and abilities, or not?

		N	Yes	No	Don't Know
Total Responding		1060	49%	36%	15%
Gender:	Male	510	43	40	17
	Female	549	55	32	13
Age:	18 to 26	226	44	42	14
	27-45	476	49	38	12
	46-64	234	52	30	18
	65 Plus	115	57	23	21
Education:	High School or Less	480	54	30	16
	Some College	289	47	40	14
	College Graduate	286	43	43	14
Ethnicity:	White	778	50	35	15
	Black	131	43	46	11
	Hispanic	90	56	29	15
Marital:	Married	575	53	34	13
	Single	311	42	43	15
	Divorced/Separated	100	49	36	16
	Widowed	70	55	19	26
Kids Under 18:	Yes	453	52	36	12
	No	607	47	36	17
Household Income:	Under $20,000	211	57	29	14
	$20,000 to $39,999	397	52	34	14
	$40,000 to $59,999	195	41	43	16
	$60,000 or more	137	43	43	15
Community:	Urban	306	48	39	13
	Suburban	395	48	38	14
	Rural	303	54	33	13
Region:	Northeast	230	48	37	15
	Midwest	246	44	41	14
	South	354	53	34	13
	Mountain	55	48	38	14
	Pacific	174	51	30	19
Born Again:	Yes	412	61	29	10
	No	648	42	40	18
Denominational Affiliation:	Protestant	589	54	34	12
	Catholic	286	52	34	15
Attended Church This Week:	Yes	576	58	33	10
	No	483	39	40	21
Read Bible This Week:	Yes	449	63	28	9
	No	611	39	42	19

TABLE 41   221

Do you you agree strongly, agree somewhat, disagree somewhat, or disagree strongly with the statement: "Men are better leaders than are women"?

		N	Agree Strongly	Agree Somewhat	Disagree Somewhat	Disagree Strongly	Don't Know
Total Responding		1060	7%	13%	26%	50%	3%
Gender:	Male	510	9	17	27	42	4
	Female	549	5	10	25	57	2
Age:	18 to 26	226	6	14	21	57	2
	27-45	476	5	13	30	51	2
	46-64	234	7	12	26	49	6
	65 Plus	115	18	17	24	35	5
Education:	High School or Less	480	10	15	26	45	4
	Some College	289	4	13	25	56	2
	College Graduate	286	6	10	28	52	4
Ethnicity:	White	778	6	15	27	48	4
	Black	131	14	8	19	54	4
	Hispanic	90	12	4	37	47	0
Marital:	Married	575	7	12	27	51	3
	Single	311	8	15	24	49	4
	Divorced/Separated	100	3	13	32	50	2
	Widowed	70	13	20	19	40	8
Kids Under 18:	Yes	453	5	13	30	51	2
	No	607	9	13	24	49	4
Household Income:	Under $20,000	211	9	9	25	52	4
	$20,000 to $39,999	397	6	16	27	48	3
	$40,000 to $59,999	195	4	16	26	52	2
	$60,000 or more	137	7	12	27	49	5
Community:	Urban	306	7	13	21	54	5
	Suburban	395	7	14	25	52	3
	Rural	303	6	15	34	43	2
Region:	Northeast	230	7	13	22	57	1
	Midwest	246	6	15	22	53	5
	South	354	9	14	31	41	5
	Mountain	55	6	9	43	43	0
	Pacific	174	6	13	21	57	2
Born Again:	Yes	412	8	16	30	44	3
	No	648	7	12	24	54	4
Denominational Affiliation:	Protestant	589	8	17	26	46	3
	Catholic	286	6	9	29	55	3
Attended Church This Week:	Yes	576	8	14	28	48	3
	No	483	7	13	24	52	4
Read Bible This Week:	Yes	449	11	15	26	45	3
	No	611	5	12	26	54	3

TABLE 42

Do you you agree strongly, agree somewhat, disagree somewhat, or disagree strongly with the statement: "Everything in life is negotiable"?

		N	Agree Strongly	Agree Somewhat	Disagree Somewhat	Disagree Strongly	Don't Know
Total Responding		1060	19%	31%	23%	23%	3%
Gender:	Male	510	24	29	19	25	3
	Female	549	15	33	26	22	4
Age:	18 to 26	226	23	43	18	16	1
	27-45	476	21	29	23	25	2
	46-64	234	19	27	23	29	3
	65 Plus	115	8	29	30	23	10
Education:	High School or Less	480	23	30	22	21	4
	Some College	289	18	34	22	23	3
	College Graduate	286	15	31	23	28	3
Ethnicity:	White	778	18	29	25	24	4
	Black	131	23	36	15	21	4
	Hispanic	90	22	39	11	25	3
Marital:	Married	575	17	28	24	28	4
	Single	311	25	38	19	17	1
	Divorced/Separated	100	18	35	25	19	2
	Widowed	70	14	23	29	24	10
Kids Under 18:	Yes	453	19	32	23	23	3
	No	607	20	30	22	24	4
Household Income:	Under $20,000	211	18	36	22	23	2
	$20,000 to $39,999	397	20	31	22	23	4
	$40,000 to $59,999	195	19	32	23	24	3
	$60,000 or more	137	22	27	24	25	2
Community:	Urban	306	20	30	21	26	4
	Suburban	395	18	37	21	21	3
	Rural	303	19	25	27	26	3
Region:	Northeast	230	24	32	22	20	2
	Midwest	246	16	30	26	24	4
	South	354	16	32	22	26	4
	Mountain	55	18	40	26	15	1
	Pacific	174	25	29	19	25	2
Born Again:	Yes	412	12	27	27	30	4
	No	648	24	34	20	19	3
Denominational Affiliation:	Protestant	589	17	29	25	25	4
	Catholic	286	22	36	19	22	2
Attended Church This Week:	Yes	576	16	26	26	27	5
	No	483	24	37	19	19	2
Read Bible This Week:	Yes	449	15	24	27	29	5
	No	611	23	36	19	20	2

TABLE 43   223

Do you you agree strongly, agree somewhat, disagree somewhat, or disagree strongly with the statement: "Most poor people are poor because they are lazy"?

		N	Agree Strongly	Agree Somewhat	Disagree Somewhat	Disagree Strongly	Don't Know
Total Responding		1060	5%	14%	28%	52%	1%
Gender:	Male	510	5	15	29	50	1
	Female	549	5	13	28	54	1
Age:	18 to 26	226	6	19	31	44	1
	27-45	476	5	14	27	53	1
	46-64	234	4	9	29	56	2
	65 Plus	115	6	14	26	53	2
Education:	High School or Less	480	7	13	28	50	2
	Some College	289	2	16	25	56	0
	College Graduate	286	4	13	32	50	1
Ethnicity:	White	778	3	15	31	50	1
	Black	131	11	7	9	70	3
	Hispanic	90	6	13	27	54	0
Marital:	Married	575	4	13	27	54	1
	Single	311	6	17	28	49	1
	Divorced/Separated	100	7	11	34	48	0
	Widowed	70	7	8	31	50	3
Kids Under 18:	Yes	453	5	16	29	50	0
	No	607	5	13	28	53	1
Household Income:	Under $20,000	211	6	13	26	54	1
	$20,000 to $39,999	397	2	12	28	56	1
	$40,000 to $59,999	195	6	19	29	46	0
	$60,000 or more	137	6	15	30	50	0
Community:	Urban	306	5	12	26	56	0
	Suburban	395	4	13	29	53	1
	Rural	303	3	18	31	47	1
Region:	Northeast	230	5	14	29	51	0
	Midwest	246	5	12	27	54	1
	South	354	5	16	31	46	2
	Mountain	55	3	12	35	51	0
	Pacific	174	3	13	21	61	0
Born Again:	Yes	412	4	12	28	54	1
	No	648	5	15	28	51	1
Denominational Affiliation:	Protestant	589	4	15	28	51	1
	Catholic	286	3	13	29	54	0
Attended Church This Week:	Yes	576	5	11	29	54	1
	No	483	5	17	27	49	1
Read Bible This Week:	Yes	449	5	12	28	54	1
	No	611	5	15	29	50	1

TABLE 44

Do you you agree strongly, agree somewhat, disagree somewhat, or disagree strongly with the statement: "The world is out of control these days"?

		N	Agree Strongly	Agree Somewhat	Disagree Somewhat	Disagree Strongly	Don't Know
Total Responding		1060	31%	33%	23%	12%	1%
Gender:	Male	510	23	33	28	15	0
	Female	549	38	33	18	9	2
Age:	18 to 26	226	29	40	22	9	0
	27-45	476	28	33	26	13	1
	46-64	234	32	31	21	16	0
	65 Plus	115	45	24	16	9	7
Education:	High School or Less	480	40	31	18	11	1
	Some College	289	29	35	21	13	2
	College Graduate	286	19	34	32	14	1
Ethnicity:	White	778	28	34	23	13	1
	Black	131	56	23	13	6	2
	Hispanic	90	28	26	33	13	0
Marital:	Married	575	29	34	22	14	1
	Single	311	32	33	25	10	0
	Divorced/Separated	100	33	31	23	12	1
	Widowed	70	40	28	18	11	3
Kids Under 18:	Yes	453	29	35	24	11	0
	No	607	32	31	22	13	2
Household Income:	Under $20,000	211	44	27	19	10	0
	$20,000 to $39,999	397	31	35	22	12	1
	$40,000 to $59,999	195	20	34	30	15	1
	$60,000 or more	137	21	36	28	14	0
Community:	Urban	306	35	27	25	12	0
	Suburban	395	27	36	23	12	2
	Rural	303	28	37	23	12	0
Region:	Northeast	230	32	31	24	12	1
	Midwest	246	32	35	18	13	1
	South	354	33	34	23	9	1
	Mountain	55	19	38	32	11	0
	Pacific	174	28	29	24	18	1
Born Again:	Yes	412	35	31	20	13	1
	No	648	29	35	24	12	1
Denominational Affiliation:	Protestant	589	35	32	20	11	2
	Catholic	286	23	36	28	13	0
Attended Church This Week:	Yes	576	32	31	22	13	2
	No	483	29	35	23	12	0
Read Bible This Week:	Yes	449	39	28	21	11	1
	No	611	25	37	24	13	1

TABLE 45 225

Do you you agree strongly, agree somewhat, disagree somewhat, or disagree strongly with the statement: "If you don't look out for your own best interests, you can be sure that no one else will, either"?

		N	Agree Strongly	Agree Somewhat	Disagree Somewhat	Disagree Strongly	Don't Know
Total Responding		1060	31%	28%	24%	16%	1%
Gender:	Male	510	30	30	23	16	0
	Female	549	32	26	25	16	1
Age:	18 to 26	226	31	34	22	13	0
	27-45	476	29	30	25	15	1
	46-64	234	31	21	29	18	1
	65 Plus	115	37	22	21	17	3
Education:	High School or Less	480	41	23	20	15	1
	Some College	289	26	29	25	18	1
	College Graduate	286	19	35	31	15	1
Ethnicity:	White	778	27	28	28	16	1
	Black	131	55	21	11	12	1
	Hispanic	90	38	27	14	19	2
Marital:	Married	575	29	28	25	17	1
	Single	311	31	33	23	13	0
	Divorced/Separated	100	37	19	24	19	1
	Widowed	70	36	21	30	11	2
Kids Under 18:	Yes	453	30	29	25	15	1
	No	607	31	27	24	16	1
Household Income:	Under $20,000	211	40	24	24	11	1
	$20,000 to $39,999	397	30	30	21	19	0
	$40,000 to $59,999	195	27	29	32	12	1
	$60,000 or more	137	23	31	28	16	1
Community:	Urban	306	30	25	27	17	1
	Suburban	395	28	31	25	16	0
	Rural	303	34	27	24	14	1
Region:	Northeast	230	25	31	25	19	0
	Midwest	246	30	27	29	14	1
	South	354	36	28	20	14	2
	Mountain	55	18	23	46	12	0
	Pacific	174	33	27	21	18	1
Born Again:	Yes	412	27	23	27	22	1
	No	648	34	31	23	11	1
Denominational Affiliation:	Protestant	589	33	26	24	16	1
	Catholic	286	26	29	29	15	1
Attended Church This Week:	Yes	576	26	25	28	20	2
	No	483	37	32	20	11	0
Read Bible This Week:	Yes	449	28	25	26	20	1
	No	611	33	30	24	12	1

TABLE 46

Do you you agree strongly, agree moderately, disagree moderately, or disagree strongly with the statement: "Participating in a boycott of products or companies doesn't really accomplish anything"?

		N	Agree Strongly	Agree Moderately	Disagree Moderately	Disagree Strongly	Don't Know
Total Responding		1060	12%	18%	35%	32%	3%
Gender:	Male	510	15	20	32	32	2
	Female	549	9	17	37	32	5
Age:	18 to 26	226	9	19	38	31	2
	27-45	476	10	19	36	34	2
	46-64	234	18	13	31	32	5
	65 Plus	115	13	23	32	24	8
Education:	High School or Less	480	14	21	35	27	4
	Some College	289	10	15	37	34	4
	College Graduate	286	11	17	33	37	2
Ethnicity:	White	778	11	18	37	30	3
	Black	131	19	22	20	35	5
	Hispanic	90	12	12	38	36	3
Marital:	Married	575	13	18	35	32	3
	Single	311	11	19	33	34	2
	Divorced/Separated	100	10	18	42	30	1
	Widowed	70	9	21	33	22	15
Kids Under 18:	Yes	453	10	20	37	30	2
	No	607	13	17	33	33	4
Household Income:	Under $20,000	211	15	17	34	28	6
	$20,000 to $39,999	397	9	19	35	35	2
	$40,000 to $59,999	195	13	19	35	29	3
	$60,000 or more	137	15	20	28	35	1
Community:	Urban	306	18	18	29	35	1
	Suburban	395	9	17	37	33	3
	Rural	303	11	21	39	26	3
Region:	Northeast	230	13	17	40	28	1
	Midwest	246	12	21	32	31	4
	South	354	12	20	34	29	4
	Mountain	55	11	15	33	35	6
	Pacific	174	9	13	34	43	1
Born Again:	Yes	412	11	18	35	32	4
	No	648	12	19	35	32	3
Denominational Affiliation:	Protestant	589	13	20	34	30	4
	Catholic	286	11	16	39	32	2
Attended Church This Week:	Yes	576	11	20	35	31	4
	No	483	13	16	35	33	3
Read Bible This Week:	Yes	449	11	18	34	32	5
	No	611	12	18	35	32	2

January 1992
Survey Tables

TABLE 47   229

Have you attended a church worship service during the last seven days?

		N	Yes	No	Don't Know
Total Responding		1013	47%	53%	0%
Gender:	Male	478	43	57	1
	Female	535	51	49	0
Age:	18 to 26	171	36	63	2
	27 to 45	402	40	60	0
	46 to 64	254	60	40	0
	65 Plus	157	54	46	0
Education:	High School or Less	666	48	52	0
	Some College	140	46	54	0
	College Graduate	201	45	55	0
Ethnicity:	White	729	46	53	0
	Black	139	52	48	0
	Hispanic	93	47	53	0
Marital:	Married	571	55	45	0
	Single	223	35	65	0
	Divorced/Separated	118	31	69	0
	Widowed	93	50	50	0
Kids Under 18:	Yes	405	46	54	0
	No	608	47	52	0
Household Income:	Under $20,000	299	48	52	0
	$20,000 to $39,999	368	44	56	0
	$40,000 to $59,999	133	46	54	0
	$60,000 or more	95	40	60	0
Job Type:	White Collar	224	45	55	0
	Blue Collar	313	45	55	0
	Not Employed	398	51	49	1
Community:	Urban	253	46	54	0
	Suburban	374	45	54	1
	Rural	290	47	53	0
Region:	Northeast	228	44	55	1
	Midwest	223	44	56	0
	South	356	55	45	0
	Mountain	54	50	50	0
	Pacific	153	36	64	0
Voter Registration:	Not	291	39	60	1
	Democrat	316	54	46	0
	Republican	210	53	47	0
	Independent	147	41	59	0
Born Again:	Yes	409	66	34	0
	No	604	34	65	0
Denominational Affiliation:	Protestant	550	53	47	0
	Baptist	209	51	49	0
	Catholic	221	54	46	0
	Lutheran	53	52	48	0
	Methodist	63	40	60	0
	Charis./Pent.	70	76	24	0
Attended Church This Week:	Yes	476	100	0	0
	No	534	0	100	0
Read Bible This Week:	Yes	479	69	31	0
	No	534	27	73	0

Have you attended a Sunday School class at a church during the last seven days?

		N	Yes	No	Don't Know
Total Responding		1013	22%	78%	0%
Gender:	Male	478	18	82	0
	Female	535	25	74	0
Age:	18 to 26	171	10	90	0
	27 to 45	402	21	79	0
	46 to 64	254	28	72	0
	65 Plus	157	26	72	1
Education:	High School or Less	666	23	77	0
	Some College	140	22	78	0
	College Graduate	201	19	81	0
Ethnicity:	White	729	23	77	0
	Black	139	22	78	0
	Hispanic	93	18	82	0
Marital:	Married	571	28	72	0
	Single	223	10	90	0
	Divorced/Separated	118	12	88	0
	Widowed	93	29	71	0
Kids Under 18:	Yes	405	25	75	0
	No	608	20	80	0
Household Income:	Under $20,000	299	26	74	0
	$20,000 to $39,999	368	20	80	0
	$40,000 to $59,999	133	23	77	0
	$60,000 or more	95	11	89	0
Job Type:	White Collar	224	20	80	0
	Blue Collar	313	22	78	0
	Not Employed	398	24	76	0
Community:	Urban	253	17	83	0
	Suburban	374	18	82	0
	Rural	290	29	70	1
Region:	Northeast	228	16	84	0
	Midwest	223	19	81	0
	South	356	31	69	1
	Mountain	54	25	75	0
	Pacific	153	15	85	0
Voter Registration:	Not	291	13	87	0
	Democrat	316	25	75	1
	Republican	210	27	73	0
	Independent	147	22	78	0
Born Again:	Yes	409	37	63	0
	No	604	12	88	0
Denominational Affiliation:	Protestant	550	29	70	0
	Baptist	209	31	69	1
	Catholic	221	9	91	0
	Lutheran	53	23	77	0
	Methodist	65	27	73	0
	Charis./Pent.	70	46	54	0
Attended Church This Week:	Yes	476	41	58	0
	No	534	5	95	0
Read Bible This Week:	Yes	479	38	61	0
	No	534	7	93	0

TABLE 49   231

Have you read part of the Bible during the last seven days?

		N	Yes	No
Total Responding		1013	47%	53%
Gender:	Male	478	43	57
	Female	535	52	48
Age:	18 to 26	171	31	69
	27 to 45	402	43	57
	46 to 64	254	54	46
	65 Plus	157	69	31
Education:	High School or Less	666	49	51
	Some College	140	50	50
	College Graduate	201	39	61
Ethnicity:	White	729	42	58
	Black	139	70	30
	Hispanic	93	50	50
Marital:	Married	571	49	51
	Single	223	33	67
	Divorced/Separated	118	48	52
	Widowed	93	72	28
Kids Under 18:	Yes	405	44	56
	No	608	49	51
Household	Under $20,000	299	59	41
Income:	$20,000 to $39,999	368	46	54
	$40,000 to $59,999	133	32	68
	$60,000 or more	95	31	69
Job Type:	White Collar	224	41	59
	Blue Collar	313	42	58
	Not Employed	398	58	42
Community:	Urban	253	44	56
	Suburban	374	40	60
	Rural	290	53	47
Region:	Northeast	228	36	64
	Midwest	223	40	60
	South	356	62	38
	Mountain	54	37	63
	Pacific	153	44	56
Voter	Not	291	40	60
Registration:	Democrat	316	56	44
	Republican	210	48	52
	Independent	147	40	60
Born Again:	Yes	409	69	31
	No	604	33	67
Denominational	Protestant	550	60	40
Affiliation:	Baptist	209	65	35
	Catholic	221	31	69
	Lutheran	53	44	56
	Methodist	65	42	58
	Charis./Pent.	70	78	22
Attended Church	Yes	476	70	30
This Week:	No	534	28	72
Read Bible	Yes	479	100	0
This Week:	No	534	0	100

Have you read part of a book, other than the Bible, during the last seven days?

		N	Yes	No	Don't Know
Total Responding		1013	67%	33%	0%
Gender:	Male	478	66	34	0
	Female	535	68	32	0
Age:	18 to 26	171	64	36	0
	27 to 45	402	72	28	0
	46 to 64	254	65	35	0
	65 Plus	157	63	35	1
Education:	High School or Less	666	59	40	0
	Some College	140	74	25	0
	College Graduate	201	86	14	0
Ethnicity:	White	729	66	33	0
	Black	139	66	34	0
	Hispanic	93	69	31	0
Marital:	Married	571	70	30	0
	Single	223	65	35	0
	Divorced/Separated	118	60	40	0
	Widowed	93	59	38	2
Kids Under 18:	Yes	405	68	32	0
	No	608	66	34	0
Household Income:	Under $20,000	299	60	40	1
	$20,000 to $39,999	368	69	30	0
	$40,000 to $59,999	133	70	30	0
	$60,000 or more	95	76	24	0
Job Type:	White Collar	224	80	20	0
	Blue Collar	313	63	37	0
	Not Employed	398	62	38	1
Community:	Urban	253	74	26	0
	Suburban	374	65	35	0
	Rural	290	68	31	0
Region:	Northeast	228	65	35	0
	Midwest	223	65	35	0
	South	356	68	31	1
	Mountain	54	69	31	0
	Pacific	153	68	32	0
Voter Registration:	Not	291	57	43	0
	Democrat	316	70	30	0
	Republican	210	65	34	1
	Independent	147	78	22	0
Born Again:	Yes	409	69	31	1
	No	604	66	34	0
Denominational Affiliation:	Protestant	550	67	32	0
	Baptist	209	65	35	0
	Catholic	221	66	33	0
	Lutheran	53	85	15	0
	Methodist	65	63	37	0
	Charis./Pent.	70	63	35	3
Attended Church This Week:	Yes	476	69	30	1
	No	534	65	35	0
Read Bible This Week:	Yes	479	73	26	1
	No	534	61	39	0

TABLE 51   233

Have you volunteered any of your free time to help a church during the last seven days?

		N	Yes	No
Total Responding		1013	24%	76%
Gender:	Male	478	23	77
	Female	535	25	75
Age:	18 to 26	171	13	87
	27 to 45	402	22	78
	46 to 64	254	31	69
	65 Plus	157	31	69
Education:	High School or Less	666	24	76
	Some College	140	25	74
	College Graduate	201	24	76
Ethnicity:	White	729	23	77
	Black	139	31	69
	Hispanic	93	23	77
Marital:	Married	571	28	72
	Single	223	12	88
	Divorced/Separated	118	23	77
	Widowed	93	29	71
Kids Under 18:	Yes	405	24	76
	No	608	24	76
Household Income:	Under $20,000	299	25	75
	$20,000 to $39,999	368	21	79
	$40,000 to $59,999	133	19	81
	$60,000 or more	95	20	80
Job Type:	White Collar	224	24	76
	Blue Collar	313	24	76
	Not Employed	398	26	74
Community:	Urban	253	18	82
	Suburban	374	24	76
	Rural	290	26	74
Region:	Northeast	228	22	78
	Midwest	223	24	76
	South	356	29	71
	Mountain	54	35	65
	Pacific	153	12	88
Voter Registration:	Not	291	19	81
	Democrat	316	26	74
	Republican	210	26	73
	Independent	147	27	73
Born Again:	Yes	409	33	67
	No	604	18	82
Denominational Affiliation:	Protestant	550	29	71
	Baptist	209	26	74
	Catholic	221	16	84
	Lutheran	53	37	63
	Methodist	65	23	77
	Charis./Pent.	70	38	62
Attended Church This Week:	Yes	476	42	58
	No	534	8	92
Read Bible This Week:	Yes	479	41	59
	No	534	9	91

Have you volunteered any of your free time to help an organization other than a church during the last seven days?

		N	Yes	No
Total Responding		1013	24%	76%
Gender:	Male	478	24	76
	Female	535	24	76
Age:	18 to 26	171	16	84
	27 to 45	402	27	73
	46 to 64	254	23	77
	65 Plus	157	25	75
Education:	High School or Less	666	20	80
	Some College	140	25	75
	College Graduate	201	35	65
Ethnicity:	White	729	24	76
	Black	139	32	68
	Hispanic	93	9	91
Marital:	Married	571	24	76
	Single	223	23	77
	Divorced/Separated	118	24	76
	Widowed	93	23	77
Kids Under 18:	Yes	405	24	76
	No	608	24	76
Household Income:	Under $20,000	299	21	79
	$20,000 to $39,999	368	22	77
	$40,000 to $59,999	133	21	79
	$60,000 or more	95	29	71
Job Type:	White Collar	224	28	72
	Blue Collar	313	22	78
	Not Employed	398	22	78
Community:	Urban	253	26	74
	Suburban	374	21	79
	Rural	290	25	74
Region:	Northeast	228	23	77
	Midwest	223	22	78
	South	356	25	75
	Mountain	54	31	69
	Pacific	153	22	78
Voter Registration:	Not	291	16	84
	Democrat	316	23	77
	Republican	210	27	73
	Independent	147	33	67
Born Again:	Yes	409	25	75
	No	604	23	77
Denominational Affiliation:	Protestant	550	25	75
	Baptist	209	26	74
	Catholic	221	19	81
	Lutheran	53	25	75
	Methodist	65	35	65
	Charis./Pent.	70	13	87
Attended Church This Week:	Yes	476	27	73
	No	534	21	79
Read Bible This Week:	Yes	479	26	74
	No	534	22	78

TABLE 53   235

Have you watched MTV during the last seven days?

		N	Yes	No	Don't Know
Total Responding		1013	30%	68%	2
Gender:	Male	478	29	70	2
	Female	535	31	67	3
Age:	18 to 26	171	36	64	0
	27 to 45	402	19	81	0
	46 to 64	254	29	68	3
	65 Plus	157	50	42	8
Education:	High School or Less	666	32	66	3
	Some College	140	30	68	2
	College Graduate	201	25	74	0
Ethnicity:	White	729	27	70	2
	Black	139	36	61	3
	Hispanic	93	40	60	0
Marital:	Married	571	25	74	1
	Single	223	39	61	0
	Divorced/Separated	118	23	76	0
	Widowed	93	45	41	14
Kids Under 18:	Yes	405	24	76	0
	No	608	34	63	3
Household Income:	Under $20,000	299	29	67	4
	$20,000 to $39,999	368	29	70	1
	$40,000 to $59,999	133	25	75	1
	$60,000 or more	95	30	70	0
Job Type:	White Collar	224	23	76	1
	Blue Collar	313	28	72	1
	Not Employed	398	37	60	4
Community:	Urban	253	29	69	1
	Suburban	374	29	71	0
	Rural	290	30	65	4
Region:	Northeast	228	30	69	1
	Midwest	223	24	74	1
	South	356	34	62	4
	Mountain	54	21	76	3
	Pacific	153	30	69	1
Voter Registration:	Not	291	30	68	2
	Democrat	316	30	67	3
	Republican	210	29	69	2
	Independent	147	29	71	0
Born Again:	Yes	409	31	67	2
	No	604	29	69	2
Denominational Affiliation:	Protestant	550	29	67	3
	Baptist	209	33	64	4
	Catholic	221	26	74	0
	Lutheran	53	45	54	1
	Methodist	65	26	67	6
	Charis./Pent.	70	22	77	2
Attended Church This Week:	Yes	476	31	66	3
	No	534	28	70	1
Read Bible This Week:	Yes	479	35	61	3
	No	534	25	74	1

TABLE 54

How important is "religion" to you? Is it very important, somewhat important, not too important, or not at all important?

		N	Very Important	Somewhat Important	Not Too Important	Not at All Important	Don't Know
Total Responding		1013	69%	23%	5%	3%	0%
Gender:	Male	478	62	26	8	4	0
	Female	535	76	20	2	2	1
Age:	18 to 26	171	54	36	6	5	0
	27 to 45	402	65	25	6	3	0
	46 to 64	254	79	17	2	1	0
	65 Plus	157	83	12	1	3	1
Education:	High School or Less	666	73	22	3	1	0
	Some College	140	66	23	6	4	0
	College Graduate	201	58	26	10	7	0
Ethnicity:	White	729	67	24	5	3	0
	Black	139	78	20	1	1	0
	Hispanic	93	65	22	9	3	0
Marital:	Married	571	72	21	4	2	1
	Single	223	53	31	9	6	0
	Divorced/Separated	118	74	22	3	1	0
	Widowed	93	84	12	2	2	0
Kids Under 18:	Yes	405	69	25	4	2	0
	No	608	69	21	5	4	1
Household Income:	Under $20,000	299	79	17	3	1	1
	$20,000 to $39,999	368	69	25	4	3	0
	$40,000 to $59,999	133	60	30	5	5	0
	$60,000 or more	95	52	21	17	9	0
Job Type:	White Collar	224	64	24	7	5	0
	Blue Collar	313	71	22	4	3	0
	Not Employed	398	74	20	4	2	1
Community:	Urban	253	65	25	6	4	0
	Suburban	374	68	23	5	4	0
	Rural	290	70	25	4	1	1
Region:	Northeast	228	61	27	6	6	0
	Midwest	223	69	22	5	3	0
	South	356	78	17	2	1	1
	Mountain	54	72	23	5	0	0
	Pacific	153	58	28	10	4	1
Voter Registration:	Not	291	64	26	5	4	0
	Democrat	316	75	19	4	1	1
	Republican	210	71	21	5	3	1
	Independent	147	65	25	6	5	0
Born Again:	Yes	409	87	12	1	0	0
	No	604	57	30	8	5	1
Denominational Affiliation:	Protestant	550	78	18	2	1	0
	Baptist	209	81	17	1	1	1
	Catholic	221	68	27	4	0	0
	Lutheran	53	72	23	4	1	0
	Methodist	65	73	22	5	0	0
	Charis./Pent.	70	90	9	0	1	0
Attended Church This Week:	Yes	476	88	11	2	0	0
	No	534	53	33	8	5	1
Read Bible This Week:	Yes	479	88	9	2	0	1
	No	534	52	34	8	5	0

TABLE 55　　　　　　　　　　237

How important is "the Bible" to you? Is it very important, somewhat important, not too important, or not at all important?

		N	Very Important	Somewhat Important	Not Too Important	Not at All Important	Don't Know
Total Responding		1013	67%	22%	8%	3%	1%
Gender:	Male	478	59	24	11	5	1
	Female	535	74	20	4	2	0
Age:	18 to 26	171	56	31	7	6	1
	27 to 45	402	63	24	9	3	1
	46 to 64	254	75	17	7	1	0
	65 Plus	157	78	16	3	3	1
Education:	High School or Less	666	74	18	6	1	0
	Some College	140	63	25	7	3	3
	College Graduate	201	45	33	13	9	0
Ethnicity:	White	729	63	25	9	3	0
	Black	139	83	10	5	1	1
	Hispanic	93	72	18	6	3	1
Marital:	Married	571	67	22	8	2	1
	Single	223	54	28	10	8	0
	Divorced/Separated	118	73	18	7	1	0
	Widowed	93	85	11	1	2	0
Kids Under 18:	Yes	405	68	22	7	3	1
	No	608	66	22	8	4	0
Household Income:	Under $20,000	299	79	15	5	1	1
	$20,000 to $39,999	368	67	22	8	2	1
	$40,000 to $59,999	133	51	34	7	8	0
	$60,000 or more	95	44	23	22	11	0
Job Type:	White Collar	224	56	25	10	7	1
	Blue Collar	313	70	21	6	2	1
	Not Employed	398	73	19	6	2	0
Community:	Urban	253	65	24	6	4	1
	Suburban	374	60	24	11	5	0
	Rural	290	70	22	7	1	0
Region:	Northeast	228	52	30	11	7	0
	Midwest	223	67	24	7	2	0
	South	356	82	13	3	1	1
	Mountain	54	52	32	10	5	0
	Pacific	153	57	23	14	4	1
Voter Registration:	Not	291	63	21	9	6	1
	Democrat	316	72	21	5	2	0
	Republican	210	69	22	7	2	1
	Independent	147	56	29	11	3	0
Born Again:	Yes	409	89	10	1	0	0
	No	604	51	30	12	5	1
Denominational Affiliation:	Protestant	550	78	17	4	0	1
	Baptist	209	83	13	3	0	1
	Catholic	221	55	34	9	1	1
	Lutheran	53	65	29	6	0	0
	Methodist	65	65	28	6	0	0
	Charis./Pent.	70	91	9	0	0	0
Attended Church This Week:	Yes	476	83	14	2	0	0
	No	534	52	29	12	6	1
Read Bible This Week:	Yes	479	90	8	1	0	0
	No	534	46	34	14	6	1

How important is "money" to you? Is it very important, somewhat important, not too important, or not at all important?

		N	Very Important	Somewhat Important	Not Too Important	Not at All Important	Don't Know
Total Responding		1013	40%	46%	10%	3%	1%
Gender:	Male	478	42	44	10	3	1
	Female	535	37	48	11	2	2
Age:	18 to 26	171	40	45	11	3	0
	27 to 45	402	35	54	10	2	0
	46 to 64	254	42	44	10	3	1
	65 Plus	157	44	35	11	4	7
Education:	High School or Less	666	45	39	12	3	1
	Some College	140	31	58	7	2	2
	College Graduate	201	27	64	7	1	1
Ethnicity:	White	729	37	49	11	2	1
	Black	139	56	35	7	1	1
	Hispanic	93	40	47	8	4	1
Marital:	Married	571	35	52	10	2	1
	Single	223	47	41	10	2	0
	Divorced/Separated	118	42	43	11	4	0
	Widowed	93	47	28	10	9	5
Kids Under 18:	Yes	405	34	53	10	2	0
	No	608	43	42	10	3	2
Household Income:	Under $20,000	299	46	33	14	6	2
	$20,000 to $39,999	368	39	50	9	1	1
	$40,000 to $59,999	133	33	57	8	1	1
	$60,000 or more	95	29	60	9	3	0
Job Type:	White Collar	224	30	60	7	2	1
	Blue Collar	313	44	42	13	1	0
	Not Employed	398	44	41	9	4	2
Community:	Urban	253	39	49	11	1	0
	Suburban	374	42	47	8	2	1
	Rural	290	36	49	10	4	1
Region:	Northeast	228	43	43	10	2	2
	Midwest	223	38	51	9	1	1
	South	356	45	40	9	4	2
	Mountain	54	29	60	11	0	1
	Pacific	153	28	54	16	3	0
Voter Registration:	Not	291	38	47	10	4	1
	Democrat	316	43	45	9	2	1
	Republican	210	31	51	14	2	2
	Independent	147	46	45	7	0	0
Born Again:	Yes	409	32	50	13	3	2
	No	604	44	44	8	2	1
Denominational Affiliation:	Protestant	550	36	49	11	2	2
	Baptist	209	41	45	10	3	1
	Catholic	221	43	47	8	2	0
	Lutheran	53	47	40	13	0	0
	Methodist	65	26	62	5	3	4
	Charis./Pent.	70	35	39	24	0	2
Attended Church This Week:	Yes	476	36	49	10	3	2
	No	534	42	44	11	2	1
Read Bible This Week:	Yes	479	40	44	11	2	2
	No	534	39	48	10	3	0

TABLE 57   239

How important is "your time" to you? Is it very important, somewhat important, not too important, or not at all important?

		N	Very Important	Somewhat Important	Not Too Important	Not at All Important	Don't Know
Total Responding		1013	78%	18%	2%	1%	1%
Gender:	Male	478	80	16	2	1	1
	Female	535	77	19	2	1	1
Age:	18 to 26	171	78	19	1	1	0
	27 to 45	402	82	17	1	0	0
	46 to 64	254	80	16	2	1	1
	65 Plus	157	66	25	4	0	5
Education:	High School or Less	666	77	19	2	1	1
	Some College	140	81	16	2	0	1
	College Graduate	201	81	15	1	0	2
Ethnicity:	White	729	75	21	2	1	2
	Black	139	90	10	0	0	0
	Hispanic	93	88	12	0	0	0
Marital:	Married	571	75	21	1	1	1
	Single	223	84	13	2	0	1
	Divorced/Separated	118	85	15	1	0	0
	Widowed	93	75	16	5	0	4
Kids Under 18:	Yes	405	82	17	1	1	0
	No	608	76	19	2	1	2
Household	Under $20,000	299	74	20	4	1	2
Income:	$20,000 to $39,999	368	80	18	0	1	0
	$40,000 to $59,999	133	81	17	0	0	2
	$60,000 or more	95	82	14	3	0	1
Job Type:	White Collar	224	86	12	1	1	1
	Blue Collar	313	79	20	1	0	0
	Not Employed	398	75	20	2	1	2
Community:	Urban	253	77	20	2	0	1
	Suburban	374	77	20	1	1	1
	Rural	290	80	16	1	1	1
Region:	Northeast	228	80	14	3	1	2
	Midwest	223	74	23	2	0	1
	South	356	79	19	0	0	1
	Mountain	54	83	15	2	0	0
	Pacific	153	79	15	3	2	1
Voter	Not	291	79	17	2	1	1
Registration:	Democrat	316	77	19	2	1	2
	Republican	210	77	19	2	0	1
	Independent	147	82	16	1	0	1
Born Again:	Yes	409	78	20	0	1	1
	No	604	79	17	3	1	1
Denominational	Protestant	550	78	20	1	0	1
Affiliation:	Baptist	209	84	15	1	1	0
	Catholic	221	81	15	1	1	2
	Lutheran	53	67	29	2	1	1
	Methodist	65	74	23	1	0	2
	Charis./Pent.	70	71	29	0	0	0
Attended Church This Week:	Yes	476	78	19	1	0	1
	No	534	79	17	2	1	1
Read Bible This Week:	Yes	479	79	17	2	1	1
	No	534	78	19	2	1	1

TABLE 58

How important is "living comfortably" to you? Is it very important, somewhat important, not too important, or not at all important?

		N	Very Important	Somewhat Important	Not Too Important	Not at All Important	Don't Know
Total Responding		1013	60%	35%	3%	1%	1%
Gender:	Male	478	60	35	4	1	1
	Female	535	59	36	3	1	1
Age:	18 to 26	171	61	36	1	2	0
	27 to 45	402	54	41	4	0	0
	46 to 64	254	59	35	4	0	3
	65 Plus	157	75	20	4	1	0
Education:	High School or Less	666	66	29	3	1	1
	Some College	140	53	43	4	0	0
	College Graduate	201	44	51	5	0	0
Ethnicity:	White	729	55	40	4	1	0
	Black	139	80	18	1	0	1
	Hispanic	93	76	22	3	0	0
Marital:	Married	571	54	40	4	1	1
	Single	223	67	31	2	0	0
	Divorced/Separated	118	64	32	4	0	0
	Widowed	93	73	21	2	2	2
Kids Under 18:	Yes	405	53	42	3	1	0
	No	608	64	31	4	0	1
Household Income:	Under $20,000	299	66	27	3	2	2
	$20,000 to $39,999	368	58	37	4	0	0
	$40,000 to $59,999	133	53	45	2	0	0
	$60,000 or more	95	44	51	5	0	0
Job Type:	White Collar	224	49	46	5	0	0
	Blue Collar	313	62	34	3	0	1
	Not Employed	398	66	29	3	0	1
Community:	Urban	253	62	33	4	0	1
	Suburban	374	58	37	4	0	1
	Rural	290	57	39	2	2	0
Region:	Northeast	228	61	32	5	0	2
	Midwest	223	59	38	1	1	0
	South	356	64	31	3	1	1
	Mountain	54	54	39	7	0	0
	Pacific	153	51	43	4	2	0
Voter Registration:	Not	291	54	41	2	2	1
	Democrat	316	67	29	4	0	1
	Republican	210	54	39	5	0	1
	Independent	147	62	35	3	0	0
Born Again:	Yes	409	57	38	5	0	0
	No	604	62	34	3	1	1
Denominational Affiliation:	Protestant	550	57	37	5	0	1
	Baptist	209	67	30	2	0	2
	Catholic	221	66	32	2	0	0
	Lutheran	53	48	44	2	0	6
	Methodist	65	52	46	2	0	0
	Charis./Pent.	70	52	41	7	0	0
Attended Church This Week:	Yes	476	58	38	4	0	0
	No	534	61	33	3	1	1
Read Bible This Week:	Yes	479	59	36	4	0	1
	No	534	60	35	3	1	1

TABLE 59   241

How important are "your friends" to you? Are they very important, somewhat important, not too important, or not at all important?

		N	Very Important	Somewhat Important	Not Too Important	Not at All Important	Don't Know
Total Responding		1013	76%	19%	3%	1%	1%
Gender:	Male	478	70	23	5	1	1
	Female	535	82	16	1	0	1
Age:	18 to 26	171	64	29	5	1	1
	27 to 45	402	71	24	4	1	1
	46 to 64	254	84	13	2	0	1
	65 Plus	157	87	9	2	0	2
Education:	High School or Less	666	77	19	3	1	1
	Some College	140	73	23	2	0	2
	College Graduate	201	77	19	3	0	0
Ethnicity:	White	729	81	16	2	0	0
	Black	139	61	28	8	0	4
	Hispanic	93	65	32	3	0	0
Marital:	Married	571	76	19	3	1	0
	Single	223	71	25	3	0	1
	Divorced/Separated	118	72	20	3	0	5
	Widowed	93	96	3	1	0	0
Kids Under 18:	Yes	405	69	26	3	1	0
	No	608	81	15	3	0	1
Household Income:	Under $20,000	299	73	18	5	1	2
	$20,000 to $39,999	368	79	17	3	0	0
	$40,000 to $59,999	133	82	17	1	0	0
	$60,000 or more	95	68	29	3	0	0
Job Type:	White Collar	224	74	24	1	1	0
	Blue Collar	313	77	19	3	0	1
	Not Employed	398	80	15	4	0	1
Community:	Urban	253	73	24	3	0	1
	Suburban	374	76	19	5	0	0
	Rural	290	80	17	1	1	1
Region:	Northeast	228	74	21	4	1	0
	Midwest	223	79	18	3	0	0
	South	356	80	15	3	0	2
	Mountain	54	69	26	1	0	4
	Pacific	153	68	26	5	2	0
Voter Registration:	Not	291	66	26	5	1	2
	Democrat	316	78	16	4	1	1
	Republican	210	81	18	1	0	0
	Independent	147	79	19	1	0	0
Born Again:	Yes	409	80	16	2	0	1
	No	604	73	21	4	1	1
Denominational Affiliation:	Protestant	550	78	18	3	0	1
	Baptist	209	79	17	3	0	1
	Catholic	221	76	20	3	1	0
	Lutheran	53	78	15	5	1	0
	Methodist	65	91	9	0	0	0
	Charis./Pent.	70	62	21	9	0	8
Attended Church This Week:	Yes	476	81	16	3	0	1
	No	534	72	23	3	1	1
Read Bible This Week:	Yes	479	79	17	2	0	2
	No	534	74	21	4	1	0

TABLE 60

How important is "family" to you? Is it very important, somewhat important, not too important, or not at all important?

		N	Very Important	Somewhat Important	Not Too Important	Not at All Important	Don't Know
Total Responding		1013	96%	3%	0%	0%	0%
Gender:	Male	478	94	4	1	0	0
	Female	535	98	1	0	0	1
Age:	18 to 26	171	93	6	1	0	0
	27 to 45	402	97	2	0	0	0
	46 to 64	254	98	2	0	0	0
	65 Plus	157	94	4	0	0	2
Education:	High School or Less	666	97	3	0	0	0
	Some College	140	95	2	0	0	1
	College Graduate	201	95	4	0	0	0
Ethnicity:	White	729	97	2	0	0	0
	Black	139	94	5	0	0	1
	Hispanic	93	95	5	0	0	0
Marital:	Married	571	98	2	0	0	0
	Single	223	91	7	1	0	1
	Divorced/Separated	118	96	3	1	0	0
	Widowed	93	95	2	0	0	2
Kids Under 18:	Yes	405	99	1	0	0	0
	No	608	95	4	0	0	1
Household Income:	Under $20,000	299	95	3	1	0	1
	$20,000 to $39,999	368	97	2	0	0	0
	$40,000 to $59,999	133	99	1	0	0	0
	$60,000 or more	95	93	7	0	0	0
Job Type:	White Collar	224	95	4	1	0	0
	Blue Collar	313	98	1	1	0	0
	Not Employed	398	95	4	0	0	1
Community:	Urban	253	95	4	0	0	1
	Suburban	374	96	3	0	0	0
	Rural	290	97	2	0	0	0
Region:	Northeast	228	99	1	0	0	0
	Midwest	223	95	4	1	0	0
	South	356	97	2	0	0	1
	Mountain	54	95	1	2	0	1
	Pacific	153	94	6	0	0	0
Voter Registration:	Not	291	94	5	0	0	1
	Democrat	316	99	1	0	0	0
	Republican	210	94	4	1	0	0
	Independent	147	98	2	1	0	0
Born Again:	Yes	409	96	3	0	0	1
	No	604	96	3	0	0	0
Denominational Affiliation:	Protestant	550	97	2	1	0	1
	Baptist	209	98	1	0	0	1
	Catholic	221	96	3	0	0	1
	Lutheran	53	91	8	0	1	1
	Methodist	65	95	2	2	0	1
	Charis./Pent.	70	97	3	0	0	0
Attended Church This Week:	Yes	476	97	2	0	0	1
	No	534	96	3	1	0	0
Read Bible This Week:	Yes	479	96	3	0	0	1
	No	534	96	3	1	0	0

TABLE 61   243

How important is "your free time" to you? Is it very important, somewhat important, not too important, or not at all important?

		N	Very Important	Somewhat Important	Not Too Important	Not at All Important	Don't Know
Total Responding		1013	64%	29%	4%	0%	2%
Gender:	Male	478	64	30	4	0	1
	Female	535	63	28	4	0	4
Age:	18 to 26	171	52	43	5	0	0
	27 to 45	402	67	29	3	0	1
	46 to 64	254	69	23	5	1	2
	65 Plus	157	60	23	6	1	10
Education:	High School or Less	666	63	29	5	0	3
	Some College	140	64	28	3	2	3
	College Graduate	201	66	30	3	0	1
Ethnicity:	White	729	61	30	5	1	3
	Black	139	73	26	1	0	1
	Hispanic	93	73	26	1	0	0
Marital:	Married	571	64	28	4	1	2
	Single	223	65	32	2	0	1
	Divorced/Separated	118	62	34	4	0	0
	Widowed	93	61	19	9	0	11
Kids Under 18:	Yes	405	61	34	4	0	0
	No	608	66	26	4	1	4
Household Income:	Under $20,000	299	55	33	7	0	4
	$20,000 to $39,999	368	69	26	3	1	1
	$40,000 to $59,999	133	65	33	1	0	0
	$60,000 or more	95	63	30	5	1	2
Job Type:	White Collar	224	70	25	4	1	1
	Blue Collar	313	65	31	3	0	1
	Not Employed	398	60	31	5	1	4
Community:	Urban	253	64	29	3	1	3
	Suburban	374	64	31	4	0	0
	Rural	290	60	31	5	0	3
Region:	Northeast	228	65	27	7	0	2
	Midwest	223	57	32	6	1	3
	South	356	67	27	2	1	3
	Mountain	54	59	37	2	1	1
	Pacific	153	67	28	3	0	2
Voter Registration:	Not	291	58	35	6	0	2
	Democrat	316	68	24	5	0	2
	Republican	210	63	29	4	1	3
	Independent	147	63	33	2	1	1
Born Again:	Yes	409	62	32	3	1	3
	No	604	65	27	5	0	2
Denominational Affiliation:	Protestant	550	63	30	3	1	4
	Baptist	209	73	21	1	1	3
	Catholic	221	66	29	5	0	0
	Lutheran	53	63	30	4	0	3
	Methodist	65	56	35	3	2	4
	Charis./Pent.	70	58	28	8	0	6
Attended Church This Week:	Yes	476	65	28	3	1	3
	No	534	62	30	6	0	2
Read Bible This Week:	Yes	479	63	28	4	1	4
	No	534	64	30	4	0	1

How important is "your career" to you? Is it very important, somewhat important, not too important, or not at all important?

		N	Very Important	Somewhat Important	Not Too Important	Not at All Important	Don't Know
Total Responding		1013	54%	26%	4%	5%	11%
Gender:	Male	478	59	26	5	3	7
	Female	535	50	26	4	7	14
Age:	18 to 26	171	67	22	2	5	4
	27 to 45	402	56	36	4	2	3
	46 to 64	254	51	25	6	5	13
	65 Plus	157	36	11	5	14	35
Education:	High School or Less	666	53	23	4	6	13
	Some College	140	54	30	5	4	8
	College Graduate	201	56	35	3	2	4
Ethnicity:	White	729	48	29	5	6	12
	Black	139	66	18	2	4	10
	Hispanic	93	67	24	1	0	8
Marital:	Married	571	51	30	5	5	10
	Single	223	66	23	3	3	5
	Divorced/Separated	118	58	29	6	4	4
	Widowed	93	38	11	2	11	38
Kids Under 18:	Yes	405	59	32	3	3	4
	No	608	51	22	5	6	15
Household Income:	Under $20,000	299	52	18	7	6	17
	$20,000 to $39,999	368	53	31	2	4	10
	$40,000 to $59,999	133	63	25	6	2	3
	$60,000 or more	95	51	38	3	4	4
Job Type:	White Collar	224	61	35	4	1	0
	Blue Collar	313	61	32	3	2	3
	Not Employed	398	44	16	6	9	25
Community:	Urban	253	54	27	4	3	11
	Suburban	374	55	28	3	6	8
	Rural	290	51	30	5	5	9
Region:	Northeast	228	51	28	6	6	9
	Midwest	223	50	28	4	6	13
	South	356	58	24	3	5	11
	Mountain	54	56	23	6	4	11
	Pacific	153	55	29	5	3	9
Voter Registration:	Not	291	59	25	4	5	6
	Democrat	316	50	26	5	5	14
	Republican	210	54	26	3	5	12
	Independent	147	55	32	4	3	6
Born Again:	Yes	409	53	29	2	4	11
	No	604	55	24	6	5	11
Denominational Affiliation:	Protestant	550	51	28	3	6	13
	Baptist	209	51	25	3	6	15
	Catholic	221	57	25	6	4	9
	Lutheran	53	49	32	5	7	8
	Methodist	65	54	23	0	9	14
	Charis./Pent.	70	56	28	3	2	12
Attended Church This Week:	Yes	476	54	26	4	4	13
	No	534	54	27	5	6	9
Read Bible This Week:	Yes	479	57	24	2	4	13
	No	534	52	28	6	6	9

How important is "health" to you? Is it very important, somewhat important, not too important, or not at all important?

		N	Very Important	Somewhat Important	Not Too Important	Not at All Important	Don't Know
Total Responding		1013	90%	9%	0%	0%	0%
Gender:	Male	478	87	11	0	0	1
	Female	535	93	7	0	0	0
Age:	18 to 26	171	84	16	0	0	0
	27 to 45	402	89	10	0	0	1
	46 to 64	254	94	6	0	0	0
	65 Plus	157	95	4	0	1	0
Education:	High School or Less	666	90	9	0	0	0
	Some College	140	91	8	0	0	0
	College Graduate	201	90	10	0	0	0
Ethnicity:	White	729	90	9	0	0	0
	Black	139	96	4	0	0	0
	Hispanic	93	87	13	0	0	0
Marital:	Married	571	90	10	0	0	0
	Single	223	92	7	0	1	0
	Divorced/Separated	118	89	11	0	0	0
	Widowed	93	91	4	0	2	3
Kids Under 18:	Yes	405	88	12	0	0	0
	No	608	92	7	0	1	1
Household Income:	Under $20,000	299	91	7	0	1	1
	$20,000 to $39,999	368	91	9	0	0	0
	$40,000 to $59,999	133	87	13	0	0	0
	$60,000 or more	95	85	13	1	1	0
Job Type:	White Collar	224	94	6	0	0	0
	Blue Collar	313	86	13	0	0	1
	Not Employed	398	93	6	0	1	0
Community:	Urban	253	89	10	0	0	0
	Suburban	374	90	9	0	0	0
	Rural	290	89	10	0	1	1
Region:	Northeast	228	91	9	0	0	0
	Midwest	223	90	8	0	0	1
	South	356	91	9	0	1	0
	Mountain	54	93	6	0	1	0
	Pacific	153	89	11	0	0	0
Voter Registration:	Not	291	84	15	0	1	0
	Democrat	316	92	7	0	0	1
	Republican	210	92	7	0	0	0
	Independent	147	95	4	0	0	0
Born Again:	Yes	409	93	7	0	0	0
	No	604	88	10	0	1	1
Denominational Affiliation:	Protestant	550	93	7	0	0	0
	Baptist	209	94	6	0	1	0
	Catholic	221	89	11	0	0	0
	Lutheran	53	94	6	0	0	0
	Methodist	65	94	6	0	0	0
	Charis./Pent.	70	86	14	0	0	0
Attended Church This Week:	Yes	476	92	8	0	0	0
	No	534	89	10	0	1	1
Read Bible This Week:	Yes	479	93	6	0	0	1
	No	534	88	11	0	1	0

How important is "your community" to you? Is it very important, somewhat important, not too important, or not at all important?

		N	Very Important	Somewhat Important	Not Too Important	Not at All Important	Don't Know
Total Responding		1013	52%	39%	4%	3%	1%
Gender:	Male	478	49	39	5	5	1
	Female	535	55	40	3	1	2
Age:	18 to 26	171	28	60	8	4	0
	27 to 45	402	48	45	3	3	0
	46 to 64	254	61	33	3	3	0
	65 Plus	157	69	17	4	3	6
Education:	High School or Less	666	55	35	4	4	1
	Some College	140	49	45	2	2	1
	College Graduate	201	43	49	6	1	1
Ethnicity:	White	729	50	41	5	3	2
	Black	139	64	29	3	5	0
	Hispanic	93	49	49	0	2	0
Marital:	Married	571	54	39	4	2	1
	Single	223	37	52	6	4	0
	Divorced/Separated	118	60	33	2	5	0
	Widowed	93	67	18	4	4	6
Kids Under 18:	Yes	405	48	45	4	3	0
	No	608	55	36	4	3	2
Household Income:	Under $20,000	299	57	31	3	6	2
	$20,000 to $39,999	368	52	43	4	2	0
	$40,000 to $59,999	133	44	47	6	2	1
	$60,000 or more	95	42	47	6	4	1
Job Type:	White Collar	224	41	51	4	3	0
	Blue Collar	313	54	39	3	4	0
	Not Employed	398	59	32	4	2	3
Community:	Urban	253	55	37	4	3	1
	Suburban	374	48	45	4	3	0
	Rural	290	56	36	4	3	1
Region:	Northeast	228	45	47	5	2	1
	Midwest	223	49	44	4	2	1
	South	356	61	30	4	3	2
	Mountain	54	56	35	3	5	1
	Pacific	153	46	44	4	6	0
Voter Registration:	Not	291	39	47	5	7	1
	Democrat	316	60	33	4	3	0
	Republican	210	55	38	4	1	2
	Independent	147	53	42	4	0	1
Born Again:	Yes	409	56	38	3	2	2
	No	604	50	40	5	4	1
Denominational Affiliation:	Protestant	550	57	35	4	3	1
	Baptist	209	62	31	4	3	0
	Catholic	221	51	45	2	1	0
	Lutheran	53	61	35	4	0	0
	Methodist	65	51	42	5	2	0
	Charis./Pent.	70	63	28	0	8	0
Attended Church This Week:	Yes	476	60	34	2	3	1
	No	534	45	44	6	3	1
Read Bible This Week:	Yes	479	60	32	3	3	1
	No	534	45	46	5	3	1

TABLE 65   247

How important is "government and politics" to you? Is it very important, somewhat important, not too important, or not at all important?

		N	Very Important	Somewhat Important	Not Too Important	Not at All Important	Don't Know
Total Responding		1013	34%	42%	13%	9%	2%
Gender:	Male	478	35	44	11	9	2
	Female	535	33	42	14	8	3
Age:	18 to 26	171	25	42	18	15	0
	27 to 45	402	30	48	14	8	0
	46 to 64	254	38	42	11	6	4
	65 Plus	157	44	29	9	9	9
Education:	High School or Less	666	34	38	14	11	3
	Some College	140	32	50	10	5	2
	College Graduate	201	32	52	12	4	0
Ethnicity:	White	729	31	43	14	8	3
	Black	139	46	38	7	9	0
	Hispanic	93	40	42	10	7	1
Marital:	Married	571	31	44	14	8	3
	Single	223	32	45	13	10	0
	Divorced/Separated	118	37	43	10	10	0
	Widowed	93	53	25	8	7	7
Kids Under 18:	Yes	405	29	45	15	11	0
	No	608	38	41	11	7	4
Household Income:	Under $20,000	299	34	30	18	14	5
	$20,000 to $39,999	368	33	44	14	7	1
	$40,000 to $59,999	133	28	58	8	6	0
	$60,000 or more	95	32	54	9	4	0
Job Type:	White Collar	224	30	53	11	5	1
	Blue Collar	313	28	44	17	9	1
	Not Employed	398	40	36	10	10	4
Community:	Urban	253	35	47	11	6	2
	Suburban	374	34	43	12	10	1
	Rural	290	33	44	12	7	3
Region:	Northeast	228	30	45	11	12	2
	Midwest	223	35	40	17	6	1
	South	356	39	41	9	6	5
	Mountain	54	41	43	7	9	0
	Pacific	153	24	45	18	13	0
Voter Registration:	Not	291	22	36	20	20	2
	Democrat	316	41	45	8	4	2
	Republican	210	38	47	11	2	2
	Independent	147	32	47	11	8	2
Born Again:	Yes	409	33	45	15	5	3
	No	604	35	41	11	11	2
Denominational Affiliation:	Protestant	550	34	43	14	7	2
	Baptist	209	36	44	10	6	4
	Catholic	221	36	46	11	5	2
	Lutheran	53	40	42	12	6	0
	Methodist	65	34	43	18	2	2
	Charis./Pent.	70	24	31	27	18	0
Attended Church This Week:	Yes	476	36	43	13	5	3
	No	534	33	42	12	12	2
Read Bible This Week:	Yes	479	40	39	12	7	3
	No	534	29	46	13	10	2

Do you agree strongly, agree moderately, disagree moderately, or disagree strongly with the statement: "Today's popular music has a negative influence on most people"?

		N	Agree Strongly	Agree Moderately	Disagree Moderately	Disagree Strongly	Don't Know
Total Responding		1013	28%	24%	24%	17%	7%
Gender:	Male	478	25	21	27	21	5
	Female	535	30	27	22	13	8
Age:	18 to 26	171	14	23	28	34	0
	27 to 45	402	26	24	29	15	6
	46 to 64	254	32	28	20	11	8
	65 Plus	157	43	22	16	10	11
Education:	High School or Less	666	32	24	22	17	6
	Some College	140	25	25	27	16	8
	College Graduate	201	15	26	31	20	8
Ethnicity:	White	729	25	24	27	18	6
	Black	139	40	27	12	13	8
	Hispanic	93	29	23	24	18	6
Marital:	Married	571	33	24	25	11	7
	Single	223	16	23	27	31	3
	Divorced/Separated	118	19	29	23	21	8
	Widowed	93	36	22	17	13	11
Kids Under 18:	Yes	405	27	24	27	17	4
	No	608	28	24	23	17	8
Household Income:	Under $20,000	299	28	26	21	17	9
	$20,000 to $39,999	368	31	27	23	15	4
	$40,000 to $59,999	133	20	23	35	18	5
	$60,000 or more	95	16	19	29	28	8
Job Type:	White Collar	224	21	23	30	20	5
	Blue Collar	313	28	28	25	14	5
	Not Employed	398	31	22	21	17	8
Community:	Urban	253	30	21	25	18	6
	Suburban	374	23	28	27	17	5
	Rural	290	28	26	23	18	5
Region:	Northeast	228	19	27	26	21	8
	Midwest	223	21	25	29	18	7
	South	356	35	25	21	13	6
	Mountain	54	33	20	29	12	7
	Pacific	153	30	19	23	21	6
Voter Registration:	Not	291	26	27	23	23	2
	Democrat	316	31	22	25	11	10
	Republican	210	34	23	20	16	6
	Independent	147	19	24	31	23	4
Born Again:	Yes	409	34	29	18	13	6
	No	604	24	21	29	20	7
Denominational Affiliation:	Protestant	550	31	27	21	14	7
	Baptist	209	37	25	17	14	7
	Catholic	221	24	21	33	14	8
	Lutheran	53	18	33	32	12	5
	Methodist	65	22	27	28	18	6
	Charis./Pent.	70	42	25	12	12	9
Attended Church This Week:	Yes	476	35	26	21	11	7
	No	534	21	23	28	22	6
Read Bible This Week:	Yes	479	34	29	17	14	7
	No	534	22	20	31	20	6

TABLE 67   249

Do you agree strongly, agree moderately, disagree moderately, or disagree strongly with the statement: "The values and life-styles shown in music videos generally reflect the ways most people live and think these days"?

		N	Agree Strongly	Agree Moderately	Disagree Moderately	Disagree Strongly	Don't Know
Total Responding		1013	14%	20%	24%	32%	9%
Gender:	Male	478	16	18	25	36	5
	Female	535	12	22	24	29	13
Age:	18 to 26	171	17	21	33	28	0
	27 to 45	402	15	19	21	38	7
	46 to 64	254	14	20	22	31	13
	65 Plus	157	12	23	16	30	20
Education:	High School or Less	666	17	23	21	29	9
	Some College	140	12	17	28	34	9
	College Graduate	201	5	13	30	43	9
Ethnicity:	White	729	10	20	23	37	9
	Black	139	29	14	28	17	13
	Hispanic	93	24	22	32	18	4
Marital:	Married	571	13	20	21	36	9
	Single	223	21	16	31	28	3
	Divorced/Separated	118	6	28	29	26	11
	Widowed	93	12	21	18	28	21
Kids Under 18:	Yes	405	17	18	23	37	5
	No	608	12	21	25	30	12
Household Income:	Under $20,000	299	18	27	20	24	11
	$20,000 to $39,999	368	15	19	24	36	6
	$40,000 to $59,999	133	8	15	32	37	9
	$60,000 or more	95	4	14	30	42	10
Job Type:	White Collar	224	8	11	28	43	9
	Blue Collar	313	19	23	23	31	5
	Not Employed	398	15	22	22	26	14
Community:	Urban	253	17	17	28	31	8
	Suburban	374	11	20	24	37	8
	Rural	290	12	25	22	32	9
Region:	Northeast	228	11	18	25	35	12
	Midwest	223	12	20	25	34	9
	South	356	16	24	20	30	10
	Mountain	54	15	10	21	36	17
	Pacific	153	18	16	31	31	4
Voter Registration:	Not	291	22	23	25	26	5
	Democrat	316	12	17	22	33	16
	Republican	210	10	22	20	40	8
	Independent	147	14	18	30	35	4
Born Again:	Yes	409	13	25	23	31	8
	No	604	15	17	25	33	10
Denominational Affiliation:	Protestant	550	12	24	21	32	11
	Baptist	209	13	28	20	28	11
	Catholic	221	15	19	29	28	10
	Lutheran	53	0	17	31	44	8
	Methodist	65	11	18	23	44	4
	Charis./Pent.	70	21	24	19	25	10
Attended Church This Week:	Yes	476	14	21	22	32	12
	No	534	14	20	26	33	7
Read Bible This Week:	Yes	479	19	22	19	28	12
	No	534	9	18	28	36	7

TABLE 68

Do you agree strongly, agree moderately, disagree moderately, or disagree strongly with the statement: "Abortion is morally wrong"?

		N	Agree Strongly	Agree Moderately	Disagree Moderately	Disagree Strongly	Don't Know
Total Responding		1013	45%	12%	15%	20%	7%
Gender:	Male	478	40	13	15	25	7
	Female	535	50	12	16	16	6
Age:	18 to 26	171	42	12	16	23	6
	27 to 45	402	41	17	20	16	6
	46 to 64	254	51	8	11	22	8
	65 Plus	157	52	8	10	22	8
Education:	High School or Less	666	51	11	12	19	7
	Some College	140	39	16	22	16	7
	College Graduate	201	30	15	21	26	7
Ethnicity:	White	729	46	12	15	20	7
	Black	139	43	14	15	22	5
	Hispanic	93	48	13	16	24	0
Marital:	Married	571	52	12	14	15	6
	Single	223	33	14	19	26	9
	Divorced/Separated	118	33	15	18	29	5
	Widowed	93	51	6	10	27	7
Kids Under 18:	Yes	405	48	15	15	16	5
	No	608	43	10	15	23	8
Household Income:	Under $20,000	299	54	11	11	15	9
	$20,000 to $39,999	368	44	10	19	23	4
	$40,000 to $59,999	133	33	22	15	21	10
	$60,000 or more	95	30	11	22	30	8
Job Type:	White Collar	224	34	14	20	25	6
	Blue Collar	313	49	14	12	18	7
	Not Employed	398	50	10	13	20	7
Community:	Urban	253	43	14	18	18	7
	Suburban	374	40	12	18	23	8
	Rural	290	51	14	14	17	4
Region:	Northeast	228	34	14	20	23	8
	Midwest	223	47	11	20	14	9
	South	356	51	14	10	21	4
	Mountain	54	50	7	12	19	11
	Pacific	153	45	9	14	24	8
Voter Registration:	Not	291	54	11	10	19	6
	Democrat	316	44	13	14	22	6
	Republican	210	43	14	17	16	10
	Independent	147	35	12	23	25	5
Born Again:	Yes	409	63	11	11	11	4
	No	604	33	13	18	26	9
Denominational Affiliation:	Protestant	550	47	13	15	16	8
	Baptist	209	43	15	18	17	6
	Catholic	221	49	12	16	20	3
	Lutheran	53	44	16	16	7	16
	Methodist	65	23	19	20	26	12
	Charis./Pent.	70	93	2	2	2	0
Attended Church This Week:	Yes	476	61	10	9	15	4
	No	534	31	14	21	25	9
Read Bible This Week:	Yes	479	58	11	11	14	6
	No	534	34	13	19	26	7

TABLE 69   251

Do you agree strongly, agree moderately, disagree moderately, or disagree strongly with the statement: "Lying is sometimes necessary"?

		N	Agree Strongly	Agree Moderately	Disagree Moderately	Disagree Strongly	Don't Know
Total Responding		1013	7%	29%	18%	44%	3%
Gender:	Male	478	10	29	16	42	2
	Female	535	5	28	19	45	3
Age:	18 to 26	171	11	40	21	28	1
	27 to 45	402	4	28	21	47	1
	46 to 64	254	4	28	12	54	2
	65 Plus	157	11	25	15	40	8
Education:	High School or Less	666	8	28	15	46	3
	Some College	140	5	30	23	40	2
	College Graduate	201	5	32	22	39	2
Ethnicity:	White	729	5	29	19	45	3
	Black	139	8	28	10	49	4
	Hispanic	93	17	30	23	30	0
Marital:	Married	571	6	24	17	51	2
	Single	223	9	40	19	31	1
	Divorced/Separated	118	12	32	17	36	3
	Widowed	93	2	25	17	44	11
Kids Under 18:	Yes	405	6	28	16	49	1
	No	608	8	29	19	41	4
Household Income:	Under $20,000	299	8	31	17	41	4
	$20,000 to $39,999	368	6	29	16	49	1
	$40,000 to $59,999	133	4	26	28	38	3
	$60,000 or more	95	10	34	18	38	1
Job Type:	White Collar	224	4	29	23	40	2
	Blue Collar	313	8	28	17	46	1
	Not Employed	398	7	29	16	44	4
Community:	Urban	253	10	27	21	40	3
	Suburban	374	7	35	20	36	2
	Rural	290	5	23	15	54	2
Region:	Northeast	228	7	37	19	34	3
	Midwest	223	3	28	21	47	1
	South	356	7	23	16	49	5
	Mountain	54	16	19	16	47	2
	Pacific	153	11	34	14	40	1
Voter Registration:	Not	291	11	35	14	37	3
	Democrat	316	7	25	20	45	3
	Republican	210	4	26	16	52	2
	Independent	147	4	26	23	45	1
Born Again:	Yes	409	3	24	17	54	2
	No	604	10	32	18	37	3
Denominational Affiliation:	Protestant	550	3	25	18	50	3
	Baptist	209	7	22	18	48	4
	Catholic	221	10	34	21	34	2
	Lutheran	53	1	47	18	32	1
	Methodist	65	2	24	25	46	3
	Charis./Pent.	70	0	18	14	66	2
Attended Church This Week:	Yes	476	5	25	17	50	4
	No	534	9	32	18	39	2
Read Bible This Week:	Yes	479	5	21	17	54	3
	No	534	9	36	18	35	2

TABLE 70

Do you agree strongly, agree moderately, disagree moderately, or disagree strongly with the statement: "Nothing can be known for certain except the things you experience in your own life"?

		N	Agree Strongly	Agree Moderately	Disagree Moderately	Disagree Strongly	Don't Know
Total Responding		1013	30%	30%	19%	17%	5%
Gender:	Male	478	32	27	18	19	4
	Female	535	28	32	19	16	5
Age:	18 to 26	171	32	39	13	11	4
	27 to 45	402	27	29	26	17	1
	46 to 64	254	33	23	13	24	6
	65 Plus	157	30	32	13	11	14
Education:	High School or Less	666	34	31	16	14	5
	Some College	140	28	28	19	20	4
	College Graduate	201	17	26	27	27	3
Ethnicity:	White	729	26	31	19	19	5
	Black	139	50	25	10	9	6
	Hispanic	93	38	24	25	13	0
Marital:	Married	571	29	29	19	19	4
	Single	223	32	32	21	11	4
	Divorced/Separated	118	25	33	21	17	4
	Widowed	93	39	21	10	20	11
Kids Under 18:	Yes	405	28	32	22	16	2
	No	608	31	28	16	18	7
Household Income:	Under $20,000	299	35	31	13	13	8
	$20,000 to $39,999	368	32	30	20	15	3
	$40,000 to $59,999	133	21	30	25	23	2
	$60,000 or more	95	27	29	17	25	3
Job Type:	White Collar	224	20	28	27	23	2
	Blue Collar	313	33	33	16	16	2
	Not Employed	398	34	28	16	13	9
Community:	Urban	253	33	30	17	16	4
	Suburban	374	29	30	22	16	4
	Rural	290	29	29	21	18	2
Region:	Northeast	228	28	32	20	16	4
	Midwest	223	30	28	21	15	5
	South	356	34	27	17	16	6
	Mountain	54	37	24	18	18	4
	Pacific	153	23	36	15	24	2
Voter Registration:	Not	291	28	35	20	13	4
	Democrat	316	38	25	15	17	5
	Republican	210	24	27	17	25	6
	Independent	147	29	30	22	15	4
Born Again:	Yes	409	27	31	14	25	4
	No	604	32	28	22	12	5
Denominational Affiliation:	Protestant	550	29	30	17	18	5
	Baptist	209	35	29	14	16	5
	Catholic	221	35	28	21	14	3
	Lutheran	53	21	42	24	11	3
	Methodist	65	23	25	28	18	5
	Charis./Pent.	70	40	28	9	19	5
Attended Church This Week:	Yes	476	29	26	17	22	6
	No	534	31	32	20	13	3
Read Bible This Week:	Yes	479	28	28	15	22	6
	No	534	32	30	21	12	4

TABLE 71 253

Do you agree strongly, agree moderately, disagree moderately, or disagree strongly with the statement: "One person can really make a difference in the world these days"?

		N	Agree Strongly	Agree Moderately	Disagree Moderately	Disagree Strongly	Don't Know
Total Responding		1013	40%	32%	15%	11%	3%
Gender:	Male	478	42	31	14	11	1
	Female	535	38	33	15	10	4
Age:	18 to 26	171	29	38	23	10	0
	27 to 45	402	42	32	15	8	2
	46 to 64	254	36	33	14	14	4
	65 Plus	157	47	25	9	13	6
Education:	High School or Less	666	39	29	17	12	4
	Some College	140	39	40	10	10	1
	College Graduate	201	42	38	12	7	1
Ethnicity:	White	729	39	34	13	12	3
	Black	139	45	26	22	7	0
	Hispanic	93	36	31	15	13	4
Marital:	Married	571	40	33	13	11	3
	Single	223	38	29	23	9	1
	Divorced/Separated	118	38	40	10	9	3
	Widowed	93	44	22	13	15	5
Kids Under 18:	Yes	405	37	33	18	10	2
	No	608	41	31	13	11	3
Household Income:	Under $20,000	299	41	24	16	13	6
	$20,000 to $39,999	368	39	35	12	13	1
	$40,000 to $59,999	133	35	36	23	5	1
	$60,000 or more	95	43	38	14	5	1
Job Type:	White Collar	224	40	35	16	8	1
	Blue Collar	313	36	34	16	10	4
	Not Employed	398	41	30	13	13	3
Community:	Urban	253	38	35	19	8	1
	Suburban	374	41	34	12	10	3
	Rural	290	40	32	15	11	3
Region:	Northeast	228	42	33	16	6	3
	Midwest	223	29	38	20	11	2
	South	356	44	29	11	13	2
	Mountain	54	41	32	14	9	4
	Pacific	153	40	30	14	12	4
Voter Registration:	Not	291	39	33	17	11	0
	Democrat	316	42	29	16	10	3
	Republican	210	41	34	9	12	5
	Independent	147	37	31	18	11	3
Born Again:	Yes	409	40	33	14	8	4
	No	604	39	32	16	12	2
Denominational Affiliation:	Protestant	550	42	31	13	10	3
	Baptist	209	48	33	6	10	3
	Catholic	221	35	32	18	12	4
	Lutheran	53	27	40	22	6	6
	Methodist	65	43	31	11	12	3
	Charis./Pent.	70	35	29	25	6	4
Attended Church This Week:	Yes	476	41	33	14	9	3
	No	534	39	31	15	12	3
Read Bible This Week:	Yes	479	43	31	14	10	3
	No	534	37	34	16	12	2

TABLE 72

Do you agree strongly, agree moderately, disagree moderately, or disagree strongly with the statement: "No matter how you feel about money, it is still the main symbol of success in life"?

		N	Agree Strongly	Agree Moderately	Disagree Moderately	Disagree Strongly	Don't Know
Total Responding		1013	24%	28%	25%	22%	1%
Gender:	Male	478	27	31	20	21	1
	Female	535	21	26	28	22	2
Age:	18 to 26	171	24	28	24	25	0
	27 to 45	402	19	30	24	27	0
	46 to 64	254	31	23	26	16	3
	65 Plus	157	26	28	28	14	3
Education:	High School or Less	666	27	29	24	18	2
	Some College	140	23	27	27	22	1
	College Graduate	201	15	27	25	32	1
Ethnicity:	White	729	19	29	26	23	2
	Black	139	49	20	20	11	0
	Hispanic	93	29	40	15	17	0
Marital:	Married	571	21	28	25	23	2
	Single	223	28	30	23	20	0
	Divorced/Separated	118	24	32	18	25	0
	Widowed	93	29	24	34	12	0
Kids Under 18:	Yes	405	23	28	22	28	0
	No	608	25	29	26	17	2
Household Income:	Under $20,000	299	29	26	24	18	3
	$20,000 to $39,999	368	22	28	24	25	1
	$40,000 to $59,999	133	21	31	27	21	0
	$60,000 or more	95	16	28	26	29	1
Job Type:	White Collar	224	18	23	29	29	1
	Blue Collar	313	28	29	22	20	1
	Not Employed	398	24	31	26	18	2
Community:	Urban	253	21	29	27	20	2
	Suburban	374	21	32	26	20	1
	Rural	290	23	26	21	27	3
Region:	Northeast	228	19	33	25	22	1
	Midwest	223	16	32	24	27	2
	South	356	33	26	24	15	2
	Mountain	54	21	17	36	26	1
	Pacific	153	23	26	23	27	1
Voter Registration:	Not	291	29	30	19	22	0
	Democrat	316	28	27	24	18	3
	Republican	210	15	32	30	23	0
	Independent	147	18	25	30	25	2
Born Again:	Yes	409	23	28	23	25	2
	No	604	25	29	26	19	1
Denominational Affiliation:	Protestant	550	24	28	25	22	2
	Baptist	209	28	30	23	16	2
	Catholic	221	22	33	25	19	1
	Lutheran	53	15	33	37	15	0
	Methodist	65	18	25	27	26	4
	Charis./Pent.	70	28	31	11	28	3
Attended Church This Week:	Yes	476	23	28	24	24	2
	No	534	25	28	25	20	1
Read Bible This Week:	Yes	479	24	27	24	24	2
	No	534	24	30	25	19	1

TABLE 73   255

Do you agree strongly, agree moderately, disagree moderately, or disagree strongly with the statement: "The Bible is the written word of God and is totally accurate in all that it teaches"?

		N	Agree Strongly	Agree Moderately	Disagree Moderately	Disagree Strongly	Don't Know
Total Responding		1013	56%	18%	12%	9%	4%
Gender:	Male	478	48	20	14	12	6
	Female	535	64	17	11	6	2
Age:	18 to 26	171	44	21	16	11	8
	27 to 45	402	52	21	15	10	3
	46 to 64	254	63	17	6	9	3
	65 Plus	157	75	7	9	4	4
Education:	High School or Less	666	67	17	8	5	4
	Some College	140	48	22	16	8	6
	College Graduate	201	28	22	24	22	5
Ethnicity:	White	729	55	19	14	8	4
	Black	139	62	15	5	13	6
	Hispanic	93	59	27	4	10	0
Marital:	Married	571	60	17	12	8	3
	Single	223	43	21	16	13	7
	Divorced/Separated	118	52	28	9	8	3
	Widowed	93	76	10	8	3	3
Kids Under 18:	Yes	405	53	21	12	10	4
	No	608	59	17	12	8	4
Household Income:	Under $20,000	299	70	15	7	5	3
	$20,000 to $39,999	368	58	19	11	10	2
	$40,000 to $59,999	133	43	21	21	11	4
	$60,000 or more	95	33	23	17	18	9
Job Type:	White Collar	224	42	20	17	15	5
	Blue Collar	313	62	17	12	7	2
	Not Employed	398	63	18	8	6	5
Community:	Urban	253	48	20	16	12	4
	Suburban	374	51	22	13	11	3
	Rural	290	66	14	10	6	3
Region:	Northeast	228	43	24	17	11	5
	Midwest	223	50	24	13	10	4
	South	356	74	8	8	5	5
	Mountain	54	45	14	8	23	9
	Pacific	153	49	26	16	8	0
Voter Registration:	Not	291	53	22	10	7	7
	Democrat	316	62	16	10	10	3
	Republican	210	58	16	15	7	4
	Independent	147	45	24	17	11	2
Born Again:	Yes	409	80	14	4	1	2
	No	604	40	22	18	14	6
Denominational Affiliation:	Protestant	550	69	14	9	5	3
	Baptist	209	79	10	6	4	1
	Catholic	221	46	29	16	7	3
	Lutheran	53	44	30	17	8	2
	Methodist	65	50	20	20	7	4
	Charis./Pent.	70	88	9	0	0	4
Attended Church This Week:	Yes	476	74	14	6	3	3
	No	534	41	23	18	14	5
Read Bible This Week:	Yes	479	77	12	5	3	3
	No	534	38	24	19	14	5

TABLE 74

Do you agree strongly, agree moderately, disagree moderately, or disagree strongly with the statement: "The Christian faith has all the answers to leading a successful life"?

		N	Agree Strongly	Agree Moderately	Disagree Moderately	Disagree Strongly	Don't Know
Total Responding		1013	41%	27%	17%	12%	3%
Gender:	Male	478	35	27	19	17	2
	Female	535	47	26	16	7	4
Age:	18 to 26	171	23	37	22	15	3
	27 to 45	402	42	25	19	12	2
	46 to 64	254	49	28	12	9	2
	65 Plus	157	51	18	15	9	7
Education:	High School or Less	666	46	26	15	9	4
	Some College	140	39	26	19	13	3
	College Graduate	201	25	29	25	19	2
Ethnicity:	White	729	39	29	18	11	3
	Black	139	52	26	13	5	5
	Hispanic	93	47	17	16	21	0
Marital:	Married	571	46	26	14	11	2
	Single	223	28	28	24	17	3
	Divorced/Separated	118	35	34	20	7	4
	Widowed	93	51	18	14	6	11
Kids Under 18:	Yes	405	40	27	20	11	2
	No	608	42	26	16	12	4
Household Income:	Under $20,000	299	49	25	13	10	3
	$20,000 to $39,999	368	42	27	17	12	2
	$40,000 to $59,999	133	30	28	26	13	3
	$60,000 or more	95	25	29	20	21	5
Job Type:	White Collar	224	31	27	23	16	3
	Blue Collar	313	46	29	14	10	1
	Not Employed	398	44	23	17	10	6
Community:	Urban	253	37	24	19	15	5
	Suburban	374	41	26	19	13	2
	Rural	290	40	30	17	9	4
Region:	Northeast	228	38	24	20	14	4
	Midwest	223	31	34	22	9	4
	South	356	52	26	13	7	2
	Mountain	54	40	30	10	13	6
	Pacific	153	36	21	20	21	2
Voter Registration:	Not	291	37	30	18	13	3
	Democrat	316	45	23	16	12	4
	Republican	210	46	28	14	9	3
	Independent	147	37	26	24	12	1
Born Again:	Yes	409	58	28	8	3	2
	No	604	30	25	23	17	4
Denominational Affiliation:	Protestant	550	50	30	13	4	3
	Baptist	209	53	32	11	4	1
	Catholic	221	35	28	20	13	4
	Lutheran	53	38	37	20	5	0
	Methodist	65	36	36	14	8	6
	Charis./Pent.	70	72	17	6	2	3
Attended Church This Week:	Yes	476	59	23	10	7	2
	No	534	26	30	24	16	4
Read Bible This Week:	Yes	479	59	20	11	6	3
	No	534	25	32	23	17	4

TABLE 75   257

Do you agree strongly, agree moderately, disagree moderately, or disagree strongly with the statement: "People's prayers do not have the power to change their circumstances"?

		N	Agree Strongly	Agree Moderately	Disagree Moderately	Disagree Strongly	Don't Know
Total Responding		1013	12%	13%	22%	49%	4%
Gender:	Male	478	11	16	24	43	6
	Female	535	12	10	20	55	3
Age:	18 to 26	171	7	19	31	38	6
	27 to 45	402	9	11	27	50	3
	46 to 64	254	15	12	16	54	4
	65 Plus	157	20	8	14	51	6
Education:	High School or Less	666	14	13	20	48	5
	Some College	140	9	12	26	52	1
	College Graduate	201	6	14	27	49	3
Ethnicity:	White	729	10	13	24	48	5
	Black	139	24	6	19	49	3
	Hispanic	93	9	15	19	57	0
Marital:	Married	571	11	11	20	56	3
	Single	223	12	21	27	36	5
	Divorced/Separated	118	19	13	27	35	6
	Widowed	93	10	6	17	60	8
Kids Under 18:	Yes	405	7	13	24	53	3
	No	608	15	13	20	46	6
Household Income:	Under $20,000	299	16	10	21	46	7
	$20,000 to $39,999	368	11	11	21	55	2
	$40,000 to $59,999	133	8	19	30	41	3
	$60,000 or more	95	3	19	25	47	6
Job Type:	White Collar	224	6	14	29	50	2
	Blue Collar	313	13	12	20	49	5
	Not Employed	398	14	12	21	47	5
Community:	Urban	253	10	15	21	54	1
	Suburban	374	13	13	24	45	4
	Rural	290	9	13	22	52	5
Region:	Northeast	228	6	18	28	44	5
	Midwest	223	13	12	26	46	3
	South	356	15	8	16	58	4
	Mountain	54	24	12	12	42	10
	Pacific	153	6	18	26	42	7
Voter Registration:	Not	291	10	16	29	39	7
	Democrat	316	16	10	16	55	3
	Republican	210	7	12	15	62	4
	Independent	147	14	15	31	38	2
Born Again:	Yes	409	9	7	14	68	2
	No	604	14	17	27	36	6
Denominational Affiliation:	Protestant	550	13	9	18	56	4
	Baptist	209	19	9	15	56	1
	Catholic	221	13	15	29	41	2
	Lutheran	53	11	18	23	46	2
	Methodist	65	8	10	29	42	10
	Charis./Pent.	70	8	5	10	70	7
Attended Church This Week:	Yes	476	13	6	14	66	2
	No	534	11	19	30	34	7
Read Bible This Week:	Yes	479	13	7	13	65	2
	No	534	10	18	30	35	7

Do you agree strongly, agree moderately, disagree moderately, or disagree strongly with the statement: "Horoscopes and astrology usually provide an accurate prediction of the future"?

		N	Agree Strongly	Agree Moderately	Disagree Moderately	Disagree Strongly	Don't Know
Total Responding		1013	2%	12%	20%	62%	4%
Gender:	Male	478	2	11	19	65	3
	Female	535	2	12	21	60	5
Age:	18 to 26	171	0	16	28	54	1
	27 to 45	402	3	8	21	66	2
	46 to 64	254	1	13	16	64	7
	65 Plus	157	5	16	17	57	6
Education:	High School or Less	666	3	15	20	57	5
	Some College	140	1	5	25	67	2
	College Graduate	201	0	5	19	74	1
Ethnicity:	White	729	2	9	20	66	3
	Black	139	4	18	27	42	9
	Hispanic	93	0	22	15	62	1
Marital:	Married	571	1	9	19	67	4
	Single	223	2	15	25	57	2
	Divorced/Separated	118	6	15	20	53	7
	Widowed	93	7	18	13	55	7
Kids Under 18:	Yes	405	1	10	24	64	2
	No	608	3	13	18	61	6
Household Income:	Under $20,000	299	3	19	18	53	7
	$20,000 to $39,999	368	2	9	20	67	3
	$40,000 to $59,999	133	3	5	21	69	1
	$60,000 or more	95	0	5	25	70	1
Job Type:	White Collar	224	0	7	19	72	2
	Blue Collar	313	3	11	22	57	7
	Not Employed	398	3	15	20	59	4
Community:	Urban	253	3	13	18	61	4
	Suburban	374	1	9	21	65	3
	Rural	290	3	11	23	60	4
Region:	Northeast	228	1	9	20	65	5
	Midwest	223	4	16	23	56	2
	South	356	3	8	22	62	5
	Mountain	54	0	5	26	62	7
	Pacific	153	1	18	12	67	2
Voter Registration:	Not	291	1	16	22	55	5
	Democrat	316	3	10	21	60	6
	Republican	210	2	8	16	72	2
	Independent	147	2	11	21	64	2
Born Again:	Yes	409	1	10	15	71	3
	No	604	3	13	24	56	5
Denominational Affiliation:	Protestant	550	3	11	17	64	5
	Baptist	209	5	12	22	55	6
	Catholic	221	1	13	23	59	4
	Lutheran	53	0	6	20	66	8
	Methodist	65	0	13	22	62	3
	Charis./Pent.	70	0	13	5	79	3
Attended Church This Week:	Yes	476	2	9	17	69	3
	No	534	3	14	23	56	5
Read Bible This Week:	Yes	479	3	12	14	66	5
	No	534	1	12	26	58	3

TABLE 77   259

Do you agree strongly, agree moderately, disagree moderately, or disagree strongly with the statement: "The Ten Commandments are not relevant for people living today"?

		N	Agree Strongly	Agree Moderately	Disagree Moderately	Disagree Strongly	Don't Know
Total Responding		1013	10%	8%	15%	64%	3%
Gender:	Male	478	9	10	18	60	3
	Female	535	11	7	12	67	4
Age:	18 to 26	171	10	19	18	50	3
	27 to 45	402	5	8	21	64	3
	46 to 64	254	12	4	6	73	5
	65 Plus	157	17	6	7	65	4
Education:	High School or Less	666	13	10	12	61	4
	Some College	140	5	5	16	73	2
	College Graduate	201	3	6	23	66	1
Ethnicity:	White	729	10	8	14	66	3
	Black	139	16	10	15	58	1
	Hispanic	93	6	13	20	53	9
Marital:	Married	571	9	6	12	68	5
	Single	223	12	18	20	49	1
	Divorced/Separated	118	11	4	22	62	2
	Widowed	93	9	6	9	76	1
Kids Under 18:	Yes	405	6	11	15	66	2
	No	608	13	6	14	62	4
Household Income:	Under $20,000	299	17	8	12	59	5
	$20,000 to $39,999	368	5	8	15	69	3
	$40,000 to $59,999	133	4	10	17	69	0
	$60,000 or more	95	5	7	30	56	2
Job Type:	White Collar	224	2	9	16	71	2
	Blue Collar	313	11	6	16	64	3
	Not Employed	398	14	9	13	59	5
Community:	Urban	253	10	11	13	63	3
	Suburban	374	8	5	18	66	3
	Rural	290	12	9	13	66	1
Region:	Northeast	228	8	7	22	61	2
	Midwest	223	12	12	14	63	0
	South	356	12	7	11	66	4
	Mountain	54	12	0	8	75	5
	Pacific	153	5	10	17	59	8
Voter Registration:	Not	291	8	15	16	54	7
	Democrat	316	12	5	13	68	2
	Republican	210	12	7	12	69	1
	Independent	147	10	7	21	61	1
Born Again:	Yes	409	7	4	9	77	3
	No	604	12	12	18	55	4
Denominational Affiliation:	Protestant	550	9	5	12	71	2
	Baptist	209	13	5	9	73	0
	Catholic	221	13	7	15	61	5
	Lutheran	53	8	9	15	68	0
	Methodist	65	6	11	12	70	1
	Charis./Pent.	70	9	3	12	65	10
Attended Church This Week:	Yes	476	11	3	9	73	4
	No	534	9	13	20	56	3
Read Bible This Week:	Yes	479	11	4	11	71	3
	No	534	9	12	18	57	4

TABLE 78

Do you agree strongly, agree moderately, disagree moderately, or disagree strongly with the statement: "The whole idea of sin is outdated"?

		N	Agree Strongly	Agree Moderately	Disagree Moderately	Disagree Strongly	Don't Know
Total Responding		1013	10%	10%	19%	57%	6%
Gender:	Male	478	12	12	19	54	3
	Female	535	8	7	18	59	8
Age:	18 to 26	171	11	12	30	40	6
	27 to 45	402	8	8	22	59	4
	46 to 64	254	8	11	11	67	3
	65 Plus	157	10	10	11	56	13
Education:	High School or Less	666	11	11	16	55	8
	Some College	140	8	6	22	64	1
	College Graduate	201	5	9	26	57	3
Ethnicity:	White	729	8	10	19	58	5
	Black	139	8	14	16	54	7
	Hispanic	93	25	1	11	54	9
Marital:	Married	571	6	10	16	63	5
	Single	223	17	9	26	44	5
	Divorced/Separated	118	12	12	24	48	5
	Widowed	93	9	9	11	59	11
Kids Under 18:	Yes	405	7	11	20	57	4
	No	608	11	9	17	56	7
Household Income:	Under $20,000	299	11	9	17	53	9
	$20,000 to $39,999	368	9	10	16	63	1
	$40,000 to $59,999	133	5	6	30	55	4
	$60,000 or more	95	12	17	22	46	3
Job Type:	White Collar	224	4	10	23	62	2
	Blue Collar	313	11	8	18	58	5
	Not Employed	398	12	9	15	54	9
Community:	Urban	253	13	11	17	55	5
	Suburban	374	12	10	21	54	3
	Rural	290	7	6	18	62	7
Region:	Northeast	228	12	10	22	48	7
	Midwest	223	12	8	22	56	2
	South	356	8	9	14	63	6
	Mountain	54	3	6	20	70	2
	Pacific	153	9	13	19	51	8
Voter Registration:	Not	291	11	14	18	51	6
	Democrat	316	8	9	17	60	6
	Republican	210	6	8	18	63	5
	Independent	147	15	7	25	50	2
Born Again:	Yes	409	5	6	10	72	7
	No	604	13	12	24	46	5
Denominational Affiliation:	Protestant	550	7	8	15	64	5
	Baptist	209	6	7	14	66	7
	Catholic	221	15	13	22	46	4
	Lutheran	53	10	7	25	57	1
	Methodist	65	7	9	22	59	3
	Charis./Pent.	70	5	15	6	69	6
Attended Church This Week:	Yes	476	8	6	13	68	5
	No	534	11	13	23	47	6
Read Bible This Week:	Yes	479	7	7	12	68	5
	No	534	12	12	25	46	6

TABLE 79   261

Do you agree strongly, agree moderately, disagree moderately, or disagree strongly with the statement: "The Bible does not command people to attend a church; that is a manmade requirement"?

		N	Agree Strongly	Agree Moderately	Disagree Moderately	Disagree Strongly	Don't Know
Total Responding		1013	23%	24%	17%	27%	9%
Gender:	Male	478	22	28	16	26	8
	Female	535	24	21	18	28	10
Age:	18 to 26	171	23	36	17	18	5
	27 to 45	402	21	26	18	28	7
	46 to 64	254	24	17	15	34	10
	65 Plus	157	26	20	17	22	15
Education:	High School or Less	666	22	23	17	30	8
	Some College	140	26	27	18	21	7
	College Graduate	201	25	28	17	19	12
Ethnicity:	White	729	24	24	17	24	10
	Black	139	18	25	11	40	5
	Hispanic	93	24	28	20	24	4
Marital:	Married	571	23	20	18	29	9
	Single	223	17	34	15	28	6
	Divorced/Separated	118	30	29	17	17	8
	Widowed	93	25	21	12	23	19
Kids Under 18:	Yes	405	23	24	20	26	6
	No	608	23	25	14	27	11
Household	Under $20,000	299	19	22	18	32	8
Income:	$20,000 to $39,999	368	26	25	17	24	8
	$40,000 to $59,999	133	17	32	20	21	9
	$60,000 or more	95	19	29	15	28	9
Job Type:	White Collar	224	20	28	15	25	11
	Blue Collar	313	23	22	21	31	4
	Not Employed	398	24	23	16	26	11
Community:	Urban	253	24	21	16	30	9
	Suburban	374	27	25	15	24	9
	Rural	290	22	27	19	27	5
Region:	Northeast	228	27	26	21	17	10
	Midwest	223	22	31	15	26	6
	South	356	20	20	18	32	9
	Mountain	54	35	14	4	33	13
	Pacific	153	20	26	14	29	11
Voter	Not	291	22	24	16	28	9
Registration:	Democrat	316	25	21	15	30	9
	Republican	210	17	24	19	31	8
	Independent	147	28	32	16	17	7
Born Again:	Yes	409	16	21	17	41	5
	No	604	28	27	17	17	11
Denominational	Protestant	550	19	23	16	34	8
Affiliation:	Baptist	209	21	26	11	36	6
	Catholic	221	32	29	18	15	6
	Lutheran	53	18	15	32	26	9
	Methodist	65	21	33	23	12	11
	Charis./Pent.	70	16	11	17	46	10
Attended Church	Yes	476	19	17	17	39	8
This Week:	No	534	26	31	17	16	10
Read Bible	Yes	479	15	20	15	42	8
This Week:	No	534	30	28	18	14	10

Do you agree strongly, agree moderately, disagree moderately, or disagree strongly with the statement: "All good people, whether they consider Jesus Christ to be their Savior or not, will live in heaven after they die on earth"?

		N	Agree Strongly	Agree Moderately	Disagree Moderately	Disagree Strongly	Don't Know
Total Responding		1013	25%	15%	16%	33%	11%
Gender:	Male	478	25	17	16	32	10
	Female	535	25	13	15	34	13
Age:	18 to 26	171	24	22	19	28	7
	27 to 45	402	25	18	17	32	8
	46 to 64	254	25	8	17	35	14
	65 Plus	157	27	10	8	37	18
Education:	High School or Less	666	26	13	15	36	10
	Some College	140	25	18	17	29	12
	College Graduate	201	23	19	17	27	14
Ethnicity:	White	729	24	16	13	34	13
	Black	139	31	7	23	32	7
	Hispanic	93	24	21	23	32	0
Marital:	Married	571	26	13	14	37	11
	Single	223	25	18	22	28	8
	Divorced/Separated	118	28	21	14	29	7
	Widowed	93	19	14	14	28	24
Kids Under 18:	Yes	405	24	17	16	35	8
	No	608	26	14	16	32	13
Household Income:	Under $20,000	299	26	14	14	34	11
	$20,000 to $39,999	368	27	11	17	35	9
	$40,000 to $59,999	133	18	24	24	23	12
	$60,000 or more	95	21	20	13	34	12
Job Type:	White Collar	224	23	14	19	31	12
	Blue Collar	313	25	15	17	36	7
	Not Employed	398	28	13	13	32	14
Community:	Urban	253	24	16	19	30	12
	Suburban	374	29	15	13	31	12
	Rural	290	21	18	14	39	10
Region:	Northeast	228	28	26	15	21	11
	Midwest	223	29	12	17	31	10
	South	356	23	9	18	41	10
	Mountain	54	26	17	4	33	21
	Pacific	153	21	16	15	36	13
Voter Registration:	Not	291	21	19	15	36	9
	Democrat	316	26	9	19	33	13
	Republican	210	21	15	16	37	11
	Independent	147	37	20	12	22	9
Born Again:	Yes	409	18	11	13	51	7
	No	604	30	18	18	21	14
Denominational Affiliation:	Protestant	550	19	11	16	44	10
	Baptist	209	21	5	18	47	9
	Catholic	221	38	27	18	9	7
	Lutheran	53	26	9	21	32	12
	Methodist	65	31	21	12	23	12
	Charis./Pent.	70	12	6	12	66	4
Attended Church This Week:	Yes	476	25	10	13	45	6
	No	534	25	19	18	22	15
Read Bible This Week:	Yes	479	21	10	13	46	9
	No	534	28	19	18	21	13

TABLE 81   263

The first commandment is "Do not worship gods other than the God described in the Bible." Does the way you live these days completely satisfy, mostly satisfy, somewhat satisfy, a little bit satisfy, or not at all satisfy that commandment?

		N	Completely	Mostly	Somewhat	A Little Bit	Not at All	Don't Know
Total Responding		1013	76%	9%	5%	3%	5%	2%
Gender:	Male	478	69	7	7	5	8	3
	Female	535	81	10	4	1	3	1
Age:	18 to 26	171	64	10	5	6	14	1
	27 to 45	402	79	8	5	3	3	2
	46 to 64	254	78	7	6	3	3	3
	65 Plus	157	80	11	4	0	3	1
Education:	High School or Less	666	78	8	5	3	5	1
	Some College	140	75	11	5	3	3	3
	College Graduate	201	70	10	6	2	8	4
Ethnicity:	White	729	77	10	5	3	4	2
	Black	139	78	7	3	3	8	2
	Hispanic	93	70	5	9	7	8	1
Marital:	Married	571	80	9	4	2	3	2
	Single	223	62	10	8	5	14	2
	Divorced/Separated	118	77	9	9	3	1	1
	Widowed	93	84	7	5	3	0	0
Kids Under 18:	Yes	405	78	8	4	3	5	2
	No	608	74	9	6	3	6	2
Household Income:	Under $20,000	299	78	8	6	2	6	0
	$20,000 to $39,999	368	76	10	5	4	3	3
	$40,000 to $59,999	133	81	8	3	2	5	0
	$60,000 or more	95	66	7	7	4	13	3
Job Type:	White Collar	224	74	9	4	3	7	3
	Blue Collar	313	76	8	5	5	3	2
	Not Employed	398	76	10	6	1	6	1
Community:	Urban	253	74	7	5	4	7	3
	Suburban	374	70	11	7	3	7	2
	Rural	290	82	9	4	4	1	1
Region:	Northeast	228	70	7	9	3	8	2
	Midwest	223	70	13	5	6	6	1
	South	356	86	6	3	1	1	2
	Mountain	54	70	10	2	9	5	4
	Pacific	153	71	11	4	1	10	2
Voter Registration:	Not	291	71	9	4	2	12	2
	Democrat	316	79	6	7	5	2	1
	Republican	210	81	12	3	1	1	2
	Independent	147	71	10	9	2	6	2
Born Again:	Yes	409	86	8	4	1	0	1
	No	604	68	10	6	5	9	3
Denominational Affiliation:	Protestant	550	83	9	4	1	2	2
	Baptist	209	86	7	4	1	0	2
	Catholic	221	80	8	7	4	1	0
	Lutheran	53	79	12	3	3	3	0
	Methodist	65	82	9	3	0	4	2
	Charis./Pent.	75	80	14	2	4	0	1
Attended Church This Week:	Yes	476	83	9	4	2	1	1
	No	534	69	9	7	4	9	2
Read Bible This Week:	Yes	479	81	9	4	1	2	2
	No	534	71	9	6	4	8	2

The next commandment is "You should not have any idols." Does the way you live these days completely satisfy, mostly satisfy, somewhat satisfy, a little bit satisfy, or not at all satisfy that commandment?

		N	Completely	Mostly	Somewhat	A Little Bit	Not at All	Don't Know
Total Responding		1013	71%	11%	8%	2%	4%	3%
Gender:	Male	478	65	10	11	4	7	3
	Female	535	77	11	6	1	2	3
Age:	18 to 26	171	53	16	11	7	12	1
	27 to 45	402	70	11	11	1	3	3
	46 to 64	254	79	8	5	2	2	3
	65 Plus	157	81	8	6	0	2	3
Education:	High School or Less	666	73	9	7	3	4	3
	Some College	140	72	12	10	0	4	3
	College Graduate	201	65	15	11	2	5	3
Ethnicity:	White	729	71	12	9	2	3	3
	Black	139	73	3	12	1	10	1
	Hispanic	93	76	9	4	4	3	4
Marital:	Married	571	75	12	8	1	2	3
	Single	223	57	13	12	6	11	0
	Divorced/Separated	118	73	7	11	1	3	5
	Widowed	93	86	4	1	3	1	4
Kids Under 18:	Yes	405	70	11	8	3	5	3
	No	608	72	10	9	2	4	3
Household Income:	Under $20,000	299	75	7	7	3	5	4
	$20,000 to $39,999	368	72	13	9	2	2	2
	$40,000 to $59,999	133	65	15	9	2	7	0
	$60,000 or more	95	65	13	14	1	6	1
Job Type:	White Collar	224	67	15	9	2	6	3
	Blue Collar	313	73	9	9	3	3	2
	Not Employed	398	72	10	8	2	5	3
Community:	Urban	253	70	11	11	1	4	3
	Suburban	374	71	10	10	3	5	2
	Rural	290	72	12	7	3	3	3
Region:	Northeast	228	64	11	12	3	6	3
	Midwest	223	69	12	8	3	7	1
	South	356	76	9	6	3	3	4
	Mountain	54	79	7	.	0	5	4
	Pacific	153	71	13	9	1	2	4
Voter Registration:	Not	291	64	13	9	2	9	4
	Democrat	316	77	9	7	3	2	2
	Republican	210	72	9	10	3	3	3
	Independent	147	70	13	11	1	3	2
Born Again:	Yes	409	80	10	4	2	2	2
	No	604	65	11	11	3	6	3
Denominational Affiliation:	Protestant	550	76	10	7	2	3	3
	Baptist	209	78	6	9	2	2	3
	Catholic	221	72	13	9	3	2	1
	Lutheran	53	75	16	5	1	3	0
	Methodist	65	70	16	8	2	3	1
	Charis./Pent.	70	88	7	1	0	3	1
Attended Church This Week:	Yes	476	81	10	5	1	2	1
	No	534	63	12	11	3	6	4
Read Bible This Week:	Yes	479	77	9	6	2	3	3
	No	534	66	12	11	2	6	3

TABLE 83   265

The next commandment is "Do not swear or misuse God's name." Does the way you live these days completely satisfy, mostly satisfy, somewhat satisfy, a little bit satisfy, or not at all satisfy that commandment?

		N	Completely	Mostly	Somewhat	A Little Bit	Not at All	Don't Know
Total Responding		1013	44%	22%	21%	7%	4%	2%
Gender:	Male	478	37	21	23	10	7	2
	Female	535	51	22	19	4	2	2
Age:	18 to 26	171	32	26	19	12	10	1
	27 to 45	402	37	24	26	7	4	1
	46 to 64	254	51	18	20	5	1	3
	65 Plus	157	64	16	15	3	1	1
Education:	High School or Less	666	51	19	18	5	4	1
	Some College	140	38	25	23	8	4	2
	College Graduate	201	25	28	29	10	6	3
Ethnicity:	White	729	40	25	22	8	4	1
	Black	139	65	13	15	1	4	1
	Hispanic	93	48	16	17	5	10	4
Marital:	Married	571	45	22	23	6	2	2
	Single	223	28	25	22	11	13	1
	Divorced/Separated	118	58	13	19	8	2	1
	Widowed	93	62	18	12	4	0	5
Kids Under 18:	Yes	405	41	22	25	7	5	1
	No	608	47	21	18	7	4	3
Household Income:	Under $20,000	299	58	16	16	4	4	2
	$20,000 to $39,999	368	43	20	25	6	3	2
	$40,000 to $59,999	133	27	30	25	10	8	1
	$60,000 or more	95	23	24	25	14	13	1
Job Type:	White Collar	224	29	25	27	11	6	2
	Blue Collar	313	43	25	21	7	3	2
	Not Employed	398	56	18	16	4	5	1
Community:	Urban	253	41	23	24	7	4	2
	Suburban	374	36	23	25	8	6	2
	Rural	290	53	21	16	7	3	1
Region:	Northeast	228	35	22	27	10	6	1
	Midwest	223	39	26	21	8	5	1
	South	356	55	18	19	4	1	3
	Mountain	54	43	24	18	7	7	2
	Pacific	153	42	23	19	7	8	2
Voter Registration:	Not	291	43	20	20	7	9	1
	Democrat	316	49	21	21	5	2	1
	Republican	210	44	21	23	8	2	1
	Independent	147	35	27	24	10	5	1
Born Again:	Yes	409	56	19	19	5	0	1
	No	604	36	23	23	8	7	2
Denominational Affiliation:	Protestant	550	51	21	20	5	1	2
	Baptist	209	57	18	19	4	1	2
	Catholic	221	38	24	23	9	4	2
	Lutheran	53	30	28	30	6	5	0
	Methodist	65	36	34	21	6	2	1
	Charis./Pent.	70	68	14	15	1	0	1
Attended Church This Week:	Yes	476	58	17	19	3	1	2
	No	534	33	25	23	10	7	2
Read Bible This Week:	Yes	479	61	18	16	2	0	2
	No	534	29	25	26	11	8	1

The next commandment is "Do not work on the day of worship." Does the way you live these days completely satisfy, mostly satisfy, somewhat satisfy, a little bit satisfy, or not at all satisfy that commandment?

		N	Completely	Mostly	Somewhat	A Little Bit	Not at All	Don't Know
Total Responding		1013	25%	20%	27%	10%	15%	3%
Gender:	Male	478	24	16	30	10	18	3
	Female	535	26	23	25	10	12	3
Age:	18 to 26	171	20	14	29	9	27	1
	27 to 45	402	23	21	29	11	14	2
	46 to 64	254	28	18	31	10	9	5
	65 Plus	157	35	26	19	9	7	4
Education:	High School or Less	666	30	18	28	9	12	2
	Some College	140	17	25	28	12	14	3
	College Graduate	201	15	21	25	12	23	4
Ethnicity:	White	729	25	20	27	12	13	2
	Black	139	29	20	27	3	17	4
	Hispanic	93	17	19	32	9	17	6
Marital:	Married	571	25	22	28	10	12	3
	Single	223	26	14	24	10	25	0
	Divorced/Separated	118	21	19	38	10	12	1
	Widowed	93	31	27	19	10	6	7
Kids Under 18:	Yes	405	23	19	29	10	17	2
	No	608	27	20	26	10	13	4
Household Income:	Under $20,000	299	32	18	28	7	11	3
	$20,000 to $39,999	368	24	18	28	11	16	3
	$40,000 to $59,999	133	16	23	28	15	17	0
	$60,000 or more	95	13	22	27	10	25	2
Job Type:	White Collar	224	16	19	28	14	20	3
	Blue Collar	313	24	22	30	9	12	3
	Not Employed	398	31	21	25	9	12	3
Community:	Urban	253	21	19	32	10	13	5
	Suburban	374	22	18	30	11	15	3
	Rural	290	29	23	23	11	14	0
Region:	Northeast	228	20	21	34	7	16	2
	Midwest	223	26	20	27	11	15	2
	South	356	31	20	27	9	9	4
	Mountain	54	26	24	17	17	13	3
	Pacific	153	17	17	24	14	24	4
Voter Registration:	Not	291	21	18	28	8	23	2
	Democrat	316	31	18	29	11	9	2
	Republican	210	22	22	25	12	15	4
	Independent	147	27	18	29	12	11	3
Born Again:	Yes	409	28	28	25	8	8	3
	No	604	23	15	29	11	19	3
Denominational Affiliation:	Protestant	550	28	23	26	10	9	3
	Baptist	209	36	25	24	7	4	5
	Catholic	221	24	21	34	10	10	1
	Lutheran	53	29	25	20	20	6	0
	Methodist	65	10	31	30	9	19	1
	Charis./Pent.	70	40	14	28	8	8	2
Attended Church This Week:	Yes	476	33	22	26	7	9	3
	No	534	18	18	29	12	19	3
Read Bible This Week:	Yes	479	32	24	25	6	9	4
	No	534	19	16	29	14	20	2

TABLE 85 267

The next commandment is "Honor your parents." Does the way you live these days completely satisfy, mostly satisfy, somewhat satisfy, a little bit satisfy, or not at all satisfy that commandment?

		N	Completely	Mostly	Somewhat	A Little Bit	Not at All	Don't Know
Total Responding		1013	77%	13%	6%	1%	0%	3%
Gender:	Male	478	74	13	9	2	0	2
	Female	535	79	13	4	0	0	3
Age:	18 to 26	171	73	17	8	1	0	1
	27 to 45	402	73	18	6	1	0	1
	46 to 64	254	86	5	5	0	0	4
	65 Plus	157	77	10	5	0	1	7
Education:	High School or Less	666	79	10	8	1	0	3
	Some College	140	75	15	7	0	0	3
	College Graduate	201	72	23	2	0	0	2
Ethnicity:	White	729	75	15	6	1	0	3
	Black	139	86	6	7	0	0	1
	Hispanic	93	73	13	13	1	0	0
Marital:	Married	571	79	14	4	0	0	3
	Single	223	72	17	8	2	0	1
	Divorced/Separated	118	73	7	17	1	0	1
	Widowed	93	81	8	4	1	2	5
Kids Under 18:	Yes	405	76	17	5	1	0	1
	No	608	77	11	7	1	0	4
Household Income:	Under $20,000	299	82	6	8	1	1	3
	$20,000 to $39,999	368	76	16	5	1	0	2
	$40,000 to $59,999	133	71	22	4	1	0	2
	$60,000 or more	95	72	19	8	0	0	1
Job Type:	White Collar	224	75	19	4	0	0	1
	Blue Collar	313	75	12	9	1	0	2
	Not Employed	398	79	10	6	0	0	4
Community:	Urban	253	80	12	6	1	0	1
	Suburban	374	73	15	9	0	0	3
	Rural	290	79	13	4	2	0	3
Region:	Northeast	228	79	11	7	1	0	1
	Midwest	223	78	13	6	0	0	2
	South	356	78	12	4	1	1	4
	Mountain	54	66	19	8	2	0	5
	Pacific	153	71	17	10	0	0	2
Voter Registration:	Not	291	74	12	9	1	1	3
	Democrat	316	82	12	4	0	0	2
	Republican	210	75	16	5	1	0	3
	Independent	147	72	17	9	1	0	2
Born Again:	Yes	409	82	10	4	1	0	3
	No	604	73	15	8	0	0	3
Denominational Affiliation:	Protestant	550	78	12	5	1	0	4
	Baptist	209	81	10	4	1	0	5
	Catholic	221	79	14	6	0	0	1
	Lutheran	53	79	17	3	1	0	0
	Methodist	65	78	15	4	0	3	1
	Charis./Pent.	70	75	5	13	2	0	5
Attended Church This Week:	Yes	476	82	11	4	1	0	3
	No	534	72	16	9	1	0	3
Read Bible This Week:	Yes	479	80	10	6	1	0	3
	No	534	74	16	7	1	0	2

TABLE 86

The next commandment is "Do not commit murder." Does the way you live these days completely satisfy, mostly satisfy, somewhat satisfy, a little bit satisfy, or not at all satisfy that commandment?

		N	Completely	Mostly	Somewhat	A Little Bit	Not at All	Don't Know
Total Responding		1013	93%	1%	2%	0%	2%	2%
Gender:	Male	478	90	2	4	1	1	2
	Female	535	95	1	0	0	2	1
Age:	18 to 26	171	88	3	4	0	4	1
	27 to 45	402	95	1	0	1	2	1
	46 to 64	254	94	1	1	0	1	3
	65 Plus	157	95	1	3	0	1	0
Education:	High School or Less	666	92	2	2	0	2	1
	Some College	140	92	3	1	1	1	2
	College Graduate	201	95	0	1	0	1	2
Ethnicity:	White	729	95	1	1	0	1	1
	Black	139	90	2	2	1	5	1
	Hispanic	93	84	4	8	0	0	4
Marital:	Married	571	96	1	1	0	1	1
	Single	223	88	2	6	1	2	0
	Divorced/Separated	118	91	3	3	0	2	1
	Widowed	93	92	1	0	0	3	4
Kids Under 18:	Yes	405	94	1	1	0	3	1
	No	608	92	2	3	0	1	2
Household Income:	Under $20,000	299	93	2	0	1	3	2
	$20,000 to $39,999	368	94	1	3	0	1	1
	$40,000 to $59,999	133	96	0	3	1	0	0
	$60,000 or more	95	89	2	7	1	1	1
Job Type:	White Collar	224	95	0	2	0	1	1
	Blue Collar	313	94	1	1	0	2	2
	Not Employed	398	91	2	3	1	2	1
Community:	Urban	253	91	1	2	0	4	2
	Suburban	374	93	2	3	0	1	2
	Rural	290	95	2	2	1	1	0
Region:	Northeast	228	95	2	1	0	1	1
	Midwest	223	93	2	1	0	3	0
	South	356	94	0	1	1	2	3
	Mountain	54	90	3	5	0	0	2
	Pacific	153	87	3	7	1	2	1
Voter Registration:	Not	291	89	2	6	0	3	1
	Democrat	316	93	1	0	1	3	2
	Republican	210	94	2	1	0	0	1
	Independent	147	97	1	1	0	0	1
Born Again:	Yes	409	97	1	0	0	1	1
	No	604	90	2	3	1	2	2
Denominational Affiliation:	Protestant	550	94	2	0	0	2	1
	Baptist	209	93	2	1	1	2	2
	Catholic	221	94	3	1	0	1	2
	Lutheran	53	95	5	0	0	0	0
	Methodist	65	91	3	1	0	4	1
	Charis./Pent.	70	98	0	0	0	2	1
Attended Church This Week:	Yes	476	95	2	0	0	1	2
	No	534	91	1	4	1	3	1
Read Bible This Week:	Yes	479	93	2	1	0	2	2
	No	534	92	1	3	1	2	1

TABLE 87   269

The next commandment is "Do not commit adultery." Does the way you live these days completely satisfy, mostly satisfy, somewhat satisfy, a little bit satisfy, or not at all satisfy that commandment?

		N	Completely	Mostly	Somewhat	A Little Bit	Not at All	Don't Know
Total Responding		1013	82%	5%	5%	2%	4%	2%
Gender:	Male	478	72	7	8	4	6	2
	Female	535	91	2	3	0	3	1
Age:	18 to 26	171	64	4	9	5	17	1
	27 to 45	402	83	6	6	2	2	2
	46 to 64	254	87	4	3	1	2	2
	65 Plus	157	91	4	4	0	0	1
Education:	High School or Less	666	82	4	5	3	5	1
	Some College	140	80	5	8	3	1	3
	College Graduate	201	83	7	3	1	4	2
Ethnicity:	White	729	87	4	4	1	3	1
	Black	139	72	5	9	1	11	2
	Hispanic	93	63	12	9	11	4	0
Marital:	Married	571	91	3	3	1	1	2
	Single	223	63	7	9	8	12	1
	Divorced/Separated	118	72	7	10	2	7	1
	Widowed	93	87	5	3	0	4	0
Kids Under 18:	Yes	405	83	3	4	2	7	2
	No	608	81	5	6	3	3	1
Household Income:	Under $20,000	299	79	5	7	2	7	0
	$20,000 to $39,999	368	84	6	4	2	3	2
	$40,000 to $59,999	133	82	7	4	4	2	2
	$60,000 or more	95	80	3	3	7	6	1
Job Type:	White Collar	224	85	4	3	2	2	3
	Blue Collar	313	81	4	6	3	5	2
	Not Employed	398	81	5	6	3	5	0
Community:	Urban	253	79	7	5	2	6	1
	Suburban	374	78	4	8	4	4	3
	Rural	290	88	4	4	1	2	0
Region:	Northeast	228	81	4	8	2	4	1
	Midwest	223	78	4	9	1	7	1
	South	356	84	5	3	1	4	2
	Mountain	54	86	0	7	5	0	2
	Pacific	153	81	8	2	6	3	1
Voter Registration:	Not	291	73	6	7	6	7	1
	Democrat	316	86	4	3	1	5	1
	Republican	210	89	4	3	1	2	1
	Independent	147	77	4	11	2	3	3
Born Again:	Yes	409	90	4	3	1	1	1
	No	604	76	5	7	3	7	2
Denominational Affiliation:	Protestant	550	86	4	4	1	4	2
	Baptist	209	86	4	3	2	2	3
	Catholic	221	83	6	7	1	3	0
	Lutheran	53	80	7	8	0	4	1
	Methodist	65	86	4	2	1	6	1
	Charis./Pent.	70	87	0	7	0	4	1
Attended Church This Week:	Yes	476	88	4	3	0	3	2
	No	534	77	5	7	4	6	1
Read Bible This Week:	Yes	479	87	4	4	1	2	2
	No	534	77	5	6	3	6	1

The next commandment is "Do not steal." Does the way you live these days completely satisfy, mostly satisfy, somewhat satisfy, a little bit satisfy, or not at all satisfy that commandment?

		N	Completely	Mostly	Somewhat	A Little Bit	Not at All	Don't Know
Total Responding		1013	86%	7%	3%	0%	2%	1%
Gender:	Male	478	77	12	6	1	3	2
	Female	535	94	3	1	0	1	1
Age:	18 to 26	171	72	12	7	2	7	1
	27 to 45	402	87	8	3	0	2	1
	46 to 64	254	91	4	3	0	0	2
	65 Plus	157	94	6	0	0	0	0
Education:	High School or Less	666	86	6	4	0	3	1
	Some College	140	87	9	2	0	0	2
	College Graduate	201	85	9	1	1	1	2
Ethnicity:	White	729	89	6	2	0	2	1
	Black	139	82	7	7	0	3	1
	Hispanic	93	72	12	11	2	3	0
Marital:	Married	571	88	6	3	0	1	1
	Single	223	76	10	8	1	4	0
	Divorced/Separated	118	88	8	1	0	1	1
	Widowed	93	94	4	0	0	3	0
Kids Under 18:	Yes	405	83	8	4	0	4	1
	No	608	88	7	3	0	1	1
Household Income:	Under $20,000	299	85	7	3	0	4	0
	$20,000 to $39,999	368	86	8	1	0	2	2
	$40,000 to $59,999	133	87	8	5	0	0	0
	$60,000 or more	95	81	5	8	3	2	1
Job Type:	White Collar	224	89	6	3	1	1	1
	Blue Collar	313	81	8	5	0	3	2
	Not Employed	398	88	7	3	1	1	0
Community:	Urban	253	82	12	4	0	0	1
	Suburban	374	83	7	5	1	2	2
	Rural	290	90	5	1	1	2	0
Region:	Northeast	228	86	9	3	0	1	0
	Midwest	223	80	7	5	2	6	0
	South	356	91	4	2	0	0	2
	Mountain	54	74	16	6	0	0	4
	Pacific	153	85	8	4	0	2	1
Voter Registration:	Not	291	77	11	6	1	4	1
	Democrat	316	90	6	3	1	1	1
	Republican	210	90	3	2	0	3	1
	Independent	147	88	8	2	0	1	1
Born Again:	Yes	409	91	6	1	1	0	1
	No	604	82	8	5	0	3	1
Denominational Affiliation:	Protestant	550	91	5	2	0	1	1
	Baptist	209	94	3	0	0	1	2
	Catholic	221	84	12	2	1	2	0
	Lutheran	53	90	3	0	0	6	0
	Methodist	65	82	11	3	0	3	1
	Charis./Pent.	70	92	2	4	0	2	1
Attended Church This Week:	Yes	476	89	7	2	0	1	1
	No	534	83	7	5	1	3	1
Read Bible This Week:	Yes	479	88	7	3	0	1	1
	No	534	84	7	4	1	3	1

TABLE 89   271

The next commandment is "Do not lie." Does the way you live these days completely satisfy, mostly satisfy, somewhat satisfy, a little bit satisfy, or not at all satisfy that commandment?

		N	Completely	Mostly	Somewhat	A Little Bit	Not at All	Don't Know
Total Responding		1013	48%	28%	17%	3%	3%	1%
Gender:	Male	478	42	29	17	4	5	2
	Female	535	53	27	16	3	1	1
Age:	18 to 26	171	28	27	26	9	8	2
	27 to 45	402	43	34	18	2	1	1
	46 to 64	254	58	22	15	3	0	2
	65 Plus	157	64	24	7	2	3	0
Education:	High School or Less	666	52	24	16	4	4	1
	Some College	140	39	36	20	3	0	2
	College Graduate	201	40	38	17	2	1	1
Ethnicity:	White	729	47	32	16	2	2	1
	Black	139	46	16	19	12	5	3
	Hispanic	93	44	27	19	4	6	0
Marital:	Married	571	51	31	14	2	1	1
	Single	223	32	29	24	6	7	2
	Divorced/Separated	118	45	25	26	3	0	1
	Widowed	93	68	15	5	8	4	0
Kids Under 18:	Yes	405	42	29	21	5	2	2
	No	608	52	27	14	3	4	1
Household Income:	Under $20,000	299	58	20	14	4	4	1
	$20,000 to $39,999	368	44	32	18	3	1	1
	$40,000 to $59,999	133	38	35	22	1	2	2
	$60,000 or more	95	41	27	17	7	7	1
Job Type:	White Collar	224	43	38	14	2	1	2
	Blue Collar	313	46	26	21	4	1	3
	Not Employed	398	53	25	12	4	5	0
Community:	Urban	253	43	32	18	6	0	1
	Suburban	374	41	27	21	4	4	2
	Rural	290	55	27	14	1	3	0
Region:	Northeast	228	44	27	21	4	4	1
	Midwest	223	43	27	21	3	5	0
	South	356	54	27	12	4	1	3
	Mountain	54	47	36	14	1	0	2
	Pacific	153	46	31	14	3	6	1
Voter Registration:	Not	291	37	30	19	6	7	2
	Democrat	316	55	24	14	4	2	1
	Republican	210	46	31	20	1	1	1
	Independent	147	51	31	13	2	2	1
Born Again:	Yes	409	53	28	15	2	1	1
	No	604	44	28	18	4	4	2
Denominational Affiliation:	Protestant	550	50	28	16	3	1	1
	Baptist	209	52	27	13	4	1	2
	Catholic	221	47	30	18	3	1	1
	Lutheran	53	51	23	18	5	3	0
	Methodist	65	40	38	18	4	0	1
	Charis./Pent.	70	61	21	13	5	0	1
Attended Church This Week:	Yes	476	57	26	13	3	1	1
	No	534	40	30	20	4	4	2
Read Bible This Week:	Yes	479	58	26	11	3	1	1
	No	534	38	30	21	4	4	2

TABLE 90

The next commandment is "Do not be jealous of the things other people have." Does the way you live these days completely satisfy, mostly satisfy, somewhat satisfy, a little bit satisfy, or not at all satisfy that commandment?

		N	Completely	Mostly	Somewhat	A Little Bit	Not at All	Don't Know
Total Responding		1013	53%	23%	13%	4%	5%	1%
Gender:	Male	478	49	21	15	6	7	2
	Female	535	57	24	12	3	3	1
Age:	18 to 26	171	38	24	18	7	13	1
	27 to 45	402	43	31	16	4	5	1
	46 to 64	254	65	15	11	5	2	2
	65 Plus	157	78	14	3	2	3	0
Education:	High School or Less	666	59	17	11	5	7	1
	Some College	140	50	27	17	3	1	2
	College Graduate	201	36	40	17	3	2	2
Ethnicity:	White	729	52	26	14	3	3	1
	Black	139	63	9	9	5	14	1
	Hispanic	93	45	21	15	11	8	0
Marital:	Married	571	56	24	12	3	3	1
	Single	223	37	24	22	7	9	0
	Divorced/Separated	118	51	23	12	3	8	3
	Widowed	93	83	10	1	2	4	0
Kids Under 18:	Yes	405	47	27	15	6	5	1
	No	608	58	20	12	3	6	2
Household Income:	Under $20,000	299	61	15	10	5	9	1
	$20,000 to $39,999	368	52	23	14	5	4	2
	$40,000 to $59,999	133	43	37	15	3	3	0
	$60,000 or more	95	41	28	24	4	2	1
Job Type:	White Collar	224	45	31	17	2	4	2
	Blue Collar	313	56	20	14	5	4	2
	Not Employed	398	58	19	9	5	7	1
Community:	Urban	253	52	22	16	4	5	2
	Suburban	374	50	25	15	4	5	2
	Rural	290	52	26	13	5	3	1
Region:	Northeast	228	49	25	17	2	6	1
	Midwest	223	45	24	16	4	9	2
	South	356	58	21	9	6	4	2
	Mountain	54	66	20	9	3	0	2
	Pacific	153	56	22	13	5	4	1
Voter Registration:	Not	291	46	21	14	7	10	1
	Democrat	316	66	18	8	2	5	1
	Republican	210	47	29	17	4	1	1
	Independent	147	44	29	18	3	4	2
Born Again:	Yes	409	57	23	10	4	4	1
	No	604	50	22	15	4	6	2
Denominational Affiliation:	Protestant	550	57	22	11	5	3	2
	Baptist	209	64	18	9	3	4	2
	Catholic	221	51	26	15	1	6	1
	Lutheran	53	41	31	12	11	3	1
	Methodist	65	63	24	9	2	1	1
	Charis./Pent.	70	73	11	5	8	3	1
Attended Church This Week:	Yes	476	57	23	12	3	3	2
	No	534	50	22	15	5	7	1
Read Bible This Week:	Yes	479	59	21	7	5	6	2
	No	534	48	24	19	3	5	1

TABLE 91   273

I'm going to read some of the beliefs people have about God. Please tell me which one of these descriptions is closest to what you, personally, believe about God.

(See legend on next page for heading descriptions)

		N	A	B	C	D	E	F	Don't Know
Total Responding		1013	2%	73%	10%	2%	6%	1%	6%
Gender:	Male	478	2	69	9	4	7	2	8
	Female	535	2	78	10	1	6	0	3
Age:	18 to 26	171	3	64	11	5	8	2	7
	27 to 45	402	2	68	12	3	8	2	6
	46 to 64	254	2	82	8	0	5	1	2
	65 Plus	157	1	83	6	1	3	0	5
Education:	High School or Less	666	2	77	8	2	5	0	5
	Some College	140	2	73	11	2	6	2	4
	College Graduate	201	3	60	14	2	9	4	7
Ethnicity:	White	729	2	73	10	2	7	1	5
	Black	139	1	81	8	0	5	0	5
	Hispanic	93	4	64	6	10	5	1	9
Marital:	Married	571	1	77	10	1	5	1	4
	Single	223	3	59	10	5	10	2	10
	Divorced/Separated	118	1	76	10	5	6	0	1
	Widowed	93	6	78	4	1	3	0	8
Kids Under 18:	Yes	405	2	70	11	1	8	2	6
	No	608	2	76	8	3	5	1	5
Household Income:	Under $20,000	299	2	78	6	4	4	0	5
	$20,000 to $39,999	368	2	74	11	1	8	1	4
	$40,000 to $59,999	133	0	67	17	2	10	2	2
	$60,000 or more	95	2	55	11	2	11	3	15
Job Type:	White Collar	224	2	68	11	2	10	3	5
	Blue Collar	313	1	79	9	2	5	1	3
	Not Employed	398	2	72	9	3	5	0	8
Community:	Urban	253	2	75	6	3	7	2	4
	Suburban	374	2	67	13	4	7	1	7
	Rural	290	1	78	10	0	6	1	4
Region:	Northeast	228	3	66	9	6	7	3	6
	Midwest	223	0	72	11	1	9	1	7
	South	356	2	82	8	1	4	1	3
	Mountain	54	5	72	7	0	8	0	8
	Pacific	153	1	68	12	3	6	1	9
Voter Registration:	Not	291	2	70	9	4	6	1	8
	Democrat	316	3	76	10	0	6	1	4
	Republican	210	1	78	9	0	7	2	3
	Independent	147	2	66	9	7	8	1	6
Born Again:	Yes	409	0	93	5	0	2	0	0
	No	604	3	60	13	4	9	2	9
Denominational Affiliation:	Protestant	550	1	83	9	1	4	0	3
	Baptist	209	0	87	9	0	3	0	1
	Catholic	221	4	71	11	4	8	1	2
	Lutheran	53	1	80	5	2	7	0	5
	Methodist	65	1	68	13	4	8	0	6
	Charis./Pent.	70	0	98	0	0	0	0	2
Attended Church This Week:	Yes	476	1	87	6	1	2	0	2
	No	534	2	61	13	4	10	2	9
Read Bible This Week:	Yes	479	2	85	6	2	2	0	3
	No	534	2	63	13	2	11	2	8

A. "Everyone is God."

B. "God is the all-powerful, all-knowing and perfect Creator of the universe, who rules the world today."

C. "God is the total realization of personal, human potential."

D. "There are many gods, each with different power and authority."

E. "God represents a state of higher consciousness that a person may reach."

F. "There is no such thing as God."

TABLE 92 275

Thinking about religion, do you consider yourself to be Christian, Jewish, Muslim, atheist, or of another religious faith?

		N	Christian	Jewish	Muslim	Atheist	None	Other	Don't Know
Total Responding		1013	88%	2%	0%	2%	3%	4%	2%
Gender:	Male	478	81	2	0	4	4	6	3
	Female	535	93	1	0	0	2	2	0
Age:	18 to 26	171	79	1	0	6	8	5	2
	27 to 45	402	87	2	0	1	3	5	2
	46 to 64	254	95	2	1	2	0	1	0
	65 Plus	157	91	2	0	0	2	3	2
Education:	High School or Less	666	90	0	0	1	3	3	2
	Some College	140	89	1	0	1	4	5	1
	College Graduate	201	80	6	1	4	2	6	1
Ethnicity:	White	729	89	2	0	2	2	2	2
	Black	139	81	0	1	0	5	13	0
	Hispanic	93	91	0	0	7	1	1	0
Marital:	Married	571	90	2	0	1	1	3	2
	Single	223	79	2	0	5	8	6	0
	Divorced/Separated	118	92	0	0	0	2	5	1
	Widowed	93	89	0	0	0	3	5	3
Kids Under 18:	Yes	405	86	1	1	2	4	5	2
	No	608	89	2	0	2	2	4	2
Household	Under $20,000	299	89	1	0	2	2	4	2
Income:	$20,000 to $39,999	368	90	1	1	1	2	4	1
	$40,000 to $59,999	133	85	1	0	2	8	2	2
	$60,000 or more	95	81	7	0	7	2	3	1
Job Type:	White Collar	224	85	4	1	3	3	4	1
	Blue Collar	313	89	0	0	1	4	3	3
	Not Employed	398	89	1	0	1	3	5	1
Community:	Urban	253	89	1	1	2	2	4	2
	Suburban	374	86	3	0	3	3	3	2
	Rural	290	89	1	0	1	3	4	2
Region:	Northeast	228	82	4	0	2	3	7	2
	Midwest	223	87	1	0	1	4	5	2
	South	356	93	1	0	1	2	1	2
	Mountain	54	88	0	0	0	6	7	0
	Pacific	153	85	3	1	5	2	3	1
Voter	Not	291	78	2	0	4	7	8	1
Registration:	Democrat	316	93	2	0	1	0	1	3
	Republican	210	94	1	0	2	1	2	0
	Independent	147	88	1	0	1	3	4	2
Born Again:	Yes	409	97	0	0	0	1	2	1
	No	604	81	3	0	3	4	6	2
Denominational	Protestant	550	100	0	0	0	0	0	0
Affiliation:	Baptist	209	100	0	0	0	0	0	0
	Catholic	221	100	0	0	0	0	0	0
	Lutheran	53	100	0	0	0	0	0	0
	Methodist	65	100	0	0	0	0	0	0
	Charis./Pent.	70	100	0	0	0	0	0	0
Attended Church	Yes	476	96	1	0	0	0	2	1
This Week:	No	534	80	2	0	4	5	6	2
Read Bible	Yes	479	93	0	0	1	0	4	2
This Week:	No	534	83	3	0	3	5	4	2

What is the denomination of the church that you attend most often? (Data represents only those denominations that include more than 5% of the church-going populaton.)

		N	Baptist	Catholic	Lutheran	Methodist	Pentecostal/ Foursquare
Total Responding		888	24%	25%	6%	7%	5%
Gender:	Male	388	20	28	7	7	5
	Female	500	26	23	5	7	4
Age:	18 to 26	134	19	31	6	8	3
	27 to 45	349	21	25	5	7	5
	46 to 64	240	26	28	10	6	5
	65 Plus	143	32	14	3	10	3
Education:	High School or Less	599	26	24	6	6	6
	Some College	125	19	27	4	10	3
	College Graduate	160	19	26	9	10	1
Ethnicity:	White	652	22	24	7	9	4
	Black	113	53	7	2	5	9
	Hispanic	84	2	62	5	0	2
Marital:	Married	517	23	25	7	8	4
	Single	176	21	27	4	6	2
	Divorced/Separated	109	31	27	4	7	8
	Widowed	83	27	17	4	10	7
Kids Under 18:	Yes	350	20	25	6	8	5
	No	539	26	25	6	7	4
Household Income:	Under $20,000	265	28	23	4	7	10
	$20,000 to $39,999	330	25	23	7	8	3
	$40,000 to $59,999	113	16	38	6	8	1
	$60,000 or more	77	10	26	11	8	2
Job Type:	White Collar	189	19	25	7	9	2
	Blue Collar	280	23	25	8	7	7
	Not Employed	352	27	25	5	7	4
Community:	Urban	225	20	28	5	8	7
	Suburban	323	22	26	9	6	3
	Rural	260	29	21	5	9	3
Region:	Northeast	186	11	48	4	6	2
	Midwest	195	18	21	15	12	1
	South	330	43	13	3	8	7
	Mountain	47	4	36	4	1	5
	Pacific	129	9	24	3	4	6
Voter Registration:	Not	228	18	26	5	4	7
	Democrat	294	33	28	3	8	4
	Republican	198	16	13	10	11	4
	Independent	130	23	34	7	5	2
Born Again:	Yes	397	32	12	5	8	9
	No	492	17	35	6	7	1
Denominational Affiliation:	Protestant	550	38	0	10	12	7
	Baptist	209	100	0	0	0	0
	Catholic	221	0	100	0	0	0
	Lutheran	53	0	0	100	0	0
	Methodist	65	0	0	0	100	0
	Charis./Pent.	70	0	0	0	0	58
Attended Church This Week:	Yes	459	23	26	6	6	7
	No	429	24	24	6	9	2
Read Bible This Week:	Yes	445	31	15	5	6	7
	No	444	16	35	7	9	2

TABLE 94 277

In a typical month, on how many weekends would you attend church worship services at a church? (Asked of people who considered themselves to be Christian.)

		N	One	Two	Three	Four or More	None	Don't Know
Total Responding		888	13%	12%	10%	41%	21%	3%
Gender:	Male	388	15	13	8	38	24	3
	Female	500	12	11	11	44	18	4
Age:	18 to 26	134	20	19	7	32	19	3
	27 to 45	349	16	14	11	33	24	1
	46 to 64	240	11	8	9	53	17	3
	65 Plus	143	4	8	9	53	16	10
Education:	High School or Less	599	13	12	9	43	20	4
	Some College	125	16	12	12	35	22	3
	College Graduate	160	13	12	10	41	22	2
Ethnicity:	White	652	14	9	10	42	22	4
	Black	113	11	21	14	38	11	5
	Hispanic	84	19	22	5	39	15	0
Marital:	Married	517	12	11	11	46	17	3
	Single	176	20	14	7	31	26	2
	Divorced/Separated	109	14	16	9	33	27	0
	Widowed	83	8	4	10	46	19	13
Kids Under 18:	Yes	350	15	14	11	39	18	2
	No	539	12	11	9	42	22	4
Household Income:	Under $20,000	265	7	11	8	47	22	4
	$20,000 to $39,999	330	16	14	12	37	19	2
	$40,000 to $59,999	113	19	15	10	39	16	2
	$60,000 or more	77	18	5	9	37	30	0
Job Type:	White Collar	189	13	16	13	35	21	2
	Blue Collar	280	19	11	10	39	20	1
	Not Employed	352	8	12	9	46	20	6
Community:	Urban	225	18	12	9	40	19	2
	Suburban	323	12	12	10	38	24	3
	Rural	260	13	11	9	43	21	2
Region:	Northeast	186	13	14	14	38	20	2
	Midwest	195	11	10	10	40	26	3
	South	330	13	13	7	47	15	5
	Mountain	47	18	5	8	38	29	2
	Pacific	129	18	9	11	34	25	2
Voter Registration:	Not	228	15	11	10	39	23	2
	Democrat	294	16	11	8	42	19	5
	Republican	198	9	8	16	47	17	4
	Independent	130	13	19	7	32	27	2
Born Again:	Yes	397	12	8	12	57	9	2
	No	492	15	15	8	29	30	4
Denominational Affiliation:	Protestant	550	12	10	12	42	20	4
	Baptist	209	11	14	8	42	20	5
	Catholic	221	18	17	4	45	12	4
	Lutheran	53	14	11	14	37	23	2
	Methodist	65	27	6	15	34	14	4
	Charis./Pent.	70	6	5	12	60	15	2
Attended Church This Week:	Yes	459	4	10	11	71	3	2
	No	429	23	14	8	9	40	5
Read Bible This Week:	Yes	445	5	12	12	59	8	4
	No	444	22	12	8	23	33	3

Which one of the following statements best describes your church attendance, not including when you are out of town? (Asked of people who consider themselves to be Christian and who attend church services in a typical month.)

		N	Always Attend Same Church Each Time	Usually Attend Same Church/Go to Others	Divide Attendance Between 2+ Churches	Don't Know
Total Responding		676	61%	29%	9%	0%
Gender:	Male	284	59	30	10	1
	Female	392	62	29	8	0
Age:	18 to 26	104	59	31	9	1
	27 to 45	262	59	29	12	0
	46 to 64	194	61	30	8	1
	65 Plus	106	70	26	3	1
Education:	High School or Less	457	61	28	11	1
	Some College	93	59	35	6	0
	College Graduate	121	62	32	5	1
Ethnicity:	White	485	64	28	7	1
	Black	95	53	31	16	0
	Hispanic	72	47	37	16	0
Marital:	Married	411	66	27	6	1
	Single	126	59	28	13	1
	Divorced/Separated	79	46	41	13	0
	Widowed	57	55	31	14	0
Kids Under 18:	Yes	278	60	31	9	0
	No	398	62	28	9	1
Household Income:	Under $20,000	195	55	29	16	0
	$20,000 to $39,999	259	64	30	6	0
	$40,000 to $59,999	93	65	29	4	2
	$60,000 or more	54	71	22	6	1
Job Type:	White Collar	145	62	30	8	1
	Blue Collar	220	58	27	15	1
	Not Employed	263	62	33	5	0
Community:	Urban	178	59	25	15	1
	Suburban	234	59	34	6	0
	Rural	199	68	28	4	0
Region:	Northeast	145	56	34	8	2
	Midwest	139	68	25	6	1
	South	265	60	31	9	0
	Mountain	33	72	25	3	0
	Pacific	94	59	26	16	0
Voter Registration:	Not	170	59	30	11	0
	Democrat	225	60	30	8	1
	Republican	157	68	26	6	0
	Independent	91	58	33	7	1
Born Again:	Yes	351	60	31	9	0
	No	324	62	28	9	1
Denominational Affiliation:	Protestant	419	63	29	8	0
	Baptist	158	64	27	10	0
	Catholic	185	57	31	11	1
	Lutheran	40	80	11	6	3
	Methodist	53	52	39	9	0
	Charis./Pent.	58	46	35	18	0
Attended Church This Week:	Yes	439	65	29%	6	1
	No	237	55	30	15	0
Read Bible This Week:	Yes	390	62	31	7	0
	No	285	60	27	12	1

TABLE 96   279

Is it likely that during the next 12 months you will change from the church you currently attend most often to a different church? (People who consider themselves to be Christian, attended church services in the last month, always or usually attend the same church.)

		N	Very Likely	Somewhat Likely	Not Too Likely	Not at All Likely	Don't Know
Total Responding		612	4%	11%	13%	71%	1%
Gender:	Male	253	5	11	13	68	3
	Female	359	4	11	13	72	0
Age:	18 to 26	94	3	12	18	66	1
	27 to 45	231	4	14	16	65	2
	46 to 64	177	4	8	10	77	1
	65 Plus	102	4	6	8	80	1
Education:	High School or Less	407	3	12	12	72	1
	Some College	88	4	10	15	69	2
	College Graduate	114	7	10	14	69	0
Ethnicity:	White	449	5	10	12	73	1
	Black	80	3	10	17	70	0
	Hispanic	60	0	20	7	69	4
Marital:	Married	383	5	8	14	73	1
	Single	109	3	12	17	68	0
	Divorced/Separated	68	4	31	8	54	3
	Widowed	49	1	8	6	82	3
Kids Under 18:	Yes	253	4	12	18	66	1
	No	359	5	11	10	74	1
Household Income:	Under $20,000	165	5	17	12	64	3
	$20,000 to $39,999	242	2	9	15	73	1
	$40,000 to $59,999	88	7	4	15	74	0
	$60,000 or more	50	7	6	11	76	0
Job Type:	White Collar	133	8	7	12	72	0
	Blue Collar	186	2	11	16	69	2
	Not Employed	247	3	13	11	72	1
Community:	Urban	150	5	11	10	72	2
	Suburban	218	3	13	16	68	0
	Rural	191	5	10	10	73	2
Region:	Northeast	131	6	18	14	61	0
	Midwest	130	2	8	10	78	2
	South	240	6	9	13	72	0
	Mountain	32	0	12	3	81	4
	Pacific	80	1	10	19	66	4
Voter Registration:	Not	151	4	19	12	65	2
	Democrat	204	1	5	16	78	0
	Republican	148	5	9	12	70	3
	Independent	84	8	19	11	60	2
Born Again:	Yes	320	4	11	15	69	2
	No	292	4	11	11	73	1
Denominational Affiliation:	Protestant	384	5	10	15	68	1
	Baptist	142	7	6	17	70	0
	Catholic	163	3	14	8	73	2
	Lutheran	37	1	3	4	91	0
	Methodist	49	3	10	17	67	3
	Charis./Pent.	48	2	15	13	63	6
Attended Church This Week:	Yes	411	4	9	13	73	2
	No	202	4	16	13	66	1
Read Bible This Week:	Yes	362	4	12	14	68	1
	No	250	4	10	11	74	1

TABLE 97

Are you currently involved in "regularly teaching a Sunday School class"?

		N	Yes	No	Don't Know
Total Responding		1013	8%	91%	0%
Gender:	Male	478	5	95	0
	Female	535	11	88	0
Age:	18 to 26	171	5	95	0
	27 to 45	402	7	92	1
	46 to 64	254	12	88	0
	65 Plus	157	8	92	0
Education:	High School or Less	666	8	92	0
	Some College	140	12	87	0
	College Graduate	201	8	92	0
Ethnicity:	White	729	7	92	0
	Black	139	12	88	0
	Hispanic	93	11	89	0
Marital:	Married	571	10	89	1
	Single	223	4	96	0
	Divorced/Separated	118	5	95	0
	Widowed	93	11	89	0
Kids Under 18:	Yes	405	11	88	1
	No	608	7	93	0
Household Income:	Under $20,000	299	6	93	1
	$20,000 to $39,999	368	9	90	0
	$40,000 to $59,999	133	6	94	0
	$60,000 or more	95	6	94	0
Job Type:	White Collar	224	9	90	1
	Blue Collar	313	8	92	0
	Not Employed	398	9	91	0
Community:	Urban	253	8	92	0
	Suburban	374	7	92	1
	Rural	290	11	89	0
Region:	Northeast	228	9	90	1
	Midwest	223	4	96	0
	South	356	10	89	0
	Mountain	54	11	89	0
	Pacific	153	7	93	0
Voter Registration:	Not	291	4	95	0
	Democrat	316	10	90	1
	Republican	210	11	89	0
	Independent	147	7	93	0
Born Again:	Yes	409	13	87	0
	No	604	5	94	0
Denominational Affiliation:	Protestant	550	10	90	0
	Baptist	209	12	88	0
	Catholic	221	3	96	1
	Lutheran	53	10	90	0
	Methodist	65	5	95	0
	Charis./Pent.	70	13	87	0
Attended Church This Week:	Yes	476	16	84	0
	No	534	2	98	0
Read Bible This Week:	Yes	479	14	86	0
	No	534	3	97	0

TABLE 98   281

Are you currently involved in "participating in a small group Bible study, fellowship group, or prayer group, other than a Sunday School class"?

		N	Yes	No	Don't Know
Total Responding		1013	25%	74%	1%
Gender:	Male	478	20	79	1
	Female	535	30	69	0
Age:	18 to 26	171	15	85	1
	27 to 45	402	22	77	1
	46 to 64	254	37	63	0
	65 Plus	157	27	72	1
Education:	High School or Less	666	26	73	0
	Some College	140	28	70	1
	College Graduate	201	21	79	0
Ethnicity:	White	729	24	76	1
	Black	139	39	60	1
	Hispanic	93	19	81	0
Marital:	Married	571	28	72	1
	Single	223	20	80	0
	Divorced/Separated	118	21	79	0
	Widowed	93	31	69	0
Kids Under 18:	Yes	405	24	75	1
	No	608	26	74	0
Household Income:	Under $20,000	299	32	67	1
	$20,000 to $39,999	368	24	76	0
	$40,000 to $59,999	133	20	80	0
	$60,000 or more	95	18	82	0
Job Type:	White Collar	224	25	73	1
	Blue Collar	313	26	73	1
	Not Employed	398	27	73	0
Community:	Urban	253	27	73	0
	Suburban	374	21	78	1
	Rural	290	28	72	0
Region:	Northeast	228	13	86	1
	Midwest	223	24	75	1
	South	356	34	65	1
	Mountain	54	26	74	0
	Pacific	153	24	76	0
Voter Registration:	Not	291	22	77	1
	Democrat	316	29	70	1
	Republican	210	27	73	0
	Independent	147	20	79	0
Born Again:	Yes	409	44	56	0
	No	604	13	86	1
Denominational Affiliation:	Protestant	550	35	64	0
	Baptist	209	33	66	1
	Catholic	221	9	90	1
	Lutheran	53	32	68	0
	Methodist	65	25	74	1
	Charis./Pent.	70	58	42	0
Attended Church This Week:	Yes	476	42	57	0
	No	534	10	89	1
Read Bible This Week:	Yes	479	43	56	0
	No	534	9	90	1

TABLE 99

Are you currently involved in "serving as a leader in the church, on a board or committee"?

		N	Yes	No	Don't Know
Total Responding		1013	13%	87%	0%
Gender:	Male	478	11	88	0
	Female	535	14	86	0
Age:	18 to 26	171	7	93	0
	27 to 45	402	11	89	0
	46 to 64	254	19	81	0
	65 Plus	157	13	87	0
Education:	High School or Less	666	11	89	0
	Some College	140	19	81	0
	College Graduate	201	14	86	0
Ethnicity:	White	729	11	88	0
	Black	139	26	74	0
	Hispanic	93	8	92	0
Marital:	Married	571	17	83	0
	Single	223	6	94	0
	Divorced/Separated	118	7	93	0
	Widowed	93	14	86	0
Kids Under 18:	Yes	405	15	85	0
	No	608	12	88	0
Household Income:	Under $20,000	299	12	88	1
	$20,000 to $39,999	368	12	88	0
	$40,000 to $59,999	133	12	88	0
	$60,000 or more	95	14	86	0
Job Type:	White Collar	224	16	83	1
	Blue Collar	313	14	86	0
	Not Employed	398	11	89	0
Community:	Urban	253	11	89	0
	Suburban	374	13	86	0
	Rural	290	16	84	0
Region:	Northeast	228	11	89	1
	Midwest	223	11	89	0
	South	356	18	82	0
	Mountain	54	16	84	0
	Pacific	153	5	95	0
Voter Registration:	Not	291	7	93	0
	Democrat	316	15	84	1
	Republican	210	17	83	0
	Independent	147	9	91	0
Born Again:	Yes	409	21	79	0
	No	604	7	93	0
Denominational Affiliation:	Protestant	550	17	83	0
	Baptist	209	18	82	0
	Catholic	221	6	93	1
	Lutheran	53	21	79	0
	Methodist	65	19	81	0
	Charis./Pent.	70	19	81	0
Attended Church This Week:	Yes	476	24	76	0
	No	534	3	97	0
Read Bible This Week:	Yes	479	22	78	0
	No	534	4	95	0

TABLE 100   283

During the past month, have you watched a religious television program?

		N	Yes	No	Don't Know
Total Responding		1013	49%	51%	0%
Gender:	Male	478	41	59	0
	Female	535	56	44	0
Age:	18 to 26	171	32	67	0
	27 to 45	402	45	54	0
	46 to 64	254	55	45	0
	65 Plus	157	69	31	0
Education:	High School or Less	666	52	48	0
	Some College	140	52	48	0
	College Graduate	201	36	63	1
Ethnicity:	White	729	47	53	0
	Black	139	71	29	0
	Hispanic	93	35	65	0
Marital:	Married	571	50	49	0
	Single	223	35	65	0
	Divorced/Separated	118	42	58	0
	Widowed	93	83	16	1
Kids Under 18:	Yes	405	46	54	0
	No	608	51	49	0
Household Income:	Under $20,000	299	59	41	0
	$20,000 to $39,999	368	48	52	0
	$40,000 to $59,999	133	36	63	1
	$60,000 or more	95	32	68	0
Job Type:	White Collar	224	41	59	0
	Blue Collar	313	48	51	1
	Not Employed	398	56	44	0
Community:	Urban	253	46	54	0
	Suburban	374	42	57	1
	Rural	290	56	44	0
Region:	Northeast	228	38	62	1
	Midwest	223	53	47	0
	South	356	64	36	0
	Mountain	54	28	72	0
	Pacific	153	33	66	0
Voter Registration:	Not	291	38	62	0
	Democrat	316	56	43	0
	Republican	210	52	47	0
	Independent	147	46	54	0
Born Again:	Yes	409	62	38	0
	No	604	40	59	0
Denominational Affiliation:	Protestant	550	60	40	0
	Baptist	209	69	31	0
	Catholic	221	36	64	0
	Lutheran	53	49	51	0
	Methodist	65	51	49	0
	Charis./Pent.	70	69	31	0
Attended Church This Week:	Yes	476	56	44	0
	No	534	43	57	0
Read Bible This Week:	Yes	479	64	36	0
	No	534	36	64	0

TABLE 101

During the past month, have you listened to Christian preaching or teaching on the radio?

		N	Yes	No	Don't Know
Total Responding		1013	39%	61%	0%
Gender:	Male	478	39	61	0
	Female	535	38	61	0
Age:	18 to 26	171	29	70	1
	27 to 45	402	36	64	0
	46 to 64	254	41	59	0
	65 Plus	157	52	47	1
Education:	High School or Less	666	43	57	0
	Some College	140	37	61	2
	College Graduate	201	27	73	0
Ethnicity:	White	729	35	65	0
	Black	139	75	25	0
	Hispanic	93	18	82	0
Marital:	Married	571	38	62	0
	Single	223	37	62	1
	Divorced/Separated	118	33	67	0
	Widowed	93	53	47	0
Kids Under 18:	Yes	405	37	63	0
	No	608	40	60	0
Household Income:	Under $20,000	299	50	49	1
	$20,000 to $39,999	368	36	64	0
	$40,000 to $59,999	133	29	71	0
	$60,000 or more	95	22	78	0
Job Type:	White Collar	224	30	70	0
	Blue Collar	313	40	60	0
	Not Employed	398	44	56	0
Community:	Urban	253	37	63	0
	Suburban	374	31	69	0
	Rural	290	45	55	0
Region:	Northeast	228	31	69	0
	Midwest	223	44	56	0
	South	356	48	52	0
	Mountain	54	25	75	0
	Pacific	153	26	73	1
Voter Registration:	Not	291	31	68	0
	Democrat	316	42	57	0
	Republican	210	43	57	0
	Independent	147	34	66	1
Born Again:	Yes	409	55	45	0
	No	604	28	72	0
Denominational Affiliation:	Protestant	550	49	51	0
	Baptist	209	58	42	0
	Catholic	221	23	77	0
	Lutheran	53	26	74	0
	Methodist	65	36	64	0
	Charis./Pent.	70	59	41	0
Attended Church This Week:	Yes	476	49	50	0
	No	534	29	70	0
Read Bible This Week:	Yes	479	53	47	0
	No	534	26	73	0

TABLE 102   285

During the past month, have you read a Christian book, other than the Bible?

		N	Yes	No	Don't Know
Total Responding		1013	34%	66%	0%
Gender:	Male	478	33	67	1
	Female	535	35	65	0
Age:	18 to 26	171	23	77	0
	27 to 45	402	32	68	0
	46 to 64	254	37	63	0
	65 Plus	157	47	52	1
Education:	High School or Less	666	34	65	0
	Some College	140	38	61	1
	College Graduate	201	30	70	0
Ethnicity:	White	729	34	66	0
	Black	139	46	54	0
	Hispanic	93	19	81	0
Marital:	Married	571	36	64	0
	Single	223	25	75	0
	Divorced/Separated	118	29	70	1
	Widowed	93	54	45	2
Kids Under 18:	Yes	405	31	68	0
	No	608	36	64	0
Household Income:	Under $20,000	299	37	62	1
	$20,000 to $39,999	368	34	66	0
	$40,000 to $59,999	133	33	67	0
	$60,000 or more	95	25	75	0
Job Type:	White Collar	224	34	65	1
	Blue Collar	313	34	66	0
	Not Employed	398	35	65	1
Community:	Urban	253	35	65	0
	Suburban	374	26	74	0
	Rural	290	39	60	1
Region:	Northeast	228	26	74	0
	Midwest	223	31	69	0
	South	356	42	57	1
	Mountain	54	33	67	0
	Pacific	153	30	70	0
Voter Registration:	Not	291	27	73	0
	Democrat	316	36	63	1
	Republican	210	39	61	0
	Independent	147	37	62	1
Born Again:	Yes	409	51	48	1
	No	604	22	78	0
Denominational Affiliation:	Protestant	550	40	59	1
	Baptist	209	46	53	1
	Catholic	221	22	78	0
	Lutheran	53	49	51	0
	Methodist	65	51	49	0
	Charis./Pent.	70	57	41	2
Attended Church This Week:	Yes	476	48	52	0
	No	534	21	78	0
Read Bible This Week:	Yes	479	53	47	0
	No	534	17	83	0

TABLE 103

During the past month, have you donated money to a Christian ministry, other than a church?

		N	Yes	No	Don't Know
Total Responding		1013	28%	71%	1%
Gender:	Male	478	26	74	1
	Female	535	30	70	1
Age:	18 to 26	171	11	89	0
	27 to 45	402	25	75	0
	46 to 64	254	36	64	0
	65 Plus	157	41	58	1
Education:	High School or Less	666	27	72	1
	Some College	140	28	71	0
	College Graduate	201	30	69	1
Ethnicity:	White	729	26	73	1
	Black	139	35	64	1
	Hispanic	93	24	76	0
Marital:	Married	571	31	68	1
	Single	223	14	86	0
	Divorced/Separated	118	29	68	2
	Widowed	93	44	56	0
Kids Under 18:	Yes	405	25	75	0
	No	608	30	69	1
Household Income:	Under $20,000	299	27	72	1
	$20,000 to $39,999	368	28	72	0
	$40,000 to $59,999	133	27	73	0
	$60,000 or more	95	28	72	0
Job Type:	White Collar	224	30	70	0
	Blue Collar	313	28	71	1
	Not Employed	398	28	71	1
Community:	Urban	253	28	70	1
	Suburban	374	29	70	0
	Rural	290	23	76	1
Region:	Northeast	228	32	65	2
	Midwest	223	25	75	0
	South	356	28	71	0
	Mountain	54	26	73	1
	Pacific	153	25	74	0
Voter Registration:	Not	291	18	80	2
	Democrat	316	33	67	0
	Republican	210	32	68	0
	Independent	147	29	71	0
Born Again:	Yes	409	40	60	0
	No	604	20	79	1
Denominational Affiliation:	Protestant	550	33	66	0
	Baptist	209	34	66	0
	Catholic	221	31	67	2
	Lutheran	53	30	70	0
	Methodist	65	20	80	0
	Charis./Pent.	70	49	51	0
Attended Church This Week:	Yes	476	40	59	1
	No	534	17	83	0
Read Bible This Week:	Yes	479	41	59	0
	No	534	16	83	1

TABLE 104   287

During the past month, have you told someone who had different beliefs about your own beliefs?

		N	Yes	No	Don't Know
Total Responding		1013	40%	58%	1%
Gender:	Male	478	42	56	1
	Female	535	39	60	1
Age:	18 to 26	171	47	53	0
	27 to 45	402	43	57	1
	46 to 64	254	36	60	4
	65 Plus	157	35	65	1
Education:	High School or Less	666	40	58	2
	Some College	140	40	59	1
	College Graduate	201	42	58	1
Ethnicity:	White	729	36	63	1
	Black	139	55	45	0
	Hispanic	93	50	45	5
Marital:	Married	571	38	61	1
	Single	223	48	52	0
	Divorced/Separated	118	40	58	2
	Widowed	93	38	56	6
Kids Under 18:	Yes	405	45	54	1
	No	608	37	61	2
Household Income:	Under $20,000	299	41	55	4
	$20,000 to $39,999	368	42	57	0
	$40,000 to $59,999	133	32	66	2
	$60,000 or more	95	45	55	0
Job Type:	White Collar	224	43	56	1
	Blue Collar	313	39	59	2
	Not Employed	398	39	59	2
Community:	Urban	253	41	58	1
	Suburban	374	39	60	1
	Rural	290	41	57	2
Region:	Northeast	228	37	62	1
	Midwest	223	38	61	0
	South	356	45	54	1
	Mountain	54	33	59	8
	Pacific	153	40	58	1
Voter Registration:	Not	291	42	58	1
	Democrat	316	42	55	2
	Republican	210	39	60	1
	Independent	147	42	56	2
Born Again:	Yes	409	50	48	2
	No	604	34	65	1
Denominational Affiliation:	Protestant	550	42	57	1
	Baptist	209	39	61	0
	Catholic	221	25	71	5
	Lutheran	53	36	64	0
	Methodist	65	31	67	2
	Charis./Pent.	70	60	38	2
Attended Church This Week:	Yes	476	45	52	2
	No	534	36	63	0
Read Bible This Week:	Yes	479	53	45	2
	No	534	29	70	1

TABLE 105

During the past month, have you listened to a radio station that was playing Christian music?

		N 1013	Yes 45%	No 55%	Don't Know 0%
Total Responding					
Gender:	Male	478	42	57	0
	Female	535	47	53	0
Age:	18 to 26	171	34	66	0
	27 to 45	402	42	58	0
	46 to 64	254	50	50	0
	65 Plus	157	58	42	0
Education:	High School or Less	666	47	53	0
	Some College	140	47	52	0
	College Graduate	201	36	64	1
Ethnicity:	White	729	41	58	0
	Black	139	83	17	0
	Hispanic	93	15	85	0
Marital:	Married	571	43	56	0
	Single	223	40	59	0
	Divorced/Separated	118	45	55	0
	Widowed	93	64	36	0
Kids Under 18:	Yes	405	44	56	0
	No	608	46	54	0
Household Income:	Under $20,000	299	54	46	0
	$20,000 to $39,999	368	42	58	0
	$40,000 to $59,999	133	35	65	0
	$60,000 or more	95	36	64	0
Job Type:	White Collar	224	40	59	1
	Blue Collar	312	44	56	0
	Not Employed	398	49	51	0
Community:	Urban	253	43	57	0
	Suburban	374	40	60	0
	Rural	290	50	50	0
Region:	Northeast	228	36	64	1
	Midwest	223	43	57	0
	South	356	59	41	0
	Mountain	54	29	71	0
	Pacific	153	35	65	0
Voter Registration:	Not	291	35	65	0
	Democrat	316	55	45	0
	Republican	210	44	56	0
	Independent	147	41	58	1
Born Again:	Yes	409	62	38	0
	No	604	33	67	0
Denominational Affiliation:	Protestant	550	59	41	0
	Baptist	209	65	35	0
	Catholic	221	22	78	0
	Lutheran	53	36	64	0
	Methodist	65	57	43	0
	Charis./Pent.	70	71	29	0
Attended Church This Week:	Yes	476	55	45	0
	No	534	36	64	0
Read Bible This Week:	Yes	479	60	40	0
	No	534	31	69	0

TABLE 106   289

During the past month, have you read a Christian magazine?

		N	Yes	No	Don't Know
Total Responding		1013	37%	62%	0%
Gender:	Male	478	34	66	1
	Female	535	41	59	0
Age:	18 to 26	171	16	84	0
	27 to 45	402	31	69	0
	46 to 64	254	50	50	0
	65 Plus	157	59	40	2
Education:	High School or Less	666	38	61	1
	Some College	140	40	60	0
	College Graduate	201	33	67	0
Ethnicity:	White	729	36	63	1
	Black	139	51	49	0
	Hispanic	93	25	75	0
Marital:	Married	571	42	58	0
	Single	223	20	80	0
	Divorced/Separated	118	32	67	1
	Widowed	93	60	40	0
Kids Under 18:	Yes	405	32	68	0
	No	608	41	58	1
Household Income:	Under $20,000	299	39	60	1
	$20,000 to $39,999	368	40	60	0
	$40,000 to $59,999	133	30	70	0
	$60,000 or more	95	27	73	0
Job Type:	White Collar	224	33	67	0
	Blue Collar	313	35	65	0
	Not Employed	398	43	56	1
Community:	Urban	253	35	64	1
	Suburban	374	33	67	0
	Rural	290	40	60	0
Region:	Northeast	228	28	72	0
	Midwest	223	37	63	0
	South	356	47	52	1
	Mountain	54	34	66	0
	Pacific	153	33	67	0
Voter Registration:	Not	291	25	75	0
	Democrat	316	48	51	1
	Republican	210	41	59	0
	Independent	147	37	63	0
Born Again:	Yes	409	51	48	0
	No	604	28	71	0
Denominational Affiliation:	Protestant	550	47	53	0
	Baptist	209	54	46	0
	Catholic	221	31	69	0
	Lutheran	53	50	50	0
	Methodist	65	33	67	0
	Charis./Pent.	70	60	40	0
Attended Church This Week:	Yes	476	55	45	0
	No	534	22	77	1
Read Bible This Week:	Yes	479	58	41	1
	No	534	19	81	0

TABLE 107

During the past month, have you volunteered your time or money to help needy people in your area?

		N	Yes	No	Don't Know
Total Responding		1013	60%	39%	0%
Gender:	Male	478	54	45	0
	Female	535	66	34	0
Age:	18 to 26	171	43	57	0
	27 to 45	402	61	38	1
	46 to 64	254	66	34	0
	65 Plus	157	68	32	0
Education:	High School or Less	666	59	41	0
	Some College	140	62	36	1
	College Graduate	201	63	36	0
Ethnicity:	White	729	62	38	0
	Black	139	63	37	0
	Hispanic	93	49	50	1
Marital:	Married	571	65	34	1
	Single	223	51	49	0
	Divorced/Separated	118	47	53	0
	Widowed	93	69	31	0
Kids Under 18:	Yes	405	62	37	1
	No	608	59	41	0
Household Income:	Under $20,000	299	55	45	1
	$20,000 to $39,999	368	60	40	0
	$40,000 to $59,999	133	67	33	0
	$60,000 or more	95	64	35	1
Job Type:	White Collar	224	63	36	0
	Blue Collar	313	60	40	1
	Not Employed	398	60	40	0
Community:	Urban	253	57	43	0
	Suburban	374	62	37	0
	Rural	290	64	35	1
Region:	Northeast	228	61	39	0
	Midwest	223	61	38	1
	South	356	63	37	0
	Mountain	54	52	48	0
	Pacific	153	54	44	1
Voter Registration:	Not	291	48	51	1
	Democrat	316	67	33	0
	Republican	210	65	34	1
	Independent	147	60	40	0
Born Again:	Yes	409	65	34	1
	No	604	57	43	0
Denominational Affiliation:	Protestant	550	65	34	1
	Baptist	209	62	38	0
	Catholic	221	53	47	0
	Lutheran	53	66	34	0
	Methodist	65	69	30	1
	Charis./Pent.	70	66	32	2
Attended Church This Week:	Yes	476	67	32	1
	No	534	54	46	0
Read Bible This Week:	Yes	479	69	30	1
	No	534	52	48	0

TABLE 108   291

During the past month, have you volunteered your time or money to help needy people in other countries?

		N	Yes	No	Don't Know
Total Responding		1013	24%	76%	0%
Gender:	Male	478	23	76	0
	Female	535	25	75	1
Age:	18 to 26	171	14	86	0
	27 to 45	402	19	80	0
	46 to 64	254	34	65	1
	65 Plus	157	31	68	1
Education:	High School or Less	666	23	77	0
	Some College	140	25	74	1
	College Graduate	201	28	72	0
Ethnicity:	White	729	25	75	1
	Black	139	30	69	1
	Hispanic	93	10	90	0
Marital:	Married	571	27	72	1
	Single	223	18	82	0
	Divorced/Separated	118	17	83	0
	Widowed	93	29	70	1
Kids Under 18:	Yes	405	20	79	1
	No	608	26	73	0
Household Income:	Under $20,000	299	23	77	0
	$20,000 to $39,999	368	24	75	0
	$40,000 to $59,999	133	21	78	1
	$60,000 or more	95	22	77	1
Job Type:	White Collar	224	26	74	1
	Blue Collar	313	20	79	1
	Not Employed	398	27	73	0
Community:	Urban	253	25	74	1
	Suburban	374	21	79	0
	Rural	290	25	75	0
Region:	Northeast	228	28	72	0
	Midwest	223	20	80	1
	South	356	25	74	1
	Mountain	54	21	79	0
	Pacific	153	22	78	0
Voter Registration:	Not	291	19	80	0
	Democrat	316	27	73	0
	Republican	210	27	72	2
	Independent	147	23	77	0
Born Again:	Yes	409	33	67	0
	No	604	18	81	1
Denominational Affiliation:	Protestant	550	27	72	1
	Baptist	209	30	69	1
	Catholic	221	17	83	0
	Lutheran	53	11	89	0
	Methodist	65	21	79	0
	Charis./Pent.	70	34	66	0
Attended Church This Week:	Yes	476	35	65	1
	No	534	14	85	0
Read Bible This Week:	Yes	479	35	65	0
	No	534	15	85	1

TABLE 109

In a typical week, during how many days, if any, would you read the Bible, not including times when you are at church?

		N	1	2	3	4	5	6	7	None	Don't Know
Total Responding		1013	14%	11%	7%	2%	5%	1%	13%	43%	4%
Gender:	Male	478	16	11	6	1	4	1	6	50	5
	Female	535	12	11	8	3	5	2	19	36	3
Age:	18 to 26	171	19	13	5	2	5	0	2	50	3
	27 to 45	402	16	14	7	2	3	1	9	47	3
	46 to 64	254	13	8	5	4	10	1	16	38	4
	65 Plus	157	8	8	11	1	1	2	33	26	9
Education:	High School or Less	666	14	12	8	2	5	1	14	39	5
	Some College	140	14	12	6	3	4	1	14	43	2
	College Graduate	201	15	8	4	2	4	1	9	55	3
Ethnicity:	White	729	14	10	7	2	4	1	12	46	3
	Black	139	9	16	7	6	5	2	22	23	10
	Hispanic	93	19	12	6	1	9	0	9	44	0
Marital:	Married	571	16	11	6	2	5	2	14	41	4
	Single	223	14	10	5	2	3	0	9	53	3
	Divorced/Separated	118	12	14	7	2	3	0	13	47	2
	Widowed	93	5	13	12	4	8	4	21	23	11
Kids Under 18:	Yes	405	18	15	6	2	6	1	7	41	3
	No	608	11	8	8	2	4	2	17	43	5
Household Income:	Under $20,000	299	13	11	7	2	7	1	17	35	6
	$20,000 to $39,999	368	15	12	7	3	4	0	13	41	3
	$40,000 to $59,999	133	15	13	5	3	3	0	5	55	1
	$60,000 or more	95	16	8	6	1	3	1	6	57	2
Job Type:	White Collar	224	16	15	4	2	4	0	8	48	3
	Blue Collar	313	19	14	6	2	5	2	8	44	1
	Not Employed	398	10	6	10	3	4	2	22	38	7
Community:	Urban	253	15	13	6	4	4	2	10	44	3
	Suburban	374	16	9	5	1	4	1	10	53	2
	Rural	290	14	13	10	3	3	2	14	36	5
Region:	Northeast	228	13	10	5	1	1	2	8	57	2
	Midwest	223	13	9	5	3	4	2	12	48	4
	South	356	15	13	10	3	8	1	18	27	6
	Mountain	54	19	9	8	4	2	1	9	47	2
	Pacific	153	14	13	5	1	5	0	12	47	3
Voter Registration:	Not	291	15	11	6	2	5	1	10	47	4
	Democrat	316	13	12	8	2	5	1	16	38	5
	Republican	210	16	11	7	3	6	2	13	38	3
	Independent	147	14	8	6	1	2	0	11	55	4
Born Again:	Yes	409	18	15	10	3	8	3	22	18	3
	No	604	12	8	5	2	2	0	7	60	5
Denominational Affiliation:	Protestant	550	16	13	8	3	7	2	17	29	5
	Baptist	209	11	16	10	3	5	1	20	23	10
	Catholic	221	16	9	5	1	2	0	4	61	1
	Lutheran	53	26	4	5	1	14	0	5	44	2
	Methodist	65	20	8	10	1	3	2	14	41	3
	Charis./Pent.	70	17	13	8	3	14	3	23	15	2
Attended Church This Week:	Yes	476	14	13	8	3	9	3	22	25	3
	No	534	14	9	5	2	1	0	5	58	5
Read Bible This Week:	Yes	479	15	15	13	4	10	3	27	11	3
	No	534	14	8	1	1	0	0	1	71	5

TABLE 110 293

Have you ever made a personal commitment to Jesus Christ that is still important in your life today?

		N	Yes	No	Don't Know
Total Responding		1013	65%	33%	2%
Gender:	Male	478	58	40	2
	Female	535	71	27	2
Age:	18 to 26	171	51	48	1
	27 to 45	402	69	29	2
	46 to 64	254	67	32	1
	65 plus	157	72	23	5
Education:	High School or Less	666	66	32	2
	Some College	140	68	31	1
	College Graduate	201	61	37	2
Ethnicity:	White	729	66	32	2
	Black	139	75	25	1
	Hispanic	93	53	44	4
Marital:	Married	571	70	28	2
	Single	223	49	50	1
	Divorced	118	71	27	3
	Widowed	93	65	28	7
Kids Under 18:	Yes	405	68	30	2
	No	608	63	35	2
Household Income:	Under $20,000	299	66	32	2
	$20,000 to $39,999	368	68	32	0
	$40,000 to $59,999	133	58	38	4
	$60,000 or more	95	51	48	2
Job Type:	White Collar	224	64	35	2
	Blue Collar	313	68	29	3
	Not Employed	398	65	33	2
Community:	Urban	253	61	35	5
	Suburban	374	63	35	2
	Rural	290	72	27	1
Region:	Northeast	228	53	43	4
	Midwest	223	68	31	1
	South	356	76	22	2
	Mountain	54	51	44	5
	Pacific	153	58	41	0
Voter Registration:	Not	291	54	45	1
	Democratic	316	68	30	2
	Republican	210	74	24	2
	Independent	147	66	33	1
Born Again:	Yes	409	100	0	0
	No	604	41	55	4
Denominational Affiliation:	Protestant	550	80	18	2
	Baptist	209	83	16	0
	Catholic	221	52	43	5
	Lutheran	53	68	32	0
	Methodist	65	75	22	3
	Charis./Pent.	70	96	4	0
Attended Church This Week:	Yes	476	77	19	3
	No	534	54	45	1
Read Bible This Week:	Yes	479	81	16	2
	No	534	50	48	2

I'm going to read six statements about life after death. Please tell me which one of these statements comes closest to describing your own belief about life after death. (Asked of people who said they had made a personal commitment to Jesus Christ.)

(See legend on next page for column heading descriptions)

		N	A	B	C	D	E	F	Don't Know
Total Responding		657	6%	9%	62%	6%	2%	11%	3%
Gender:	Male	275	4	10	63	3	3	15	3
	Female	382	7	9	62	9	1	9	4
Age:	18 to 26	87	1	6	59	5	8	20	2
	27 to 45	277	4	10	63	9	2	10	3
	46 to 64	170	9	7	69	3	0	10	2
	65 Plus	113	7	13	53	7	2	9	9
Education:	High School or Less	438	5	8	63	6	3	11	3
	Some College	96	6	9	65	6	0	10	5
	College Graduate	122	6	14	57	8	1	11	3
Ethnicity:	White	481	5	9	65	5	2	10	4
	Black	104	8	8	54	7	0	19	2
	Hispanic	49	8	16	49	10	5	11	0
Marital:	Married	402	6	8	63	7	3	10	3
	Single	110	2	12	60	4	0	19	3
	Divorced/Separated	83	7	14	61	7	3	7	2
	Widowed	60	4	9	62	4	0	11	10
Kids Under 18:	Yes	275	7	7	59	9	4	13	2
	No	382	5	11	65	5	1	10	4
Household Income:	Under $20,000	198	2	10	65	4	3	10	6
	$20,000 to $39,999	250	6	9	63	9	2	10	1
	$40,000 to $59,999	77	5	9	61	10	0	12	2
	$60,000 or more	48	4	8	67	2	5	10	3
Job Type:	White Collar	143	3	8	67	7	4	8	3
	Blue Collar	214	4	6	67	6	3	12	2
	Not Employed	257	8	13	56	6	1	12	5
Community:	Urban	153	3	8	61	5	0	18	5
	Suburban	237	6	11	55	11	3	10	3
	Rural	210	4	6	71	3	3	9	3
Region:	Northeast	121	6	19	55	6	2	10	2
	Midwest	151	5	6	57	10	3	18	2
	South	269	7	5	71	4	0	8	4
	Mountain	27	9	20	50	7	2	4	8
	Pacific	89	1	10	58	6	7	14	4
Voter Registration:	Not	158	7	8	60	5	9	8	4
	Democrat	216	9	8	62	3	0	13	4
	Republican	155	3	9	68	6	0	11	3
	Independent	97	2	15	53	13	0	14	3
Born Again:	Yes	409	0	0	100	0	0	0	0
	No	248	15	24	0	16	6	30	9
Denominational Affiliation:	Protestant	440	6	5	73	4	2	8	2
	Baptist	174	8	6	74	4	0	6	2
	Catholic	115	7	24	42	10	0	16	2
	Lutheran	36	16	7	59	7	0	11	1
	Methodist	49	2	9	61	6	0	14	7
	Charis./Pent.	67	0	0	88	0	7	4	0
Attended Church This Week:	Yes	368	7	7	73	4	3	4	2
	No	289	4	12	48	9	1	20	5
Read Bible This Week:	Yes	389	6	7	72	5	3	5	3
	No	268	5	13	48	8	1	20	4

TABLE 111 (COLUMN HEADINGS)   295

A. "When you die you will go to heaven because you have tried to obey the Ten Commandments."

B. "When you die you will go to heaven because you are basically a good person."

C. "When you die you will go to heaven because you have confessed your sins and have accepted Jesus Christ as your Savior."

D. "When you die you will go to heaven because God loves all people and will not let them perish."

E. "When you die you will not go to heaven."

F. "You do not know what will happen after you die."

TABLE 112

In the past 30 days, did you make a contribution to a charitable organization?

		N	Yes	No	Don't Know
Total Responding		1013	46%	53%	1%
Gender:	Male	478	44	55	1
	Female	535	47	52	1
Age:	18 to 26	171	26	74	0
	27 to 45	402	47	53	0
	46 to 64	254	55	43	2
	65 Plus	157	51	47	2
Education:	High School or Less	666	37	61	1
	Some College	140	57	42	2
	College Graduate	201	66	34	0
Ethnicity:	White	729	51	48	1
	Black	139	32	68	0
	Hispanic	93	28	72	0
Marital:	Married	571	52	47	1
	Single	223	33	67	0
	Divorced/Separated	118	41	59	0
	Widowed	93	43	55	2
Kids Under 18:	Yes	405	44	56	0
	No	608	47	51	2
Household Income:	Under $20,000	299	35	64	2
	$20,000 to $39,999	368	45	54	0
	$40,000 to $59,999	133	58	39	2
	$60,000 or more	95	62	37	1
Job Type:	White Collar	224	61	38	1
	Blue Collar	313	44	56	0
	Not Employed	398	38	60	2
Community:	Urban	253	44	56	1
	Suburban	374	52	47	1
	Rural	290	45	54	1
Region:	Northeast	228	46	53	1
	Midwest	223	53	44	3
	South	356	39	61	0
	Mountain	54	56	44	0
	Pacific	153	47	53	0
Voter Registration:	Not	291	31	68	1
	Democrat	316	46	52	2
	Republican	210	56	44	0
	Independent	147	55	44	1
Born Again:	Yes	409	48	51	1
	No	604	44	55	1
Denominational Affiliation:	Protestant	550	48	51	1
	Baptist	209	38	61	1
	Catholic	221	46	53	1
	Lutheran	53	68	29	3
	Methodist	65	51	46	3
	Charis./Pent.	70	39	61	0
Attended Church This Week:	Yes	476	53	45	1
	No	534	39	60	1
Read Bible This Week:	Yes	479	51	48	1
	No	534	41	58	1

TABLE 113   297

During the past 30 days, did you make a contribution by responding to "a direct mail appeal"? (Asked of people who said they had made a charitable contribution during the past 30 days.)

		N	Yes	No	Don't Know
Total Responding		464	31%	69%	0%
Gender:	Male	211	24	76	0
	Female	253	36	63	0
Age:	18 to 26	44	18	82	0
	27 to 45	189	24	76	0
	46 to 64	139	35	65	0
	65 Plus	80	47	53	0
Education:	High School or Less	249	32	68	0
	Some College	79	29	71	0
	College Graduate	132	30	69	1
Ethnicity:	White	370	31	69	0
	Black	44	44	56	0
Marital:	Married	298	29	70	0
	Single	73	29	71	0
	Divorced	49	28	71	1
	Widowed	40	50	50	0
Kids Under 18:	Yes	178	21	78	0
	No	286	36	63	0
Household Income:	Under $20,000	104	37	63	0
	$20,000 to $39,999	167	25	75	0
	$40,000 to $59,999	77	26	72	2
	$60,000 or more	59	33	67	0
Job Type:	White Collar	136	22	77	1
	Blue Collar	138	24	76	0
	Not Employed	145	45	55	0
Community:	Urban	111	32	68	0
	Suburban	194	30	70	1
	Rural	129	29	70	0
Region:	Northeast	105	49	51	0
	Midwest	119	26	73	1
	South	138	28	72	0
	Pacific	72	20	79	1
Voter Registration:	Not	91	28	72	0
	Democrat	144	31	69	1
	Republican	117	35	64	1
	Independent	80	22	78	0
Born Again:	Yes	198	35	65	1
	No	266	28	72	0
Denominational Affiliation:	Protestant	257	31	69	0
	Baptist	80	40	59	1
	Catholic	101	29	71	0
Attended Church This Week:	Yes	254	32	68	0
	No	210	29	71	1
Read Bible This Week:	Yes	245	32	68	0
	No	218	29	71	0

TABLE 114

During the past 30 days, did you make a contribution by responding to "a telephone appeal"? (Asked of people who said they had made a charitable contribution during the past 30 days.)

		N	Yes	No	Don't Know
Total Responding		464	12%	88%	0%
Gender:	Male	211	13	86	0
	Female	253	12	88	0
Age:	18 to 26	44	9	91	0
	27 to 45	189	15	85	0
	46 to 64	139	11	89	0
	65 Plus	80	12	88	0
Education:	High School or Less	249	10	90	0
	Some College	79	15	84	1
	College Graduate	132	16	84	0
Ethnicity:	White	370	14	85	0
	Black	44	2	98	0
Marital:	Married	298	11	89	0
	Single	73	15	85	0
	Divorced	49	12	87	1
	Widowed	40	19	81	0
Kids Under 18:	Yes	178	12	88	0
	No	286	13	87	0
Household Income:	Under $20,000	104	8	92	0
	$20,000 to $39,999	167	12	88	0
	$40,000 to $59,999	77	17	82	1
	$60,000 or more	59	13	87	0
Job Type:	White Collar	136	16	84	0
	Blue Collar	138	10	90	0
	Not Employed	145	12	88	0
Community:	Urban	111	15	85	0
	Suburban	194	12	87	0
	Rural	129	13	87	0
Region:	Northeast	105	14	86	0
	Midwest	119	15	85	0
	South	138	10	90	0
	Pacific	72	10	90	0
Voter Registration:	Not	91	11	89	0
	Democrat	144	15	85	0
	Republican	117	14	85	0
	Independent	80	8	92	0
Born Again:	Yes	198	12	88	0
	No	266	13	87	0
Denominational Affiliation:	Protestant	257	11	89	0
	Baptist	80	7	93	0
	Catholic	101	12	88	0
Attended Church This Week:	Yes	254	11	89	0
	No	210	14	86	0
Read Bible This Week:	Yes	245	11	89	0
	No	218	14	86	0

TABLE 115 299

During the past 30 days, did you make a contribution by responding to "a church collection or temple donation"? (Asked of people who said they had made a charitable contribution during the past 30 days.)

		N	Yes	No
Total Responding		464	69%	31%
Gender:	Male	211	69	31
	Female	253	69	31
Age:	18 to 26	44	58	42
	27 to 45	189	64	36
	46 to 64	139	74	26
	65 Plus	80	78	22
Education:	High School or Less	249	70	30
	Some College	79	71	29
	College Graduate	132	68	32
Ethnicity:	White	370	66	34
	Black	44	84	16
Marital:	Married	298	76	24
	Single	73	51	49
	Divorced	49	56	44
	Widowed	40	65	35
Kids Under 18:	Yes	178	74	26
	No	286	66	34
Household	Under $20,000	104	70	30
Income:	$20,000 to $39,999	167	64	36
	$40,000 to $59,999	77	76	24
	$60,000 or more	59	67	33
Job Type:	White Collar	136	69	31
	Blue Collar	138	65	35
	Not Employed	145	75	25
Community:	Urban	111	65	35
	Suburban	194	72	28
	Rural	129	65	35
Region:	Northeast	105	69	31
	Midwest	119	67	33
	South	138	78	22
	Pacific	72	59	41
Voter	Not	91	64	36
Registration:	Democrat	144	77	23
	Republican	117	67	33
	Independent	80	63	37
Born Again:	Yes	198	80	20
	No	266	62	38
Denominational	Protestant	257	73	27
Affiliation:	Baptist	80	74	26
	Catholic	101	83	17
Attended Church	Yes	254	92	8
This Week:	No	210	42	58
Read Bible	Yes	245	82	18
This Week:	No	218	56	44

TABLE 116

During the past 30 days, did you make a contribution by responding to "a person-to-person appeal"? (Asked of people who said they had made a charitable contribution during the past 30 days.)

		N	Yes	No	Don't Know
Total Responding		464	39	61	0
Gender:	Male	211	41	59	0
	Female	253	37	62	1
Age:	18 to 26	44	39	61	0
	27 to 45	189	38	62	0
	46 to 64	139	37	63	0
	65 Plus	80	41	57	1
Education:	High School or Less	249	39	60	0
	Some College	79	34	65	1
	College Graduate	132	40	60	0
Ethnicity:	White	370	40	59	0
	Black	44	29	69	2
Marital:	Married	298	39	60	1
	Single	73	35	65	0
	Divorced	49	39	61	0
	Widowed	40	40	60	0
Kids Under 18:	Yes	178	41	58	1
	No	286	37	62	0
Household Income:	Under $20,000	104	34	65	1
	$20,000 to $39,999	167	43	57	1
	$40,000 to $59,999	77	35	65	0
	$60,000 or more	59	35	65	0
Job Type:	White Collar	136	34	66	0
	Blue Collar	138	43	56	1
	Not Employed	145	41	58	1
Community:	Urban	111	39	61	0
	Suburban	194	38	62	0
	Rural	129	42	57	1
Region:	Northeast	105	44	56	0
	Midwest	119	42	57	1
	South	138	36	63	1
	Pacific	72	35	65	0
Voter Registration:	Not	91	34	66	0
	Democrat	144	37	62	0
	Republican	117	41	59	0
	Independent	80	42	57	1
Born Again:	Yes	198	40	60	1
	No	266	38	62	0
Denominational Affiliation:	Protestant	257	41	58	1
	Baptist	80	45	55	0
	Catholic	101	35	65	0
Attended Church This Week:	Yes	254	35	64	1
	No	210	43	57	0
Read Bible This Week:	Yes	245	38	62	0
	No	218	40	60	0

TABLE 117   301

During the past 30 days, did you make a contribution by responding to "a television, radio, or print advertisement"? (Asked of people who said they had made a charitable contribution during the past 30 days.)

		N	Yes	No	Don't Know
Total Responding		464	13%	87%	0%
Gender:	Male	211	13	87	0
	Female	253	12	87	0
Age:	18 to 26	44	18	82	0
	27 to 45	189	8	92	0
	46 to 64	139	13	87	0
	65 Plus	80	19	81	1
Education:	High School or Less	249	14	86	0
	Some College	79	13	86	1
	College Graduate	132	11	89	0
Ethnicity:	White	370	11	89	0
	Black	44	37	63	0
Marital:	Married	298	11	89	0
	Single	73	15	85	0
	Divorced	49	21	79	0
	Widowed	40	13	86	1
Kids Under 18:	Yes	178	9	91	0
	No	286	15	85	0
Household Income:	Under $20,000	104	21	79	0
	$20,000 to $39,999	167	10	89	0
	$40,000 to $59,999	77	12	88	0
	$60,000 or more	59	6	94	0
Job Type:	White Collar	136	9	91	0
	Blue Collar	138	11	89	0
	Not Employed	145	18	82	0
Community:	Urban	111	14	86	0
	Suburban	194	9	91	0
	Rural	129	11	89	0
Region:	Northeast	105	14	86	0
	Midwest	119	14	86	0
	South	138	12	88	0
	Pacific	72	12	88	0
Voter Registration:	Not	91	16	84	0
	Democrat	144	9	91	0
	Republican	117	10	90	0
	Independent	80	14	86	0
Born Again:	Yes	198	14	85	0
	No	266	11	89	0
Denominational Affiliation:	Protestant	257	13	87	0
	Baptist	80	18	82	0
	Catholic	101	8	92	0
Attended Church This Week:	Yes	254	13	87	0
	No	210	13	87	0
Read Bible This Week:	Yes	245	16	84	0
	No	218	9	91	0

During the past 30 days, did you make a contribution by responding to "through an automatic deduction from your paycheck"? (Asked of people who said they had made a charitable contribution during the past 30 days.)

		N	Yes	No	Don't Know
Total Responding		464	24%	75%	1%
Gender:	Male	211	27	73	1
	Female	253	22	76	1
Age:	18 to 26	44	27	73	0
	27 to 45	189	33	67	0
	46 to 64	139	22	77	1
	65 Plus	80	5	91	4
Education:	High School or Less	249	20	78	2
	Some College	79	28	72	0
	College Graduate	132	31	69	0
Ethnicity:	White	370	22	77	1
	Black	44	26	70	4
Marital:	Married	298	26	74	0
	Single	73	27	71	2
	Divorced	49	21	79	0
	Widowed	40	7	84	9
Kids Under 18:	Yes	178	33	67	0
	No	286	19	79	2
Household Income:	Under $20,000	104	12	84	4
	$20,000 to $39,999	167	27	72	1
	$40,000 to $59,999	77	33	67	0
	$60,000 or more	59	27	73	0
Job Type:	White Collar	136	29	71	0
	Blue Collar	138	30	70	0
	Not Employed	145	10	87	4
Community:	Urban	111	22	75	3
	Suburban	194	30	69	1
	Rural	129	22	78	0
Region:	Northeast	105	16	80	3
	Midwest	119	30	70	0
	South	138	28	72	0
	Pacific	72	15	82	3
Voter Registration:	Not	91	26	74	0
	Democrat	144	25	72	3
	Republican	117	20	78	1
	Independent	80	26	74	0
Born Again:	Yes	198	25	75	0
	No	266	24	74	2
Denominational Affiliation:	Protestant	257	26	73	1
	Baptist	80	22	73	4
	Catholic	101	25	75	0
Attended Church This Week:	Yes	254	25	74	1
	No	210	24	75	1
Read Bible This Week:	Yes	245	20	79	1
	No	218	29	69	2

TABLE 119   303

Are you registered to vote at your current address?

		N	Yes	No	Don't Know
Total Responding		1013	71%	28%	1%
Gender:	Male	478	70	29	1
	Female	535	72	27	0
Age:	18 to 26	171	42	55	3
	27 to 45	402	73	27	0
	46 to 64	254	81	19	0
	65 plus	157	84	16	0
Education:	High School or Less	666	66	33	1
	Some College	140	80	20	1
	College Graduate	201	81	19	0
Ethnicity:	White	729	75	25	0
	Black	139	69	27	4
	Hispanic	93	53	47	0
Marital:	Married	571	77	22	0
	Single	223	54	43	2
	Divorced	118	65	35	0
	Widowed	93	84	16	0
Kids Under 18:	Yes	405	66	32	2
	No	608	75	25	0
Household Income:	Under $20,000	299	66	32	2
	$20,000 to $39,999	368	71	29	0
	$40,000 to $59,999	133	77	22	1
	$60,000 or more	95	77	23	0
Job Type:	White Collar	224	79	20	1
	Blue Collar	313	70	30	0
	Not Employed	398	70	29	1
Community:	Urban	253	74	25	0
	Suburban	374	71	29	0
	Rural	290	74	26	0
Region:	Northeast	228	67	33	0
	Midwest	223	78	20	2
	South	356	75	25	0
	Mountain	54	67	33	0
	Pacific	153	59	40	1
Voter Registration:	Not	291	0	98	2
	Democratic	316	100	0	0
	Republican	210	100	0	0
	Independent	147	100	0	0
Born Again:	Yes	409	77	23	1
	No	604	67	32	1
Denominational Affiliation:	Protestant	550	78	22	0
	Baptist	209	81	19	0
	Catholic	221	73	27	0
	Lutheran	53	80	20	0
	Methodist	65	86	14	0
	Charis./Pent	70	65	35	0
Attended Church This Week:	Yes	476	76	24	0
	No	534	67	32	1
Read Bible This Week:	Yes	479	75	24	0
	No	534	67	31	1

Are you registered as a Democrat, as a Republican, or are you independent? (Asked of registered voters.)

		N	Democrat	Republican	Independent	Other Party	Don't Know
Total Responding		722	44%	29%	20%	0%	6%
Gender:	Male	334	41	30	24	1	4
	Female	387	46	28	17	0	9
Age:	18 to 26	72	35	24	36	0	5
	27 to 45	292	39	33	24	0	3
	46 to 64	207	53	24	17	1	5
	65 Plus	132	48	31	10	0	12
Education:	High School or Less	442	49	27	18	0	6
	Some College	112	40	31	22	1	6
	College Graduate	163	33	34	25	1	7
Ethnicity:	White	547	38	35	21	0	6
	Black	96	74	3	15	0	9
	Hispanic	49	56	19	17	0	8
Marital:	Married	442	42	33	18	0	7
	Single	121	41	23	32	0	3
	Divorced	77	40	21	32	1	5
	Widowed	79	59	23	7	0	10
Kids Under 18:	Yes	268	40	34	21	1	5
	No	454	46	27	20	0	7
Household Income:	Under $20,000	197	53	18	23	0	6
	$20,000 to $39,999	260	43	30	20	1	6
	$40,000 to $59,999	102	41	35	19	1	5
	$60,000 or more	73	35	40	24	0	2
Job Type:	White Collar	177	36	33	23	1	7
	Blue Collar	220	41	28	24	0	6
	Not Employed	277	52	26	16	0	7
Community:	Urban	189	48	27	20	0	5
	Suburban	264	39	33	21	1	6
	Rural	216	45	28	20	0	7
Region:	Northeast	154	41	27	25	1	6
	Midwest	174	28	36	27	0	9
	South	268	57	24	15	0	4
	Mountain	36	35	36	29	0	0
	Pacific	90	42	34	13	1	11
Voter Registration:	Not	0	0	0	0	0	0
	Democratic	316	100	0	0	0	0
	Republican	210	0	100	0	0	0
	Independent	147	0	0	100	0	0
Born Again:	Yes	315	43	33	16	0	8
	No	407	45	26	24	1	5
Denominational Affiliation:	Protestant	427	44	34	15	0	6
	Baptist	169	58	19	18	0	5
	Catholic	161	51	16	27	1	5
	Lutheran	43	23	48	21	0	8
	Methodist	56	40	38	13	0	10
	Charis./Pent	45	51	38	9	0	2
Attended Church This Week:	Yes	362	47	31	17	0	6
	No	359	41	28	24	0	7
Read Bible This Week:	Yes	362	49	28	16	0	7
	No	360	39	30	25	0	6

TABLE 121   305

Would knowing a presidential candidate's position on "women's rights" be very important, somewhat important, not too important, or not at all important in your decision of which candidate to support in November 1992? (Asked of registered voters.)

		N	Very Important	Somewhat Important	Not Too Important	Not At All Important	Don't Know
Total Responding		722	49%	36%	8%	4%	2%
Gender:	Male	334	48	40	8	4	0
	Female	387	51	33	9	4	4
Age:	18 to 26	72	48	45	6	1	0
	27 to 45	292	50	37	8	3	2
	46 to 64	207	47	41	7	6	0
	65 Plus	132	52	23	13	6	6
Education:	High School or Less	442	49	35	8	5	3
	Some College	112	48	39	9	4	0
	College Graduate	163	50	38	9	2	1
Ethnicity:	White	547	46	39	9	5	1
	Black	96	71	19	7	0	3
	Hispanic	49	48	27	8	8	8
Marital:	Married	442	46	39	8	5	2
	Single	121	55	38	5	0	1
	Divorced	77	62	32	4	2	0
	Widowed	79	47	21	16	7	8
Kids Under 18:	Yes	268	45	42	8	3	2
	No	454	52	33	8	5	2
Household Income:	Under $20,000	197	51	29	8	6	5
	$20,000 to $39,999	260	51	37	8	4	0
	$40,000 to $59,999	102	45	41	11	2	0
	$60,000 or more	73	38	49	8	4	1
Job Type:	White Collar	177	51	41	5	3	1
	Blue Collar	220	50	41	6	2	2
	Not Employed	277	49	29	11	7	4
Community:	Urban	189	58	31	6	4	1
	Suburban	264	46	43	7	3	1
	Rural	216	49	35	9	4	3
Region:	Northeast	154	49	39	6	1	4
	Midwest	174	50	38	7	3	2
	South	268	52	32	9	6	1
	Mountain	36	36	52	10	1	1
	Pacific	90	45	32	12	6	5
Voter Registration:	Not	0	0	0	0	0	0
	Democratic	316	56	33	6	4	1
	Republican	210	37	43	12	5	2
	Independent	147	56	35	7	2	1
Born Again:	Yes	315	44	39	9	4	4
	No	407	54	33	7	4	1
Denominational Affiliation:	Protestant	427	47	38	10	3	2
	Baptist	169	55	29	10	4	2
	Catholic	161	54	32	6	5	3
	Lutheran	43	26	63	7	4	0
	Methodist	56	43	46	6	3	1
	Charis./Pent.	45	51	35	12	0	2
Attended Church This Week:	Yes	362	45	41	9	3	3
	No	359	54	31	8	5	2
Read Bible This Week:	Yes	362	49	33	10	5	3
	No	360	50	39	6	3	2

Would knowing a presidential candidate's position on "abortion" be very important, somewhat important, not too important, or not at all important in your decision of which candidate to support in November 1992? (Asked of registered voters.)

		N	Very Important	Somewhat Important	Not Too Important	Not At All Important	Don't Know
Total Responding		722	56%	30%	4%	5%	5%
Gender:	Male	334	54	32	5	6	4
	Female	387	57	28	4	5	6
Age:	18 to 26	72	53	31	6	9	1
	27 to 45	292	55	35	4	2	4
	46 to 64	207	57	27	3	5	8
	65 Plus	132	57	20	5	11	6
Education:	High School or Less	442	56	28	3	7	6
	Some College	112	57	32	5	3	3
	College Graduate	163	53	33	8	2	4
Ethnicity:	White	547	55	31	6	4	4
	Black	96	54	27	1	14	4
	Hispanic	49	66	17	0	0	17
Marital:	Married	442	58	29	5	3	5
	Single	121	54	31	4	7	4
	Divorced	77	56	31	3	6	4
	Widowed	79	45	28	3	14	10
Kids Under 18:	Yes	268	53	37	5	3	3
	No	454	57	25	4	7	6
Household Income:	Under $20,000	197	59	20	5	6	10
	$20,000 to $39,999	260	57	31	3	5	3
	$40,000 to $59,999	102	53	38	5	3	1
	$60,000 or more	73	45	40	8	5	2
Job Type:	White Collar	177	51	35	7	4	4
	Blue Collar	220	56	31	3	4	6
	Not Employed	277	60	24	3	7	6
Community:	Urban	189	54	34	5	3	5
	Suburban	264	54	33	3	5	4
	Rural	216	59	28	6	5	3
Region:	Northeast	154	51	35	4	4	7
	Midwest	174	53	34	5	4	3
	South	268	61	25	3	6	5
	Mountain	36	59	31	8	1	1
	Pacific	90	51	27	6	6	10
Voter Registration:	Not	0	0	0	0	0	0
	Democratic	316	58	27	4	6	5
	Republican	210	54	30	6	4	6
	Independent	147	53	36	2	6	3
Born Again:	Yes	315	60	27	4	3	6
	No	407	53	32	5	7	4
Denominational Affiliation:	Protestant	427	54	30	4	6	5
	Baptist	169	56	25	2	9	7
	Catholic	161	56	29	4	4	7
	Lutheran	43	45	33	10	4	9
	Methodist	56	40	44	4	10	2
	Charis./Pent	45	83	14	2	1	0
Attended Church This Week:	Yes	362	64	24	3	4	5
	No	359	47	36	6	6	5
Read Bible This Week:	Yes	362	64	22	3	6	5
	No	360	48	37	6	5	4

TABLE 123   307

Would knowing a presidential candidate's position on "taxes" be very important, somewhat important, not too important, or not at all important in your decision of which candidate to support in November 1992? (Asked of registered voters.)

		N	Very Important	Somewhat Important	Not Too Important	Not At All Important	Don't Know
Total Responding		722	66%	27%	3%	2%	2%
Gender:	Male	334	68	27	2	3	0
	Female	387	65	27	4	1	3
Age:	18 to 26	72	59	35	1	4	0
	27 to 45	292	64	31	2	1	2
	46 to 64	207	71	22	2	3	1
	65 Plus	132	69	20	6	1	4
Education:	High School or Less	442	70	22	3	3	2
	Some College	112	65	30	3	1	1
	College Graduate	163	57	39	3	0	1
Ethnicity:	White	547	66	28	3	1	1
	Black	96	73	24	0	3	0
	Hispanic	49	66	15	2	8	8
Marital:	Married	442	64	29	3	2	2
	Single	121	71	26	1	2	0
	Divorced	77	78	21	1	0	0
	Widowed	79	63	20	6	5	6
Kids Under 18:	Yes	268	61	32	3	2	2
	No	454	69	24	3	2	2
Household Income:	Under $20,000	197	68	21	3	4	4
	$20,000 to $39,999	260	72	25	2	1	0
	$40,000 to $59,999	102	61	32	5	1	0
	$60,000 or more	73	53	42	3	1	1
Job Type:	White Collar	177	63	31	5	0	1
	Blue Collar	220	72	21	1	3	3
	Not Employed	277	65	28	3	3	2
Community:	Urban	189	71	26	2	1	1
	Suburban	264	68	29	2	1	1
	Rural	216	62	30	4	2	1
Region:	Northeast	154	63	31	2	2	2
	Midwest	174	63	28	4	3	2
	South	268	71	24	2	2	0
	Mountain	36	67	27	4	0	1
	Pacific	90	65	26	3	1	6
Voter Registration:	Not	0	0	0	0	0	0
	Democratic	316	69	25	2	3	1
	Republican	210	65	28	4	2	2
	Independent	147	66	29	3	1	1
Born Again:	Yes	315	66	28	2	1	2
	No	407	66	26	3	3	1
Denominational Affiliation:	Protestant	427	67	28	3	1	1
	Baptist	169	73	23	1	1	2
	Catholic	161	73	18	1	5	3
	Lutheran	43	66	29	5	0	0
	Methodist	56	68	25	4	3	1
	Charis./Pent	45	70	24	6	0	0
Attended Church This Week:	Yes	362	65	28	3	2	1
	No	359	67	26	2	2	2
Read Bible This Week:	Yes	362	63	30	3	2	2
	No	360	69	24	3	2	2

Would knowing a presidential candidate's position on "environmental policy" be very important, somewhat important, not too important, or not at all important in your decision of which candidate to support in November 1992? (Asked of registered voters.)

		N	Very Important	Somewhat Important	Not Too Important	Not At All Important	Don't Know
Total Responding		722	57%	32%	3%	1%	6%
Gender:	Male	334	60	32	3	1	3
	Female	387	55	32	4	1	8
Age:	18 to 26	72	67	26	3	3	1
	27 to 45	292	58	34	3	1	5
	46 to 64	207	53	37	5	3	3
	65 Plus	132	57	26	5	0	13
Education:	High School or Less	442	58	29	3	1	9
	Some College	112	53	39	5	1	2
	College Graduate	163	57	35	4	1	2
Ethnicity:	White	547	54	35	4	1	6
	Black	96	68	23	1	1	7
	Hispanic	49	55	25	3	8	8
Marital:	Married	442	52	37	4	1	6
	Single	121	68	29	2	1	1
	Divorced	77	71	20	5	0	3
	Widowed	79	57	21	1	5	16
Kids Under 18:	Yes	268	57	35	3	1	4
	No	454	57	31	4	2	7
Household Income:	Under $20,000	197	60	17	5	4	14
	$20,000 to $39,999	260	60	36	2	1	1
	$40,000 to $59,999	102	54	40	4	1	1
	$60,000 or more	73	49	43	5	1	2
Job Type:	White Collar	177	58	34	5	1	1
	Blue Collar	220	60	31	1	1	7
	Not Employed	277	56	30	4	2	9
Community:	Urban	189	64	30	3	0	3
	Suburban	264	56	37	2	1	4
	Rural	216	54	31	5	0	9
Region:	Northeast	154	63	31	2	0	4
	Midwest	174	56	33	5	1	6
	South	268	59	29	3	3	6
	Mountain	36	50	32	11	0	7
	Pacific	90	47	43	2	1	8
Voter Registration:	Not	0	0	0	0	0	0
	Democratic	316	62	26	3	2	7
	Republican	210	45	47	4	1	3
	Independent	147	65	26	4	2	4
Born Again:	Yes	315	50	37	5	1	7
	No	407	62	28	2	2	5
Denominational Affiliation:	Protestant	427	55	35	4	1	5
	Baptist	169	54	34	4	1	7
	Catholic	161	62	28	3	3	4
	Lutheran	43	66	31	3	0	0
	Methodist	56	63	32	2	1	2
	Charis./Pent	45	68	25	3	0	4
Attended Church This Week:	Yes	362	51	35	5	2	7
	No	359	63	29	2	1	5
Read Bible This Week:	Yes	362	54	35	3	2	6
	No	360	60	30	4	1	6

TABLE 125   309

Would knowing a presidential candidate's position on "public education" be very important, somewhat important, not too important, or not at all important in your decision of which candidate to support in November 1992? (Asked of registered voters.)

		N	Very Important	Somewhat Important	Not Too Important	Not At All Important	Don't Know
Total Responding		722	78%	18%	1%	1%	2%
Gender:	Male	334	79	20	1	1	0
	Female	387	77	17	1	1	4
Age:	18 to 26	72	80	20	0	0	0
	27 to 45	292	79	18	1	0	2
	46 to 64	207	77	18	1	2	3
	65 Plus	132	77	17	1	1	5
Education:	High School or Less	442	82	14	0	1	3
	Some College	112	78	20	1	1	1
	College Graduate	163	68	28	2	0	2
Ethnicity:	White	547	75	22	1	1	1
	Black	96	94	6	0	0	0
	Hispanic	49	76	8	0	0	17
Marital:	Married	442	76	20	1	1	2
	Single	121	81	19	0	0	0
	Divorced	77	84	15	1	0	0
	Widowed	79	78	10	0	0	12
Kids Under 18:	Yes	268	80	17	1	0	2
	No	454	77	19	1	1	3
Household Income:	Under $20,000	197	78	15	1	0	6
	$20,000 to $39,999	260	82	17	0	1	0
	$40,000 to $59,999	102	81	18	1	0	0
	$60,000 or more	73	61	33	2	2	1
Job Type:	White Collar	177	75	22	2	0	1
	Blue Collar	220	82	14	0	2	2
	Not Employed	277	78	18	1	0	4
Community:	Urban	189	77	19	1	1	1
	Suburban	264	76	21	1	1	1
	Rural	216	84	16	1	0	0
Region:	Northeast	154	76	22	0	0	2
	Midwest	174	73	24	1	2	1
	South	268	84	12	1	0	2
	Mountain	36	79	17	2	0	1
	Pacific	90	73	19	1	1	6
Voter Registration:	Not	0	0	0	0	0	0
	Democratic	316	86	11	1	0	2
	Republican	210	68	27	1	2	2
	Independent	147	77	22	0	0	1
Born Again:	Yes	315	78	18	1	1	2
	No	407	78	18	1	1	3
Denominational Affiliation:	Protestant	427	78	19	1	1	1
	Baptist	169	85	12	1	1	1
	Catholic	161	76	18	0	0	6
	Lutheran	43	73	24	3	0	0
	Methodist	56	66	32	0	1	1
	Charis./Pent	45	92	8	0	0	0
Attended Church This Week:	Yes	362	76	20	1	1	3
	No	359	80	16	1	1	2
Read Bible This Week:	Yes	362	79	17	1	0	3
	No	360	77	19	1	1	2

TABLE 126

Would knowing a presidential candidate's position on "crime" be very important, somewhat important, not too important, or not at all important in your decision of which candidate to support in November 1992? (Asked of registered voters.)

		N	Very Important	Somewhat Important	Not Too Important	Not At All Important	Don't Know
Total Responding		722	78%	17%	2%	2%	2%
Gender:	Male	334	73	20	4	2	0
	Female	387	81	13	1	1	4
Age:	18 to 26	72	69	24	6	0	1
	27 to 45	292	74	22	2	0	2
	46 to 64	207	79	14	1	2	3
	65 Plus	132	87	5	2	4	2
Education:	High School or Less	442	83	10	2	2	2
	Some College	112	79	19	1	1	1
	College Graduate	163	62	33	3	0	2
Ethnicity:	White	547	75	20	2	1	1
	Black	96	84	8	3	5	0
	Hispanic	49	81	2	0	0	17
Marital:	Married	442	77	18	2	1	2
	Single	121	73	22	4	0	1
	Divorced	77	87	10	2	0	0
	Widowed	79	80	5	2	6	6
Kids Under 18:	Yes	268	75	21	1	1	2
	No	454	80	14	2	2	2
Household Income:	Under $20,000	197	84	7	2	2	5
	$20,000 to $39,999	260	78	17	2	3	0
	$40,000 to $59,999	102	76	21	3	0	0
	$60,000 or more	73	57	37	3	1	2
Job Type:	White Collar	177	67	29	2	1	1
	Blue Collar	220	81	15	1	0	2
	Not Employed	277	83	9	3	3	2
Community:	Urban	189	78	18	2	2	1
	Suburban	264	77	20	2	0	1
	Rural	216	79	16	2	2	1
Region:	Northeast	154	74	20	3	2	1
	Midwest	174	73	23	1	1	1
	South	268	85	9	1	3	2
	Mountain	36	78	15	4	2	1
	Pacific	90	71	20	3	0	5
Voter Registration:	Not	0	0	0	0	0	0
	Democratic	316	81	11	3	3	2
	Republican	210	76	22	1	1	1
	Independent	147	75	21	2	1	1
Born Again:	Yes	315	80	16	1	1	2
	No	407	76	17	3	2	2
Denominational Affiliation:	Protestant	427	78	17	2	2	1
	Baptist	169	83	9	2	5	1
	Catholic	161	80	13	1	1	6
	Lutheran	43	71	27	2	0	0
	Methodist	56	61	32	4	2	1
	Charis./Pent	45	93	7	0	0	0
Attended Church This Week:	Yes	362	77	17	3	1	3
	No	359	79	16	1	2	2
Read Bible This Week:	Yes	362	79	14	2	3	3
	No	360	76	19	2	1	2

TABLE 127 311

Would knowing a presidential candidate's position on "military and defense spending" be very important, somewhat important, not too important, or not at all important in your decision of which candidate to support in November 1992? (Asked of registered voters.)

		N	Very Important	Somewhat Important	Not Too Important	Not At All Important	Don't Know
Total Responding		722	51%	34%	7%	3%	5%
Gender:	Male	334	54	31	8	4	2
	Female	387	49	36	6	2	7
Age:	18 to 26	72	53	33	12	2	0
	27 to 45	292	48	40	7	2	3
	46 to 64	207	48	36	6	5	5
	65 Plus	132	63	18	6	3	9
Education:	High School or Less	442	53	29	7	4	7
	Some College	112	48	41	9	1	1
	College Graduate	163	48	43	6	2	1
Ethnicity:	White	547	51	35	8	2	4
	Black	96	49	34	7	8	2
	Hispanic	49	57	20	2	3	17
Marital:	Married	442	50	35	8	3	4
	Single	121	53	35	6	5	0
	Divorced	77	59	30	5	1	5
	Widowed	79	45	30	7	2	17
Kids Under 18:	Yes	268	47	40	9	2	2
	No	454	53	31	6	4	6
Household Income:	Under $20,000	197	54	22	7	5	12
	$20,000 to $39,999	260	54	37	6	2	1
	$40,000 to $59,999	102	48	38	10	3	1
	$60,000 or more	73	42	50	4	2	1
Job Type:	White Collar	177	48	43	6	3	1
	Blue Collar	220	50	35	7	4	4
	Not Employed	277	53	28	8	3	8
Community:	Urban	189	48	41	8	1	2
	Suburban	264	53	36	6	3	2
	Rural	216	52	31	8	4	5
Region:	Northeast	154	47	39	9	2	3
	Midwest	174	47	38	7	4	4
	South	268	55	31	6	4	4
	Mountain	36	52	36	4	0	8
	Pacific	90	56	28	9	0	7
Voter Registration:	Not	0	0	0	0	0	0
	Democratic	316	55	32	6	1	5
	Republican	210	50	36	8	3	3
	Independent	147	44	39	7	8	2
Born Again:	Yes	315	47	38	7	3	5
	No	407	55	31	7	3	4
Denominational Affiliation:	Protestant	427	51	36	6	2	4
	Baptist	169	55	33	4	3	5
	Catholic	161	51	33	9	1	6
	Lutheran	43	56	34	9	1	0
	Methodist	56	48	37	11	0	4
	Charis./Pent	45	49	43	1	0	7
Attended Church This Week:	Yes	362	46	36	9	3	5
	No	359	56	32	5	3	4
Read Bible This Week:	Yes	362	49	34	8	4	5
	No	360	53	34	6	3	4

Would knowing a presidential candidate's position on "the budget deficit" be very important, somewhat important, not too important, or not at all important in your decision of which candidate to support in November 1992? (Asked of registered voters.)

		N	Very Important	Somewhat Important	Not Too Important	Not at All Important	Don't Know
Total Responding		722	64%	26%	3%	1%	5%
Gender:	Male	334	67	26	3	1	3
	Female	387	62	26	3	1	7
Age:	18 to 26	72	55	40	4	0	1
	27 to 45	292	60	33	3	1	2
	46 to 64	207	68	21	2	3	5
	65 Plus	132	71	11	2	1	15
Education:	High School or Less	442	65	23	2	2	8
	Some College	112	68	24	5	2	1
	College Graduate	163	60	34	3	1	2
Ethnicity:	White	547	66	26	3	1	4
	Black	96	57	29	4	0	11
	Hispanic	49	53	27	2	10	8
Marital:	Married	442	62	29	3	1	4
	Single	121	66	26	3	0	5
	Divorced	77	80	17	1	1	1
	Widowed	79	59	16	0	5	20
Kids Under 18:	Yes	268	58	36	3	1	3
	No	454	68	20	3	2	7
Household Income:	Under $20,000	197	67	18	1	3	11
	$20,000 to $39,999	260	64	29	3	1	3
	$40,000 to $59,999	102	66	29	5	0	1
	$60,000 or more	73	55	36	5	2	2
Job Type:	White Collar	177	61	35	2	1	1
	Blue Collar	220	62	29	2	1	6
	Not Employed	277	68	18	3	2	9
Community:	Urban	189	64	28	3	1	4
	Suburban	264	70	24	3	0	2
	Rural	216	64	30	2	1	4
Region:	Northeast	154	69	23	4	1	4
	Midwest	174	67	28	2	2	2
	South	268	62	26	2	2	8
	Mountain	36	67	28	0	4	1
	Pacific	90	59	27	5	0	10
Voter Registration:	Not	0	0	0	0	0	0
	Democratic	316	63	27	3	2	5
	Republican	210	66	26	3	1	4
	Independent	147	64	28	1	0	6
Born Again:	Yes	315	64	27	2	1	6
	No	407	65	26	3	2	5
Denominational Affiliation:	Protestant	427	65	25	3	1	6
	Baptist	169	63	25	3	1	8
	Catholic	161	63	26	3	4	4
	Lutheran	43	66	26	4	1	2
	Methodist	56	68	23	3	3	3
	Charis./Pent	45	82	14	0	0	4
Attended Church This Week:	Yes	362	64	26	3	2	6
	No	359	65	26	3	1	5
Read Bible This Week:	Yes	362	67	22	3	2	7
	No	360	62	30	2	1	4

TABLE 129   313

Would knowing a presidential candidate's position on "health care" be very important, somewhat important, not too important, or not at all important in your decision of which candidate to support in November 1992? (Asked of registered voters.)

		N	Very Important	Somewhat Important	Not Too Important	Not at All Important	Don't Know
Total Responding		722	75%	20%	2%	0%	3%
Gender:	Male	334	75	22	2	0	1
	Female	387	76	18	1	0	5
Age:	18 to 26	72	67	33	0	0	0
	27 to 45	292	74	22	2	1	2
	46 to 64	207	79	16	3	0	2
	65 Plus	132	80	12	0	0	8
Education:	High School or Less	442	81	13	1	0	4
	Some College	112	72	24	2	0	1
	College Graduate	163	61	34	2	1	2
Ethnicity:	White	547	74	23	2	0	1
	Black	96	84	7	0	0	9
	Hispanic	49	60	20	0	3	17
Marital:	Married	442	74	22	2	0	1
	Single	121	75	24	0	0	0
	Divorced	77	89	9	1	0	1
	Widowed	79	72	6	1	0	20
Kids Under 18:	Yes	268	71	24	2	1	2
	No	454	78	17	1	0	4
Household Income:	Under $20,000	197	87	6	0	0	6
	$20,000 to $39,999	260	77	20	2	0	2
	$40,000 to $59,999	102	68	29	3	0	0
	$60,000 or more	73	54	41	2	0	2
Job Type:	White Collar	177	66	28	4	1	1
	Blue Collar	220	79	18	1	0	2
	Not Employed	277	79	14	0	0	6
Community:	Urban	189	80	18	1	0	1
	Suburban	264	71	25	2	1	1
	Rural	216	78	18	2	0	3
Region:	Northeast	154	74	20	2	0	4
	Midwest	174	72	26	2	0	0
	South	268	79	15	1	1	4
	Mountain	36	67	24	9	0	1
	Pacific	90	75	18	1	0	6
Voter Registration:	Not	0	0	0	0	0	0
	Democratic	316	83	13	1	0	3
	Republican	210	62	32	4	1	2
	Independent	147	81	17	1	0	1
Born Again:	Yes	315	74	20	2	1	4
	No	407	76	20	1	0	3
Denominational Affiliation:	Protestant	427	76	21	1	0	2
	Baptist	169	84	12	0	1	3
	Catholic	161	78	14	2	0	6
	Lutheran	43	59	37	4	0	0
	Methodist	56	67	29	3	0	1
	Charis./Pent	45	87	11	0	0	2
Attended Church This Week:	Yes	362	73	22	2	0	3
	No	359	78	17	1	0	4
Read Bible This Week:	Yes	362	74	19	2	0	4
	No	360	76	20	1	0	2

Would knowing a presidential candidate's position on "welfare and unemployment policies" be very, somewhat, not too, or not at all important in your decision of which candidate to support in November 1992? (Asked of registered voters.)

		N	Very Important	Somewhat Important	Not Too Important	Not At All Important	Don't Know
Total Responding		722	63%	29%	3%	1%	4%
Gender:	Male	334	61	33	4	1	1
	Female	387	65	25	3	1	6
Age:	18 to 26	72	52	38	10	0	0
	27 to 45	292	62	33	1	1	2
	46 to 64	207	67	25	4	1	3
	65 Plus	132	64	21	4	1	9
Education:	High School or Less	442	70	21	4	1	5
	Some College	112	60	34	4	1	1
	College Graduate	163	48	47	2	1	2
Ethnicity:	White	547	62	31	4	1	2
	Black	96	69	24	3	0	4
	Hispanic	49	62	21	0	0	17
Marital:	Married	442	61	32	3	1	2
	Single	121	61	32	5	1	0
	Divorced	77	80	14	1	1	5
	Widowed	79	62	20	3	0	15
Kids Under 18:	Yes	268	59	36	2	1	2
	No	454	65	25	4	1	4
Household Income:	Under $20,000	197	65	21	5	1	8
	$20,000 to $39,999	260	67	27	2	2	1
	$40,000 to $59,999	102	56	40	3	0	1
	$60,000 or more	73	52	44	1	1	1
Job Type:	White Collar	177	59	35	3	2	1
	Blue Collar	220	68	26	3	0	3
	Not Employed	277	64	26	4	1	6
Community:	Urban	189	59	36	3	1	2
	Suburban	264	63	32	3	0	1
	Rural	216	67	26	3	2	2
Region:	Northeast	154	64	28	4	0	4
	Midwest	174	65	30	2	2	2
	South	268	63	28	4	1	4
	Mountain	36	72	22	5	0	1
	Pacific	90	57	35	2	1	5
Voter Registration:	Not	0	0	0	0	0	0
	Democratic	316	64	27	4	1	4
	Republican	210	61	32	3	2	3
	Independent	147	65	30	3	1	1
Born Again:	Yes	315	66	26	3	1	3
	No	407	61	31	4	1	4
Denominational Affiliation:	Protestant	427	63	29	3	1	3
	Baptist	169	66	25	4	1	3
	Catholic	161	60	29	5	1	5
	Lutheran	43	59	34	3	0	4
	Methodist	56	64	30	0	1	5
	Charis./Pent	45	74	21	4	0	2
Attended Church This Week:	Yes	362	64	28	2	1	4
	No	359	62	29	4	1	3
Read Bible This Week:	Yes	362	66	26	3	1	4
	No	360	61	32	3	1	3

TABLE 131   315

Would knowing a presidential candidate's position on "the separation of church and state" be very important, somewhat important, not too important, or not at all important in your decision of which candidate to support in November 1992? (Asked of registered voters.)

		N	Very Important	Somewhat Important	Not Too Important	Not At All Important	Don't Know
Total Responding		722	50%	32%	9%	4%	6%
Gender:	Male	334	57	29	8	5	2
	Female	387	44	35	9	3	10
Age:	18 to 26	72	38	43	12	7	1
	27 to 45	292	44	37	10	4	5
	46 to 64	207	61	26	5	3	6
	65 Plus	132	53	25	10	2	10
Education:	High School or Less	442	52	29	7	3	8
	Some College	112	50	34	9	4	3
	College Graduate	163	43	38	13	4	3
Ethnicity:	White	547	48	34	10	4	5
	Black	96	59	27	4	4	7
	Hispanic	49	46	27	7	3	17
Marital:	Married	442	52	30	9	4	5
	Single	121	45	39	9	5	1
	Divorced	77	47	41	7	1	4
	Widowed	79	44	26	7	2	22
Kids Under 18:	Yes	268	49	33	11	5	3
	No	454	50	32	8	3	8
Household Income:	Under $20,000	197	52	27	6	3	11
	$20,000 to $39,999	260	51	33	7	6	3
	$40,000 to $59,999	102	48	34	14	1	2
	$60,000 or more	73	43	43	8	4	2
Job Type:	White Collar	177	41	41	14	3	1
	Blue Collar	220	59	27	5	3	6
	Not Employed	277	49	30	7	5	9
Community:	Urban	189	47	38	8	5	2
	Suburban	264	46	37	9	4	3
	Rural	216	54	24	10	3	8
Region:	Northeast	154	45	33	12	3	7
	Midwest	174	44	39	8	4	5
	South	268	56	26	8	4	6
	Mountain	36	49	34	8	1	8
	Pacific	90	50	34	5	4	7
Voter Registration:	Not	0	0	0	0	0	0
	Democratic	316	54	28	7	3	8
	Republican	210	50	35	9	3	3
	Independent	147	43	37	13	6	1
Born Again:	Yes	315	56	31	6	2	7
	No	407	45	33	11	5	6
Denominational Affiliation:	Protestant	427	53	31	8	3	5
	Baptist	169	57	25	7	5	7
	Catholic	161	42	34	13	2	9
	Lutheran	43	44	32	16	7	1
	Methodist	56	54	32	6	4	5
	Charis./Pent	45	73	19	2	0	6
Attended Church This Week:	Yes	362	56	29	8	2	6
	No	359	43	35	10	5	6
Read Bible This Week:	Yes	362	55	29	5	3	7
	No	360	44	35	12	4	5

Would knowing a presidential candidate's position on "drug enforcement" be very important, somewhat important, not too important, or not at all important in your decision of which candidate to support in November 1992? (Asked of registered voters.)

		N	Very Important	Somewhat Important	Not Too Important	Not At All Important	Don't Know
Total Responding		722	78%	15%	2%	2%	2%
Gender:	Male	334	77	17	3	4	0
	Female	387	80	13	2	0	4
Age:	18 to 26	72	70	25	2	3	1
	27 to 45	292	76	19	2	1	2
	46 to 64	207	81	11	3	2	3
	65 Plus	132	87	4	3	4	2
Education:	High School or Less	442	84	9	1	2	3
	Some College	112	78	19	2	2	0
	College Graduate	163	63	28	5	2	2
Ethnicity:	White	547	77	17	3	2	1
	Black	96	82	10	0	5	3
	Hispanic	49	81	2	0	0	17
Marital:	Married	442	80	14	3	1	2
	Single	121	72	21	3	4	1
	Divorced	77	84	15	1	0	0
	Widowed	79	75	7	1	6	11
Kids Under 18:	Yes	268	78	16	2	1	2
	No	454	78	14	3	2	3
Household Income:	Under $20,000	197	85	7	2	1	5
	$20,000 to $39,999	260	79	16	2	3	0
	$40,000 to $59,999	102	77	21	2	0	0
	$60,000 or more	73	59	26	7	6	2
Job Type:	White Collar	177	68	24	4	3	1
	Blue Collar	220	85	10	1	2	2
	Not Employed	277	81	11	2	2	4
Community:	Urban	189	83	13	3	1	1
	Suburban	264	75	21	2	1	1
	Rural	216	81	12	3	2	2
Region:	Northeast	154	72	19	4	1	4
	Midwest	174	78	16	3	3	1
	South	268	82	12	2	2	2
	Mountain	36	84	13	0	2	1
	Pacific	90	76	15	1	3	5
Voter Registration:	Not	0	0	0	0	0	0
	Democratic	316	81	11	3	3	2
	Republican	210	79	17	2	2	1
	Independent	147	74	21	3	1	1
Born Again:	Yes	315	81	13	2	0	3
	No	407	76	16	2	4	2
Denominational Affiliation:	Protestant	427	81	14	2	2	1
	Baptist	169	79	14	1	4	2
	Catholic	161	78	13	3	0	6
	Lutheran	43	78	17	2	4	0
	Methodist	56	73	24	0	3	1
	Charis./Pent	45	94	3	2	0	0
Attended Church This Week:	Yes	362	80	15	3	0	3
	No	359	77	15	2	4	2
Read Bible This Week:	Yes	362	80	13	2	1	3
	No	360	76	16	3	3	2

TABLE 133   317

Would knowing a presidential candidate's position on "human rights protection" be very important, somewhat important, not too important, or not at all important in your decision of which candidate to support in November 1992? (Asked of registered voters.)

		N	Very Important	Somewhat Important	Not Too Important	Not at All Important	Don't Know
Total Responding		722	66%	26%	2%	1%	4%
Gender:	Male	334	67	28	3	2	0
	Female	387	66	24	2	0	8
Age:	18 to 26	72	58	40	2	0	0
	27 to 45	292	63	30	2	2	3
	46 to 64	207	70	24	2	1	4
	65 Plus	132	73	13	4	1	9
Education:	High School or Less	442	71	20	1	1	6
	Some College	112	62	31	5	1	1
	College Graduate	163	55	39	3	1	2
Ethnicity:	White	547	62	31	3	1	3
	Black	96	87	7	2	0	4
	Hispanic	49	64	19	0	0	17
Marital:	Married	442	63	29	2	1	5
	Single	121	65	32	2	0	0
	Divorced	77	81	14	4	1	0
	Widowed	79	71	9	2	4	14
Kids Under 18:	Yes	268	64	31	2	1	3
	No	454	68	23	3	1	5
Household Income:	Under $20,000	197	73	13	3	1	9
	$20,000 to $39,999	260	71	25	1	1	2
	$40,000 to $59,999	102	60	36	3	0	1
	$60,000 or more	73	42	52	3	2	1
Job Type:	White Collar	177	58	37	3	1	2
	Blue Collar	220	70	25	2	1	3
	Not Employed	277	72	17	3	1	7
Community:	Urban	189	74	22	2	0	2
	Suburban	264	63	33	2	0	2
	Rural	216	64	26	3	2	5
Region:	Northeast	154	63	30	2	0	6
	Midwest	174	65	27	3	3	2
	South	268	71	21	2	1	5
	Mountain	36	75	16	7	1	1
	Pacific	90	56	37	1	1	5
Voter Registration:	Not	0	0	0	0	0	0
	Democratic	316	75	19	1	1	4
	Republican	210	55	38	3	1	3
	Independent	147	67	26	4	1	2
Born Again:	Yes	315	63	29	2	1	5
	No	407	69	24	3	1	4
Denominational Affiliation:	Protestant	427	65	29	2	1	4
	Baptist	169	69	22	2	0	7
	Catholic	161	69	21	3	1	6
	Lutheran	43	61	38	1	0	0
	Methodist	56	58	34	1	3	3
	Charis./Pent	45	87	12	2	0	0
Attended Church This Week:	Yes	362	65	25	3	1	6
	No	359	67	27	2	2	3
Read Bible This Week:	Yes	362	68	23	2	2	5
	No	360	65	29	2	1	3

TABLE 134

Would knowing a presidential candidate's position on "the economy" be very important, somewhat important, not too important, or not at all important in your decision of which candidate to support in November 1992? (Asked of registered voters.)

		N	Very Important	Somewhat Important	Not Too Important	Not at All Important	Don't Know
Total Responding		722	76%	19%	1%	1%	3%
Gender:	Male	334	77	20	1	2	1
	Female	387	76	18	0	0	6
Age:	18 to 26	72	76	24	0	0	0
	27 to 45	292	72	25	0	0	2
	46 to 64	207	82	14	2	0	2
	65 Plus	132	76	9	0	4	11
Education:	High School or Less	442	76	18	0	1	5
	Some College	112	80	16	2	1	1
	College Graduate	163	74	24	0	0	1
Ethnicity:	White	547	79	18	1	0	2
	Black	96	72	19	0	5	4
	Hispanic	49	45	38	0	0	17
Marital:	Married	442	76	21	1	0	2
	Single	121	84	16	0	0	0
	Divorced	77	74	21	0	0	5
	Widowed	79	69	12	0	6	12
Kids Under 18:	Yes	268	74	24	0	0	2
	No	454	78	16	1	1	4
Household Income:	Under $20,000	197	78	12	0	0	9
	$20,000 to $39,999	260	78	20	0	2	0
	$40,000 to $59,999	102	78	20	2	0	0
	$60,000 or more	73	66	32	1	0	1
Job Type:	White Collar	177	77	21	1	0	1
	Blue Collar	220	81	16	1	0	2
	Not Employed	277	72	20	0	2	7
Community:	Urban	189	76	19	1	0	3
	Suburban	264	75	23	0	0	1
	Rural	216	80	18	0	0	1
Region:	Northeast	154	78	19	1	0	2
	Midwest	174	76	21	0	0	2
	South	268	75	19	0	2	4
	Mountain	36	93	4	2	0	1
	Pacific	90	70	22	1	0	8
Voter Registration:	Not	0	0	0	0	0	0
	Democratic	316	76	17	1	2	5
	Republican	210	77	21	0	0	1
	Independent	147	78	21	0	0	1
Born Again:	Yes	315	78	19	0	0	2
	No	407	75	19	1	1	4
Denominational Affiliation:	Protestant	427	75	21	0	1	2
	Baptist	169	76	18	0	3	3
	Catholic	161	79	15	1	0	5
	Lutheran	43	68	32	0	0	0
	Methodist	56	80	17	1	0	3
	Charis./Pent	45	78	20	0	0	2
Attended Church This Week:	Yes	362	77	18	1	0	4
	No	359	76	20	0	1	2
Read Bible This Week:	Yes	362	75	18	0	1	5
	No	360	78	20	1	0	2

TABLE 135   319

Would knowing a presidential candidate's position on "mass transportation" be very important, somewhat important, not too important, or not at all important in your decision of which candidate to support in November 1992? (Asked of registered voters.)

		N	Very Important	Somewhat Important	Not Too Important	Not at All Important	Don't Know
Total Responding		722	26%	46%	16%	6%	7%
Gender:	Male	334	28	46	17	7	1
	Female	387	23	45	16	4	11
Age:	18 to 26	72	15	59	15	11	1
	27 to 45	292	20	51	22	5	2
	46 to 64	207	28	48	14	5	5
	65 Plus	132	40	24	11	5	21
Education:	High School or Less	442	29	42	12	7	10
	Some College	112	21	51	20	4	3
	College Graduate	163	18	52	25	3	2
Ethnicity:	White	547	21	48	20	6	5
	Black	96	39	40	7	5	8
	Hispanic	49	30	44	9	0	17
Marital:	Married	442	23	49	19	5	5
	Single	121	18	54	16	10	2
	Divorced	77	38	37	11	7	8
	Widowed	79	40	26	8	4	22
Kids Under 18:	Yes	268	17	55	19	6	3
	No	454	31	40	15	5	9
Household Income:	Under $20,000	197	41	27	10	7	16
	$20,000 to $39,999	260	22	54	18	5	2
	$40,000 to $59,999	102	14	56	22	7	1
	$60,000 or more	73	16	56	21	6	1
Job Type:	White Collar	177	16	53	22	8	1
	Blue Collar	220	27	48	15	8	3
	Not Employed	277	31	38	13	3	14
Community:	Urban	189	26	49	20	5	1
	Suburban	264	24	52	15	5	3
	Rural	216	28	41	17	4	10
Region:	Northeast	154	29	48	12	4	6
	Midwest	174	23	48	20	5	3
	South	268	28	42	13	7	9
	Mountain	36	18	44	28	4	6
	Pacific	90	19	47	20	7	7
Voter Registration:	Not	0	0	0	0	0	0
	Democratic	316	33	47	12	2	7
	Republican	210	20	42	25	7	6
	Independent	147	16	52	15	13	3
Born Again:	Yes	315	20	44	19	7	10
	No	407	30	47	14	5	4
Denominational Affiliation:	Protestant	427	25	44	18	6	7
	Baptist	169	29	46	11	5	9
	Catholic	161	27	52	13	2	6
	Lutheran	43	25	54	17	4	0
	Methodist	56	22	39	21	12	7
	Charis./Pent	45	42	30	17	1	10
Attended Church This Week:	Yes	362	23	43	19	5	10
	No	359	28	48	14	6	4
Read Bible This Week:	Yes	362	31	38	16	4	10
	No	360	20	53	16	7	3

Barna Research Group
L i m i t e d

ABOUT BARNA RESEARCH GROUP

The Barna Research Group was launched by George and Nancy Barna in 1984. Conceived as a company dedicated to serve Christian ministries by providing quality state-of-the-art marketing research, the firm has become a leader in providing research-based ministry insights concerning the challenges and opportunities facing churches and other Christian organizations.

Since its inception, the Barna Research Group has served more than 100 ministries in English-speaking nations, ranging from large parachurch ministries to small churches. Parachurch clients have included the Billy Graham Evangelistic Association, World Vision, Focus on the Family, The Navigators, Campus Crusade for Christ, Youth for Christ, Compassion International, American Bible Society, Gospel Light Publications, Dallas Theological Seminary, Fuller Theological Seminary, Biola University, Salvation Army, CBN and Moody Bible Institute. Churches served represent more than a dozen denominations.

Also numbered among its clients are a broad range of for-profit organizations. Those clients have included Visa, The Disney Channel, Associates Financial Services, J. Walter Thompson Advertising, Rapp Collins Marcoa, Russ Reid Company and others.

To achieve its vision of providing Christian ministries with current, accurate information that will facilitate better decision-making and more effective ministry, Barna Research produces many publications based on self-funded, national research projects. Some of the publications currently available include the following:

Books
The Barna Report 1992-1993, George Barna, Regal Books, 1992.
The Power of Vision, George Barna, Regal Books, 1992.
A Step-by-Step Guide to Church Marketing: Breaking Ground for the Harvest,
     George Barna, Regal Books, 1992.
What Americans Believe, George Barna, Regal Books, 1991.
User Friendly Churches, George Barna, Regal Books, 1991.
The Frog in the Kettle, George Barna, Regal Books, 1990.
Marketing the Church, George Barna, NavPress, 1988.

Newsletter
Ministry Currents, published quarterly.

Reports
The Church Today: Insightful Statistics and Commentary, published 1990.
Today's Teenagers: A Generation in Transition, published 1991.
Never on a Sunday: The Challenge of the Unchurched, published 1990.
Born Again: A Look at Christians in America, published 1990.

For further information about these or other resources from Barna Research, or to get information about other research services provided by the Barna Research Group, Ltd., please write to them at: P.O. Box 4152, Glendale, CA 91222-0152, or call 818-241-9300.

INDEX

abortion(s), 19-20, 23, 32, 34, 73, 82, 84, 135, 143, 145-146, 147, 175, 177, 250, 306
Abraham, 119
adultery, 111, 113, 115, 116, 176, 269
AIDS, 19, 30
assumptions, 13, 18, 58, 67, 70, 72, 133, 157, 161
astrology, 43, 54, 55, 56, 154, 176, 258
attend, 34, 36, 47-48, 52-54, 56, 67, 70, 82, 89, 92, 94, 117, 126, 128, 148, 168, 173, 175-176, 261, 276-279
baby boomer(s), 27, 29, 31-32, 44, 46, 48, 74, 78, 80, 89, 92, 94, 96, 105, 106, 114-115, 124, 125, 130, 132, 139, 155-156, 166
baby busters, 27, 31-39, 44, 46, 48, 53-54, 74, 78, 80, 105, 106, 113-115, 117, 118, 119, 123-126, 130, 139, 146, 166
Baptist(s), 34, 38, 47, 52, 54, 60, 61, 62-63, 65, 82, 83, 89-90, 92, 108, 114, 132, 135, 139, 173, 229-273, 275-294, 296-319
behavior, 11, 20, 31-32, 48, 57, 82, 86, 96, 117, 119-121, 126, 128, 154, 161
Bible, 13-14, 19-21, 23-29, 31-32, 36, 38, 41, 43-45, 46-48, 52-54, 56-58, 63-64, 70, 73, 76, 81, 84, 86, 90, 92, 99-100, 104-113, 117, 121, 123-124, 126-128, 132, 154, 156, 168, 173, 175-177, 229-273, 275-294, 296-319, 321
biblical, 14, 43, 54, 56-57, 70, 148, 150
book(s), 7, 12-14, 20-21, 41, 57, 82, 99, 104-105, 107, 121, 123-124, 128, 133, 150, 161-163, 166, 168, 171, 175-177, 232, 285, 322
born again, 26-27, 34, 38, 47, 49, 50, 51, 52, 54, 56, 59, 63-64, 68, 73-74, 76, 77, 78, 79, 80, 82, 86, 89, 92, 100, 102, 104-105, 108, 111, 113, 115, 117, 119, 123, 126, 128, 130, 132, 135, 137, 138, 140, 141, 145-146, 147, 148, 167, 229-273, 275-294, 296-319, 322
boycott(s), 135, 148, 149
budget deficit, 142-143, 145, 177, 312
Bush, George, 30, 135, 142
career, 24-29, 31-32, 74, 175, 244
Catholic(s), 15, 32, 35, 38, 47-48, 52-54, 61, 62-65, 66, 71, 72, 76, 79, 80, 82, 83, 89-90, 92, 94, 108, 126, 132, 135, 137, 138, 139, 150, 168, 173, 229-273, 275-294, 296-319
Christ, 7, 9-13, 21, 26, 43, 50, 51, 52, 56, 58, 67, 74, 76, 78, 81-82, 86, 90, 119-120, 133, 151,

154, 156, 162, 167, 177, 262, 293-295, 321
church(es), 7, 9, 20-22, 32, 34, 36, 38-39, 41-43, 47-48, 52-54, 56-60, 62-64, 66-68, 69, 70, 72-73, 76, 79, 80-82, 84, 86-87, 89-90, 91-97, 99, 104-105, 107-110, 114-115, 117, 120-121, 123-124, 126, 127, 128, 130, 131, 132-135, 137, 139-140, 143, 145-148, 150-151, 154-156, 161, 168, 170-171, 173-178, 229-273, 275-294, 296-319, 321-322
comfortably, 19, 23-25, 26-29, 31-32, 36, 175, 240
community, 24, 25-27, 29, 41, 70, 82, 87, 92, 96-97, 130, 131, 133, 150, 161-162, 167, 175, 229-273, 275-294, 296-319
conservative(s), 114, 135, 137
contextualization, 10
control, 18, 20, 23, 36, 38, 174
crime, 20, 84, 115, 135, 142-145, 177, 310
Democrat(s), 52, 62-63, 73, 84, 85, 135, 137, 139-142, 144-146, 168, 173, 229-273, 275-294, 296-319
donation(s), 132-133, 177, 299
drug(s), 20, 84, 135, 142-145, 147, 178, 316
economic(s), 20, 30, 38, 146
education, 20, 34, 36, 44, 48, 53, 78, 84, 108, 117, 135, 137, 139, 142-146, 164, 166, 177, 229-273, 275-294, 296-319
environmental, 142-143, 145-147, 177, 308
evangelicals, 73, 81-83, 84-86
evangelism, 58, 72, 86, 103, 133-134
evangelistic, 13, 15, 58, 72, 76, 104, 156, 321
family, 19-20, 23-28, 30-32, 39, 72, 74, 102, 115, 154, 175, 242, 321
friends, 7, 13-14, 19-20, 23-28, 29, 31-32, 52, 58, 72, 82, 123, 128, 130-131, 174-175, 241
Gallup, 11, 112
Germany, 19
God, 7, 9-15, 21, 41-48, 52, 54, 56, 58, 72-76, 78, 81-82, 86, 90, 97, 108, 110-114, 117, 119-121, 154, 156, 161, 175-176, 255, 263, 265, 273-274, 295
gods, 21, 74, 75, 111, 113-114, 116, 176, 263, 274
gospel, 10, 12, 58, 76
government, 23, 25, 26, 29, 34, 68, 137, 175, 247
health care, 20, 84, 135, 142-145, 177, 313
health, 19-20, 23-28, 30, 32, 39, 74, 84, 135,

142-145, 175, 177, 245, 313
human rights, 142-143, 145, 147, 178, 317
idol(s), 113-114, 116, 176, 264
illiteracy, 20, 123, 133
jealousy, 117
Jesus, 9-10, 12, 26, 50-52, 56, 67, 72, 74, 76, 78, 81, 112, 119, 154-156, 167, 177, 262, 293-295
Johnson, Magic, 19, 30
leader(s), 10, 23, 32, 34, 38-39, 52, 64, 70, 86, 96-97, 110, 124, 146, 150, 174
leadership, 38, 58, 60, 68, 84, 89, 96, 110, 143
lie, 19, 23, 113, 117, 176, 271
Lutheran(s), 32, 47, 52, 54, 61-65, 82, 90, 108, 114, 140, 173, 229-273, 275-294, 296, 303-319
lying, 21, 32, 111, 116-118, 120, 175, 251
magazine(s), 21, 84, 99, 104-105, 107, 176-177, 289
mainline, 82, 89-90, 135, 137, 139
mass transportation, 143, 147, 148, 178, 319
Methodist(s), 36, 47, 52-53, 61-65, 76, 82, 83, 90, 108, 137, 140, 173, 229-273, 275-294, 296, 303-319
ministry(ies), 7-9, 12-14, 39, 41-42, 59-60, 64, 66, 68, 70, 72, 82, 87, 96-97, 104-105, 107, 110, 133-134, 138, 155-157, 161-162, 177, 286, 321-322
modeling, 41
money, 7, 11, 19, 23-29, 31-32, 34, 82, 104-105, 107, 114, 123, 130, 132, 134, 153, 175, 177, 238, 254, 286, 290-291
moral, 22, 32, 34, 120, 154-155
Mormon, 61-65, 174
MTV, 123-125, 128, 175, 235
murder, 111, 113, 115, 116, 176, 268
needy, 105, 107, 177, 290-291
New Age, 54, 74, 84, 86
orthodox, 21, 56, 76
parent(s), 39, 66, 113, 115-117, 132, 140, 174, 176, 267
Persian Gulf, 19
Pharisees, 10, 112
politics, 23, 25, 26, 29, 135-151, 175, 247
prayer, 7, 21, 41, 43, 53, 86, 96, 99-100, 105-106, 154, 281
pre-boomer(s), 29, 31, 80, 105, 106, 132, 139
preaching, 99-100, 105, 107, 284
Presbyterian(s), 61-65, 90, 173, 190
Protestant(s), 15, 22, 48, 59, 64, 66-70, 72, 76,

79-80, 82, 89-90, 128, 130, 135, 137-139, 148, 168, 174, 229-273, 275-294, 296-319
public education, 84, 135, 142-145, 177, 309
radio, 21, 82, 99-102, 105, 107-108, 126, 132, 176-177, 284, 288, 301
random sample, 14, 163
relationships, 14, 29, 39, 41, 72, 133, 174
religion(s), 10, 19, 21, 23-29, 31-32, 82, 84, 100, 126, 133, 154, 156, 175, 236, 275
religious, 10, 20-21, 24, 26-27, 29, 31, 41, 44, 54, 60, 62, 73, 76, 81-82, 90, 99-102, 105, 107-108, 110, 123, 126, 128, 130, 148, 154, 173, 175-177, 275, 283
Republican(s), 52, 54, 62-63, 73, 84-85, 135, 137, 139-142, 144, 146, 148, 168, 173, 229-273, 275-294, 296-319
Sabbath, 114, 116
Salvation Army, 60, 62-63, 173, 321
salvation, 21, 44, 48, 52, 58, 76, 78, 86, 156, 173
senior citizen(s), 15, 29, 31, 36-38, 44, 46, 48, 55, 63, 80, 105-106, 132
sin, 21, 43, 48-50, 56-58, 112, 115, 117, 120, 154, 260
small groups, 21, 105, 107, 128, 150
Soviet Union, 19, 30
success, 19, 23-24, 34, 41, 53, 58, 74, 89, 117, 175, 254
Sunday School, 21, 82, 96, 126-127, 150, 173, 175-176, 230, 280-281
swearing, 21, 111, 114, 116, 120
taxes, 142-143, 145, 167, 177, 307
television, 21, 99-102, 107, 115, 124, 126, 132, 283, 301
Ten Commandments, 20-21, 43, 47-48, 56, 78, 111-121, 154, 176, 259, 295
truth, 13-14, 17, 19, 21, 34, 36, 41, 50, 57-58, 117, 154-155, 157
values, 10-11, 17, 19-20, 23-42, 70, 78, 151, 161, 175, 249
volunteers, 96
vote, 20, 34, 39, 84, 118, 132, 135-138, 144, 150-151, 166, 168, 177, 303
welfare, 73, 84, 142-143, 145-147, 178, 314
women's rights, 143, 145, 147, 148, 177, 305
worship, 9, 21, 41, 72, 82, 92, 93, 110-111, 113-114, 124, 126, 133, 170-171, 229, 263, 266, 277